D0474576

PRENTICE-HALL FOUNDATIONS OF PHILOSOPHY SERIES

| | |
|---|---|
| *Virgil Aldrich* | Philosophy of Art |
| *William Alston* | Philosophy of Language |
| *Stephen Barker* | Philosophy of Mathematics |
| *Roderick Chisholm* | Theory of Knowledge |
| *William Dray* | Philosophy of History |
| *Joel Feinberg* | Social Philosophy |
| *William Frankena* | Ethics |
| *Martin Golding* | Philosophy of Law |
| *Carl Hempel* | Philosophy of Natural Science |
| *John Hick* | Philosophy of Religion |
| *David Hull* | Philosophy of Biological Science |
| *James McClellan* | Philosophy of Education |
| *Willard Van Orman Quine* | Philosophy of Logic |
| *Richard Rudner* | Philosophy of Social Science |
| *Wesley Salmon* | Logic |
| *Jerome Shaffer* | Philosophy of Mind |
| *Richard Taylor* | Metaphysics |

*Elizabeth and Monroe Beardsley, editors*

# PHILOSOPHY
# OF EDUCATION

James E. McClellan
STATE UNIVERSITY OF NEW YORK AT ALBANY

*PRENTICE-HALL, INC.*
*Englewood Cliffs, New Jersey*

*Library of Congress Cataloging in Publication Data*

McClellan, James Edward, 1922–
   Philosophy of education.

   (Prentice-Hall foundations of philosophy series)
   Bibliography: p.
   Includes index.
   1. Education—Philosophy.  I. Title.
LB885.M2216     370.1     75-33008
ISBN  0-13-663302-1
ISBN  0-13-663294-7 pbk.

10  9  8  7  6  5  4  3  2

PRENTICE-HALL INTERNATIONAL, INC., London
PRENTICE-HALL OF AUSTRALIA, PTY., Sydney
PRENTICE-HALL OF CANADA, LTD., Toronto
PRENTICE-HALL OF INDIA PRIVATE LIMITED, New Delhi
PRENTICE-HALL OF JAPAN, INC., Tokyo
PRENTICE-HALL OF SOUTHEAST ASIA (PTE.) LTD., Singapore

*To Paul Joseph Dietl, 1932–1972*

"If all we get are students who perform according to rules, students who do not see the point of what they are doing, then we will not have all we want anymore than we will if we get students who are civil to one another but do not see the good of it at all—no love, no anger, no pride, no shame."

# FOUNDATIONS OF PHILOSOPHY

Many of the problems of philosophy are of such broad relevance to human concerns, and so complex in their ramifications, that they are, in one form or another, perennially present. Though in the course of time they yield in part to philosophical inquiry, they may need to be rethought by each age in the light of its broader scientific knowledge and deepened ethical and religious experience. Better solutions are found by more refined and rigorous methods. Thus, one who approaches the study of philosophy in the hope of understanding the best of what it affords will look for both fundamental issues and contemporary achievements.

Written by a group of distinguished philosophers, the Foundations of Philosophy Series aims to exhibit some of the main problems in the various fields of philosophy as they stand at the present stage of philosophical history.

While certain fields are likely to be represented in most introductory courses in philosophy, college classes differ widely in emphasis, in method of instruction, and in rate of progress. Every instructor needs freedom to change his course as his own philosophical interests, the size and makeup of his classes, and the needs of his students vary from year to year. The seventeen volumes in the Foundations of Philosophy Series—each complete in itself, but complementing the others—offer a new flexibility to the instructor, who can create his own textbook by combining several volumes as he wishes, and can choose different combinations at different times. Those volumes that are not used in an introductory course will be found valuable, along with other texts or collections of readings, for the more specialized upper-level courses.

*Elizabeth Beardsley* / *Monroe Beardsley*

# CONTENTS

# 4

**THE ACTS
OF TEACHING,** 87

# 5

**MORAL EDUCATION:
THE MORALITY
OF TEACHING VS.
THE TEACHING
OF MORALITY,** 122

# PREFACE

This book is intended for readers who've had some personal acquaintance with schools but no specific training in philosophy of education. Thus it might be of some use in introductory courses, especially if read in conjunction with Plato's *Meno*.

So far as I know, this book contains not a single original idea. Its value, if any, consists in giving reasonably concise expression to a rich but scattered body of philosophical thought, only a part of which is cited in the text. It is a pleasure to acknowledge my dependence on the tradition in which this book stands, but strictly speaking, I cannot be grateful to those whose ideas I have come to believe. For gratitude implies a gift and gift implies ownership, and all that belies the truth that "Die Gedanken sind frei." No one who holds a true belief is in the least diminished by my sharing his idea. And if the shared belief be false, then both of us will be the better for the criticism which, we may hope, its appearance here will attract.

But I am grateful to those who have given of their time and thought to try to make this book intelligible: to colleagues and graduate students at Cornell, Syracuse, Temple, and SUNY Albany, to Elizabeth and Monroe Beardsley, and to my wife and colleague, Dorothy McClellan. I'm also grateful to my son Bruce, who gave me six months of his adolescence as a private pupil, diligently teaching me what "learning" means.

*James E. McClellan*

# CHAPTER ONE

# What Is Philosophy of Education

Many otherwise sensible men and women turn quite silly when they try to answer that question.[1] I've no reason to think that I shall succeed where others have failed, but I'm obliged to make the effort. For I fear that this little book will fail to make its point unless we are first agreed on what sort of point it's trying to make. So . . .

**A PHILOSOPHY OF A PRACTICE**     Let us begin with the obvious: philosophy of education is simply one among those branches of philosophy dealing with a distinctive practice in human life, where the word "practice" is used, following John Rawls, to mean "any form of activity specified by a system of rules which defines offices, roles, moves, penalties, defences and so on, and which gives the activity its structure."[2] In those terms, law is clearly a practice, so are

[1] See Christopher J. Lucas, ed., *What is Philosophy of Education?* (New York: The Macmillan Company, 1969), 313 pp. Also same author and respondent, "The Demise of Educational Philosophy," *The School Review,* 79:2 (February 1971), 269–281.

[2] John Rawls, "Justice as Fairness," in Peter Laslett and W. G. Runciman, eds., *Phil-*

engineering, medicine, mathematics, science, religion, war, sport, business, politics, and many other things. Neither art nor the criticism of art is clearly a practice, though the latter is perhaps more like a practice than the former. Love is unequivocally *not* a practice, though it is often perverted into a facsimile of one or more practices. Schooling is unmistakably a practice. Is education? Yes, for ideal as well as actual practices will have to be allowed in Rawls' universe of practices. But schooling and education are not the same practice.

The expression "philosophy of," when prefixed to the name of a practice, denotes something which is somewhat, but not exactly, like a practice. A philosophy of _____ (any practice) does have rules, but it's hard to say exactly what those rules are, once you get beyond the fundamental principles of ethics and logic. A philosophy of _____ does have a structure, that provided by the history of philosophical reflection on that practice, as well as by the history of the practice itself. But I shouldn't think that a philosophy of _____ has or needs such things as "offices, roles, moves, penalties, defences, and so on." Those things are appropriate to activities in which individuals have interests, even vested interests, that conflict with one another. A philosophy of _____ is not quite like that; it is defined by a purpose in which anyone who wishes may join as a cooperative partner.

And what is the purpose that defines the philosophy of a practice? It is an effort to discover the distinctive form which human reason assumes in that practice. That inquiry has two complementary aspects, which we may call the "revelatory" and the "critical," without, I hope, taking either name too seriously. We are engaged in philosophy of Y from its revelatory aspect when we try to reveal some general feature(s) of human reason as exemplified in the practice of Y, from its critical aspect when we test the "system of rules" that defines the practice of Y at a given historical moment against more fundamental canons of what it is to think and act rationally. It doesn't require philosophy to point out that each of us can follow a story, a proof, and a lawyer's advice. We are engaged in philosophy of history, mathematics, and law from their revelatory aspects when we (try to) uncover the presupposed canons of reason which make "following" in each case a rational activity. We are engaged in the practice of those philosophies of _____ from their critical aspects when we (try to) examine the presupposed canons of those practices (as they are practiced among us) against the most general canons of rationality we can discern.

The terms "logic" and "ethics" are used throughout this book (though

---

*osophy, Politics and Society*, 2d Series (Oxford: Basil Blackwell & Mott Ltd., 1962), p. 132 n. Reprinted from *Philosophical Review*, 1958).

not, I think, by most logicians and moral philosophers) to designate those most general canons of rational thought and action discernible at our present level of cultural development. The continued tension between ethics and logic on one hand and the philosophies of practices on the other is among the necessary conditions for continued cultural development.

That view of philosophy has at least one advantage: it accounts for the fact that the philosophies of some practices, such as mathematics, law, science, religion, and education, are alive and flourishing, while other practices associated with them, such as engineering, business, sport, war, and schooling, do not receive sustained philosophical inquiry despite the frequent complaint that they are most particularly in need of it. Each of the first set of practices, when seen from the inside, seems to be built on rules or principles which reveal some *distinctive* form that human reason can assume. To understand exactly what happens when we follow a scientific explanation is to understand something that is both distinctive to science and, at the same time, revelatory of a general capacity of the human mind. On the other hand the most abstruse calculation in a business transaction, whether that calculation is carried out in a businessman's head or in the corporation's computer, is only an elaborated version of the same *form* of reasoning that each of us engages in when we choose between fork and spoon at dessert. The means-end form of reasoning is certainly general enough, but studying the practice of business, or engineering, or war, or schooling reveals no distinctive *form* of reason—nothing we cannot learn more easily from the study of the behavior of simpler species of animals.

The practice of medicine over the past century has been enormously advanced by the assumption that it, too, embodies nothing but means-end reasoning based on causal laws. More recently, of course, that assumption has been challenged in all sorts of ways. Medical ethics has come to be the subject of sustained inquiry; just over the horizon lies a general recognition that the practice of medicine is a form of human interaction in which doctor and patient attempt cooperatively to extend the effectiveness of reason in promoting health. Under that description, philosophy of medicine is a most promising inquiry and, like philosophy of education, a most difficult one. Whenever we encounter a form of reason which appears distinctively in the *inter*action of human beings, we are dealing with something more elusive, less easily pinned down than the arguments, descriptions, theories, explanations, judicial decisions, and so on, which take on an independent existence when penned onto paper and there fixed for study. Electronic recording devices make it possible to reproduce the visual and auditory vibrations of a time-slice of reality in which human interaction occurs, but just what in that time-slice is *really* the practice of medicine or teaching is a question which the recording device, however sophisticated, cannot answer. But a philosophy of medicine or education must at least try.

And that's how I see philosophy of education: as an inquiry into the distinctive form that human reason takes in the practice of education—that is, in the interaction that generates the particular acts of teaching and learning. In its revelatory aspect, philosophy of education is an attempt to re-present the general features of human reason discernible in that practice. In its critical aspects it tries to discover whether the rules and presuppositions which define the practice of education at a given historical moment are authentic versions or corrupt perversions of human reason.

When we think about the practice of education today, our first thought is of schools, and, if we happen to be citizens of the United States (or of any heavily industrialized, capitalistic society, more or less), to think of schools is to think of the concatenating arrangements by which individual schools are linked together to form a national system of schooling, which we'll call "the System" for short.[3] Thus we would think that to look for the operative philosophy of education of our own time and place is to look for the philosophical principles and presuppositions which guide the actions of those in the System.

But today, for reasons that many have tried to grasp and communicate, philosophy seems to have lost its force—its power to charm or entice or whatever—in influencing the ideas and beliefs that permeate the System. Perhaps it's that academic philosophy has come to appear too arcane, too technical, to be of use to educators who want to think seriously and deeply about their work. Perhaps it's that we have lost our faith that radical thinking can have a positive effect in reforming our inherited institutions. However it is, the impression I get from participating in the credentialing services of the System is that very few even bother to regret that philosophy has ceased to be a significant force in our thinking about education. Both those who hold power and those who teach philosophy of education agree on one point: the study of philosophy is only a luxury, a little extra finishing touch for teachers and administrators. Philosophy has nothing to do with what they will *really* need to be effective functionaries in their assigned tasks.

As you probably anticipated, I disagree profoundly with that view.

[3] Efforts to institute rational planning for education on a national scale have required a detailed analysis of the various mechanisms—accreditation, admission standards, graduation requirements, certification, credentials, and so on—by which schools, colleges, and universities maintain an ordered relation to one another. "System" is merely a technical term designating all and only those institutions thus ordered. See Thomas F. Green and Emily Haynes: "Notes Toward a General Theory of Educational Systems," Educational Policy Research Center, Syracuse University, October 1972, 47 pp.

When philosophy of education, as defined above, loses its place in the intellectual life of our teachers and administrators, it is not, unfortunately, replaced by native, common-sense beliefs as guides to the practice of schooling. What happens is that the practice of schooling tends to generate its own operative "philosophy," which is a parody rather than a paradigm of philosophical reasoning. Right now, the parody of philosophy fashionable among the officeholders in our system of schools is behaviorism. Let us digress (briefly) from the main track of this discussion to see what "behaviorism" might mean. Then we shall return to the serious question of the relation of philosophy of education to the practice of schooling.

**VARIETIES**
**OF BEHAVIORISM**

The term "behaviorism" is about as open-textured as any you can find. It can be, and has been, cut up in all sorts of shapes.[4] The schema presented here has only one advantage: it makes clear the difference between the admirable and contemptible ideas that can be labeled "behaviorism." Contexts make clear what sense is intended as the term appears from time to time in the succeeding chapters.

Most basic, I suppose, is metaphysical behaviorism: the belief that for any possible agent A, and any possible action of that agent X, the only reality to which any statement "A did X" could refer is a physically observable movement of a physically locatable body. Metaphysical behaviorism is not an unattractive belief, especially if it is seen, as Gilbert Ryle saw it, as the only alternative to a metaphysical dualism, "postulating mysterious actions and reactions to correspond with certain familiar biographical episodic words."[5]

It's surely better to restrict one's metaphysics to behaviorism than to invent Ghosts in the Machines of whom we predicate unseen actions to explain those actions we do observe. Metaphysical behaviorism has its problems, but it is innocuous compared with certain other varieties of behaviorism. Ryle was not trying to change our use of "familiar biographical episodic words." He was arguing, rather, that our use of such words does not commit us to the belief in the reality of entities other

---

[4] See T. W. Wann, ed., *Behaviorism and Phenomenology: Contrasting Bases for Modern Psychology* (Chicago: University of Chicago Press, 1964), esp. articles by B. F. Skinner, Norman Malcolm, and Michael Scriven. For brief historical background, see Howard Racklin, *Introduction to Modern Behaviorism* (San Francisco: W. H. Freeman and Company Publishers, 1970), chap. I, bibliography. *The Encyclopedia of Philosophy*, ed. Paul Edwards, 1967, contains two informative, analytical articles on behaviorism: "Behaviorism" by Arnold S. Kaufman (I, 268–273) and "Psychological Behaviorism" by Charles Taylor (VI, 516–520).

[5] Gilbert Ryle, *The Concept of Mind* (New York: Barnes & Noble, 1949), p. 153.

than physical bodies and their observable behavior. The problems in Ryle's view are as nothing compared to those in the view it attacked. (Which is not to say that anyone actually held the view Ryle attacked.)

Epistemological behaviorism is not so easily characterized and evaluated. We may distinguish here, as at many other points in this book, between benign and malignant varieties of the belief we're considering. The benign variety of epistemological behaviorism is related to and supportive of metaphysical behaviorism. The sort of evidence that comes closest to being conclusive warrant for any statement of the form "A did X" is observation of A's movements. The alternative would be, or at least seem to be, some form of mysticism. Whether A's knowledge of "A did X" is grounded in observation is a philosophically controversial point. But if he wishes to become or remain sane, A would be well advised to check from time to time to see that his belief that he did X (and not Y, or not merely dreamed it, or whatever) is confirmed by competent external observers. Thus, epistemological behaviorism may not capture a universal truth, but it does embody sound advice. (We shall discover other philosophical doctrines that are best understood as good advice.)

The malignant version of epistemological behaviorism shades into semantic behaviorism, which is a real, albeit not the worst, villain in the piece. The doctrine is: to know that A did X is to know that A made certain movements; or, semantically speaking, the meaning of "A did X" is exhausted by a complex claim "A made movements $M_1, M_2 \ldots M_n$, at times-places, $t_1 - p_1, t_2 - p_2, \ldots$." Now semantic behaviorism is not, as the earlier mentioned varieties are, compatible with our ordinary speech habits. By the canons of semantic behaviorism, the following three statements all mean the same thing:

A looked toward the sign.
A saw the sign.
A read the sign.

But they don't mean the same thing in English. So the semantic behaviorist must embark on a program to change our speech habits in order to preserve his thesis. The most obvious (and, if properly limited, admirable) program can reasonably be attributed to B. F. Skinner: simply purge the language of all those ways of talking about human action that don't analyze easily and unambiguously into talk about observable movements. Thus, one would not be allowed to say: "Karen is studying the board, trying to decide how to answer her opponent's knight gambit." One could say: "Karen's forehead is wrinkling, the forefinger on her left hand is moving up and down with no discernible rhythm, her shoulders . . . and so on." The Skinnerian excision, in effect, takes out of the language the most natural and normal ways of talking about human action, namely second-person questions and first-person answers. In ordinary speech, "A did X," a third-person report, takes its meaning from an actual or possible question to A, "What were you doing?" answered by A's saying, "I was Xing." After the Skinnerian amputation, "A did X" takes what meaning it has from reports about observable movements of various parts of A's anatomy.

The vocabulary permitted after a Skinnerian purging is lean and clean, excellent for reporting changes in behavior under different schedules of reinforcement. A language of pure behaviorism also has distinct advantages in thinking about certain limited sorts of pedagogical encounters, particularly those in which learners are being brought to do things which the learners have not chosen to do.[6] What the language of Skinnerian behaviorism obviously *cannot* do is to serve as the medium for arguing that its restrictions ought to apply to all social and political discourse. But how else is the Skinnerian going to achieve his program of semantical behaviorism except by arguing for it in social and political discourse? Thus the Skinnerian must be either hypocritical or inconsistent if he undertakes to convince us that *all* language should be purged of "I and Thou" discourse—the sort of discourse in which actions such as arguing for things can be carried on.

The Skinnerian-type program may be labeled the purgative; it is aimed simply at purging the language of action predicates which do not satisfy semantic behaviorism. The purgative program fits very well with methodological behaviorism in experimental psychology. The costs and benefits of that "science" and its linguistic vehicle are being debated at length these days and need no comment here.

In contrast to the open (and necessarily limited) purgative program of semantic behaviorism is the concealed tyranny of the reductionist program. The latter program would allow us (how gracious of them!) to retain in our language all the action predicates of ordinary English but insist that we (re-)define them, using only terms that refer to observable movements. Thus the reductionist would allow such a statement as "Karen is studying the board, trying to figure out her move" but insist that the meaning of the statement is to be found in the conjunction of statements about the observed movements of various parts of Karen's body.

Apart from its connection with a crude verificationism (the doctrine that the meaning of any empirical statement is to be found in the set of

6 Cf. "B. F. Skinner's Philosophy of Human Nature" in B. P. Komisar and C. J. B. Macmillan, eds., *Psychological Concepts in Education* (Chicago: Rand McNally & Company, 1967), pp. 224–247. It should be noted that Skinner would probably not be content with the minimal and admirable program I have called Skinnerian.

statements verifying it), the program of reductionist behaviorism would seem to have nothing at all to recommend it. But in fact reductionism is thriving because of its political fusion with the last and vilest form of behaviorism, pedagogical behaviorism: the doctrine that teaching can be defined and described in terms which are purely behavioral in reference. The political strength of pedagogical behaviorism lies in a complex of bureaucrats and testers who understand education as something that can be predicted, measured, and controlled through mechanisms of political power. The dangers as well as conceptual confusion inherent in pedagogical behaviorism are obviously enormous, but they have been catalogued elsewhere and need no comment here.[7]

The relation of pedagogical behaviorism to philosophy of education is the point that does need making. Behaviorism stands to philosophy of education as nihilism to metaphysics, skepticism to epistemology, or cynicism to ethics. One's philosophical theory is always in danger of being reduced to a denial of exactly what it started out to account for. Philosophy of education is an attempt to reveal the distinctive form which human reason takes in the teaching encounter. If, in the course of attempting to provide a general theory of the teaching encounter, the philosopher multiplies entities that Occam's razor can scrape away, he may find that his account does not reveal but implicitly denies the function of reason in teaching. He hasn't escaped behaviorism; his account comes down to the description of physical movements. It has not, to my knowledge, ever occurred, but it could happen that one philosopher of education should do a Humean critique of another's theory, showing that the theory attacked could be reduced to behaviorism. To this point, theories in philosophy of education have not been stated with the degree of precision that would permit a reductionist analysis.

What is vile is to rest comfortably with pedagogical behaviorism and to enlist political support to make an antirational theory the official, operating philosophy of our institutions of schooling. The virtues that behaviorism is supposed to achieve—clarity in means-end discourse most prominent among them—do not require semantic reductionism at all. The closer one gets to the source of pedagogical behaviorism, the more one is inclined to believe that it is mostly a reflection of the nihilistic, skeptical, cynical system of power in our society. One is also inclined to regard persons who advocate pedagogical behaviorism as either knaves or fools, either persons who are grasping for power or willing helpers of others who are. Those inclinations must be understood and then transcended, for behaviorists, even pedagogical behaviorists, are human

---

[7] See Ralph A. Smith, ed., *Regaining Educational Leadership: Critical Essays . . .* (New York: John Wiley & Sons, Inc., 1975), especially editor's introduction and essays by Mauritz Johnson, Huge Petrie, Leonard Waks, Harry Broudy, and Donald Arnstine.

beings whose only crime is holding a set of false and confused beliefs. The situation calls not for hostility but for careful, cooperative thinking.

**PHILOSOPHY**          In sum, the correct treatment for a vile philosophy
**AND SCHOOLING**       of education is to bring it back into the main-
                        stream of philosophical thought and wash it clean.
For no philosophy of education (or of any other practice) can be sustained with integrity apart from a continuous and mutual involvement with other branches of philosophy. All of which is but to reiterate a simple truth which has been expressed often and convincingly by others.[8] It may not be clear how a particular theory in philosophy of education articulates with theories in another branch of the discipline; my arguments on the epistemology of learning (Chapter Three), for example, may not be as transparent to others as they seem to me. But overall, the relation of philosophy of education to the rest of philosophy is clear enough.

What is not clear at all is the relationship between philosophy of education and institutions of schooling. Here are my own views on the nature of that relationship, to be taken (if taken at all) only as a personal and possibly idiosyncratic basis for engaging in this branch of philosophy.

I know of no reliable studies on the question, but I should judge that most of the actual work done in philosophy of education in this country today is done in some relation to the credentialing services of the System. That relation may be quite direct and obvious—as when one is teaching a course in philosophy of education for people who must complete that course, among others, for a license to teach. Other work in philosophy of education may bear a much less direct relation to the System. But it would be foolish indeed to ignore the fact that of all the branches of philosophy, only philosophy of education has grown into its present form as part of a training program for institutional functionaries.

That historical accident has affected our conception of the nature of philosophy of education in many and profound ways. We have tended to include in the scope of philosophy of education *all* the philosophy that school teachers and administrators might find it valuable to know, but that, of course, includes all of philosophy. Which explains why the large textbooks in the field used to contain a mélange of everything.[9]

More insidiously, the connection between philosophy of education and

8 For example, by Israel Scheffler in his introduction to *Philosophy of Education: Modern Readings,* 2d ed. (Boston: Allyn & Bacon, Inc., 1966), pp 1–14.

9 The genre shamelessly perdures. See Charles D. Marler, *Philosophy and Schooling* (Boston: Allyn & Bacon, Inc., 1975).

the training functions of the System has influenced the way we tend to think about the concepts central to philosophy of education itself. Consider the concept of teaching: philosophical analyses have proceeded under the real, but mostly tacit, constraint that any theory of teaching must be tested against what happens in public school classrooms. But that constraint makes philosophy impossible. It's as if a philosophical analysis of justice had to accord with what happens in police courts.

In short, the historical accident that connected philosophy of education to the training and credentialing functions of the System has complicated things. But does that connection make it impossible to do honest work in this branch of philosophy? Let's see: there are obvious dangers of corruption and cynicism in any system of credentialing (and in the System as a whole, which is stuck together by the concrete power of credentials), but is the principle involved inherently immoral? What principle? Let us consider the case of teaching in a credentialing program in, say, the State of New York. The people of this state have decreed (through cumbersome, bureaucratic, legal, constitutional processes) that those who are to administer and teach in their public schools shall be rewarded if they have some acquaintance with philosophy of education. Like most state education authorities, those in New York find it difficult to determine whether "acquaintance" shall be defined as exposure in a course or as competence displayed either on examinations or in real (or simulated) field situations. That question, however, doesn't affect the principle we're following.

Now the principle: the people of the State of New York have also decreed that all children in this state shall attend school regardless of their or their parents' wishes on the matter. For most children, that decree is a decree to attend public schools. Under those conditions, to encourage teachers and administrators to study philosophy of education is to make it more likely that they will come to see education as a philosophically complex idea. And *that* principle seems eminently reasonable. The alternative is that schooling will come to be seen as an end in itself or that education will come to be identified (behavioristically) as training which serves the dominant classes in the society.

I don't believe that this principle was understood very well by those who founded the System and initiated the idea that normal preparation for service in schools should include an admixture of philosophy of education. It seems incontestable that the System-builders regarded "philosophy" as simply another name for a program to indoctrinate would-be teachers and administrators in the social, political, and pedagogical orthodoxies of their time and place. It also seems incontestable that those teachers and writers who were qualified by temperament and training to do *philosophy* of education simply would not, perhaps could not, take on the role of indoctrinators. The last quarter of the nineteenth century was not only the era which saw the structure of the System firmly riveted together; it was also an era of educational upheaval, one in which John Dewey emerges as *primus inter pares* in a large company of educators who saw philosophy not as a tool of indoctrination but as a standpoint for the radical reconstruction of schools as well as other political and economic institutions of American life.[10]

The rhetoric, if not the reality, of the System has thus been shaped in large part by a tradition of philosophical thought. And that is one reason, among others, for denying that philosophy of education is properly thought of as a mere luxury in the training of teachers and administrators in the System. If that tradition of philosophical thinking is not kept alive in the critical consciousness of the men and women who serve as teachers and administrators in the System, they will inevitably come to identify the concept of "education" with the ostensible goals of the System; they will identify "teaching" with what is done by those who have the role of teacher in the System; they will identify "learning" with a child's conforming to the System's expectations. Such identifications are totally pernicious. Those who are concerned about education should look upon the System as a band of early Christians might have looked upon the temple of a despised pagan god: it's a damned poor structure for the kind of interaction we engage in. Eventually, we'll want to tear it down, preserving only those materials we can use for our own purposes. In the meantime, it beats standing out in the rain.

Assuming that we wish to make philosophy of education an intellectually honest branch of the discipline and, at the same time, a source of practical guidance in pedagogical activities, our wisest course is to forget the System entirely and to inquire directly into the meaning of "education," "teaching," and "learning." Only when those concepts are understood does it make sense to ask what, if anything, should be done with the System. Let us begin with "education."

**EDUCATION
AS A CONCEPT
IN SOCIAL SCIENCE**

Looked at one way, education is simply a natural phenomenon, like any other natural phenomenon, subject to study by the methods of natural science. Education is a necessary condition for the survival of the human species: marvelous as our genetic processes are, they do not insure the learning of the myriad skills, knowledge, and other dispositions which make it possible for people to live in societies. And

---

[10] See Lawrence A. Cremin, *The Transformation of the School* (New York: Alfred A. Knopf, Inc., 1961). Also M. I. Berger, *The Settlement, The Immigrant and the Public School* (unpublished Ph.D. thesis, Columbia University, 1956).

people either live in societies, or they do not live at all. If we mean by "education" whatever happens to a bunch of human protoplasm such that it eventually becomes a person-in-society (and we have to put it that broadly to account for the succession of social roles that constitute being a person-in-society, the first stage of which begins well before birth), then education is clearly an object for study by the social sciences. Indeed, an understanding of education, thus broadly defined, is the major concern of all the social sciences. In principle, then, everything we might want to know about education should be found (eventually) in or by some branch of the social sciences.

One must avoid even the hint of condescension here. Many and important things about education have been discovered by research in the social sciences. There are many more things that it would be important to learn from that kind of research. Whether one is studying great global questions such as how the human species learned to use language, or small personal questions such as how one happened to learn to prefer one kind of music to another, one is well advised to follow the canons of all social science: keep your attention firmly fixed on what people (including yourself) actually *do*. Remember that what people say is often best understood by looking at what they are doing in (or by) saying it. Then try to understand how doing *that* would be reinforced by its "natural" consequences in the environment. Try to see what survival value for the social group (in some determinate environment) would attend a general tendency to act that way. Try to see how that way of acting (with attendant beliefs and feelings) in one sort of situation *fits* with the way one acts or is expected to act in other sorts of situations.

There is something immediately liberating in trying to think like a scientist about any human phenomenon, including education. To the extent that one succeeds in understanding one's own behavior in that way, one is likely to find it therapeutic as well.

But there is nothing of particular philosophical interest in looking at education as the social scientist looks at it. There are, of course, second-order philosophical questions about the theories and techniques of the social scientist, but these same questions arise whether the social scientist is studying education or toothaches. Both are, more or less, omnipresent concomitants of human existence. The difference is this: whatever else might occasion our interest in toothaches (it might be a practical concern to reduce their occurrence; it might be a purely intellectual curiosity about varied cultural responses to intense but usually nonlethal pain; and so on), interest could not arise from the meaning of "toothache." But "education" is sometimes puzzling in the distinctively philosophical way that terms such as "real" and "meaningless" and "value" and others are puzzling. And for much the same reasons.

What reasons? Let us look at "toothache" and "education" a bit more closely. The difference is not that judgments about toothaches are infallible while those about education are not. "I have a toothache" can go wrong in several ways. It might be said by a lying malingerer. It might be a mistake of a person who has an abscessed jawbone. It might be a linguistic error: a Spaniard who has learned English imperfectly might say "toothache" as a translation of "dolor de la cabeza." Or a person might have grown up with such great good fortune that he never had a toothache, consequently he wouldn't know what "toothache" means (in the sense that people who have suffered toothaches know what the term means): thus he might say "I have a toothache" to describe the momentary discomfort of a spoon scraping a canine. The point is this: although the sentence "I have a toothache" can go wrong in several different ways, we have no difficulty in sorting out those ways or in deciding which (one or combination) of them applies in any particular case in which the sentence does go wrong.

But with "education" it is different. *If* we use the term just as the social scientist might use it (first paragraph of this section), *then* a sentence constructed on the model "B is an educated person" can go wrong in only two ways: (i) the name for "B" does not designate a person at all, or (ii) the name for "B" designates some feral person who has no role whatsoever in any human society. [There is a historically sanctioned use of the term "person" in which (ii) is simply an instance of (i).] In either case, if two persons should disagree on whether B is an educated person, their dispute would be equivalent to disagreement on whether B is a person-in-society. But that simply is not what we ordinarily mean when we affirm or deny that a person is educated. Thus the broad definition of "education," useful as it may be in the social sciences, does not capture the nuances of the use of "education" in ordinary discourse, including the practical discourse of teachers, parents, legislators, and others who make decisions about education.

This disparity between the neutral, scientific use of "education" and other uses of the term sometimes leads the social scientist to coin other words to make his meaning clearer. Thus he may say "acculturation," or "enculturation," or "socialization," or he may use all those terms and stipulate distinctions among them. The time may come when the term "education" is used exclusively in its neutral, scientific sense. This has happened to "culture" already. Every human society, we now recognize, possesses a culture, its distinctive "cup of life" as one of Ruth Benedict's respondents once put it. However primitive or sophisticated, however deprived or privileged the group, each has its own culture. To say of the primitive or deprived person that he lacks culture is obviously to be guilty of ethnocentrism. The sin does not lie in making a norma-

tive judgment but in the fact that the normative judgment is not consciously and deliberately *that*—more specifically, that the grounds or
bases of the normative judgment are not rendered in explicit, critical
form.

So also with "education." When we talk about education, we ordinarily mean a particular *way of becoming* a person-in-society. When we
say that a person is educated or uneducated, we ordinarily mean that
he's one *kind* of person-in-society or that he's not. If the word "education" were neutralized, we should still need to make those distinctions;
very likely we would borrow or invent other terms for that purpose. If
what follows is read as a discourse on the meaning of the English *word*
"education," then it fails its purpose. It is concerned rather with certain
fundamental evaluations that lie at the very center of our communal
life. We shall find that analysis of the word "education" will take us
only to the starting point of the inquiry, but to make the right start on
a fundamental question is itself no mean achievement.

**EDUCATION**
**AS A PROCESS?**

Debate on whether or not to make education the
preferred or socially favored form of child rearing
could not get started, then, if "education" meant
any way of bringing up children that happened to be followed by some
social group. No one is likely to make *that* conceptual error—to praise
or condemn education while stipulating that absolutely any old way of
bringing up children is to be labeled "education." But there is a somewhat similar error which lots of people, including those who should
know better, make all the time: that error is to assume that one underlying process really *is* education, which process any actual form of dealing with children approximates or promotes, more or less. Since this
notion of *process* is going to reappear in many guises throughout
this book—as in the phrases "process of teaching," "process of learning," "*the* teaching-learning process"—it's well to scotch the mistake as
soon as possible. To do that, let me again distinguish between a benign
and a malignant use of an expression—in this case, the expression "process of education."

(a) *Benign.* At right angles to the distinction between the (supposedly)
value-neutral context of the social sciences and other contexts in which
"education" appears we can draw another distinction between "education as product" and "education as process." On the one hand we can
say: "By her twenty-first birthday she had acquired an Ivy-league education and a second-hand Ford." On the other hand we can say: "Her
education is coming along splendidly, thank you, but I'm concerned

about her digestion." It is the second of these which Max Black had in mind when he wrote of "a conception of 'education' as activity . . . a doing something."[11]

That process-product distinction is simple and clear enough. I find it hard to believe that failure to make that distinction actually brings about failure of communication. But it might happen, if not in the use of "education" then in the use of "revolution" or "alienation" or certain other very general concepts in respect to which the same distinction should be made.

It is still within the realm of the benign to ask which of those uses is primary and which derivative. It's an enlightening exercise in the history of educational thought to ask of major educational thinkers whether they gave primacy to the product or process of education in their theories. Sometimes it seems to be one, sometimes the other. Plato in the *Republic* seems to put major emphasis on the product—the peculiar combination of knowledge and attitudes which must be instilled in each member of the guardian class if that class is to be equipped to carry out its political function. At other times, as in the *Theaetetus*, Plato wrote as if a quite specific intellectual activity or process were the true essence of education. Invoking the distinction between education as process and as product can help to increase the clarity of our understanding of any significant educational theorist, up to a point. But beyond that point, it's

(b) *Malignant.* For directly one takes the sentence "Education is a process" as saying something *about* education—as opposed to noting one half of a simple distinction—one is on the road to confusion. For one is tempted to ask, "What, exactly, *is* a process?" and "What kind of process, exactly, is education?" All that one could mean sensibly by saying that education is a process is something that cannot be rendered exactly; it's merely to note that we can use the word "education" to mean something happening in and through time, something people engage in or do—as well as something they have or (substituting the past participle "educated" for "education") have come to be.

But in certain contexts the word "process" does mean something exact. Photosynthesis is a process; so are radioactive decay, classical conditioning, digestion, and thousands of other things as studied in various sciences. We could say exactly what it is about each of these things that makes the term "process" appropriate, but it is quite a difficult, technical task to do so. We might begin by saying:

F is a process if and only if F consists of an ordered sequence of transformations in the conditions, $C_1, C_2, . . ., C_n$, of a structure of elements, $e, e', . . . ,$ *and* there

11 Max Black, *Critical Thinking* (New York: Prentice-Hall, Inc., 1946), p. 177.

exists a set of laws, L, such that according to L, if $C_1$ obtains at $t_1$, then the properties of $e, e', \ldots,$ make it necessary that at $t_2$, $C_2$ obtains; at $t_3$, $C_3$ and so on to $C_T$, the terminating condition of F.

But that definition of F is only the beginning. What it *asserts* is the regularity in an ordered sequence of transformations; what it *presupposes* is that there are still more fundamental regularities as captured in L. Thus the laws of chemistry, by virtue of which we explain photosynthesis and digestion as processes, are, relative to the biology of these processes, more fundamental in a sense that is fairly obvious but enormously difficult to state with precision. We have to be able to abstract the elements in each $C_1$, $C_2$, $\ldots$, $C_n$ from any particular, existential circumstances, such as photosynthesis from a leaf, digestion from the bowels, conditioning from the laboratory, and so on.

Further, to *explain* process F is to show the logical necessity in the ordered sequence of transformations in F from $C_1$ to $C_T$—that is, from the initial to the terminating set of conditions. If L contains any description of stages or sequences or the like, the explanation of F is essentially incomplete, for one would then have to show, relative to still more fundamental laws, the logical necessity of the transformations in L. Photosynthesis *can* be recounted as a story: "First there is this green stuff, then the sun shines on it, then. . . ." But if photosynthesis is to be explained *as a process,* the elements of which green stuff is made up must be described in chemical terms to which *non*processual chemical laws can be applied.[12]

The remarks just above constitute only the prologue, not the analysis, of the concept of process in its full, technical sense. But enough has been said, I hope, to justify the one point for which this talk about process was introduced: when we use such expressions as "the process of education," the "process of teaching," ". . . of learning," ". . . of development," ". . . of growth," "the teaching-learning process," and so on, we are not talking about, or referring to, or presupposing the existence of, any *process* in the full, technical sense. When we use those expressions in such a way as to suggest that there *is* some specific process we're talking about, the term "process" is malignant and should be excised. For example:

Q: Has Joanne learned the square of opposition yet?
A₁ (Benign use of "process"): No, but she's in the process of doing so.
A₂ (Malignant use of "process"): No, but she's engaged in the learning process.
A₃ (A₂ after surgery): No, but she's trying to learn it.

So, is education a process? The most sensible way to deal with that

12 Cf. Ernest Nagel, *The Structure of Science* (New York: Harcourt Brace Jovanovich, Inc., 1961), pp. 428–446.

question is to ask that it be recast. Education is something that happens in and over time; it is something that people engage in, more or less deliberately. It is also something that people try to achieve by doing other things (for example, by going to college) and in doing things to other people (for example, in teaching philosophy). In sum, nothing is to be gained by either affirming or denying that education is a process.

**CRITERIA**       As long as the word "education" served chiefly a
**OF A DEFINITION**   ceremonial function at graduation exercises and
**OF EDUCATION**    budget hearings, no very precise meaning needed
to be attached to it. Whatever it might be, education was a good thing and more of it a better thing. Now we're not so sure. A pervasive skepticism about the value of education can be felt everywhere. I don't mean merely among the snobs who today, as always, deplore giving education to the masses on the grounds that doing so dilutes Culture and spoils the minds of those who must toil for their bread. Such *gusanos* are found more or less everywhere; they must be invited to leave the woodwork and re-educate themselves.[13]

Nor is the skepticism found only among those who doubt that the System can become (again?) an effective mechanism for bringing education to those who need or want it. The System, admittedly, is out of control; or, to say the same thing in other words, no matter who or how many may believe it, no thought or idea can significantly alter the activities carried on in schools. Those administrators charged with keeping things going from day to day have their hands and minds full of doing just that. Those at the highest political levels who are charged with thinking about the future of the institution are afflicted with boredom, cynicism, and chronic triviality. Harry Broudy, a major architect of contemporary philosophy of education as well as a devoted friend of the System, compares the forty-six million Americans who are involved, one way or another, with schools to a vast army on a centuries-long campaign with no general—or, more realistically, "to thousands of herds of varying sizes, all moving more or less in the same general direction at different speeds over a vast terrain."[14]

But even if, by some miracle, we could direct the System toward education, would that be what we really want to do? Put this way, the

---

13 The problem is serious, for under- and unemployed holders of advanced degrees (both arts and professional degrees) were easy converts to Fascism during the 1930's. See Karl Mannheim, *Man and Society in an Age of Reconstruction* (London: Routledge and Kegan Paul Ltd., 1951), pp. 98–108.

14 *The Real World of the Public Schools* (New York: Harcourt Brace Jovanovich, Inc., 1972), p. 23.

question begins to touch deeper veins of skepticism among us. Some might put it that education is too cognitive, that our pedagogical efforts should be directed more toward the affective life of children. Others might put it, more sensibly, that (liberal) education is and, given its intractable, historical roots, must be essentially literary and aristocratic in character, hence inappropriate as a way of initiating youth into the technical, egalitarian culture which alone gives the human species any chance of surviving this century. The more we ponder arguments such as these, the more we doubt that we are quite clear on what education really is, once we have distinguished it from schooling and from the extraneous, social-class-striped mannerisms that come in varying degree with years of schooling.

A recent and serious proposal to separate education from schooling, institutionally as well as conceptually, is Carl Bereiter's *Must We Educate?*[15] His thesis is deceptively simple: schools would be OK places if they restricted their activities to child care and skill training, both of which they could do well if they gave up the effort to provide education. And they ought to give up trying to educate anyway, for teachers have no *right* to educate other people's children. What does Bereiter mean by "education"?

Education is a matter of purpose and focus. To educate a child is to act with the purpose of influencing the child's development as a whole person. What you do may vary. You may teach him, you may play with him, you may structure his environment, you may censor his television viewing, or you may pass laws to keep him out of bars.[16]

So you may. But does doing any one or combination of those things mean that you are engaged in education? Not necessarily, acknowledges Bereiter, for "you may do any of these things for purposes other than to educate the child." But when *do* those things constitute education? Answer: When done by those who deliberately "set out to influence in [a] profound way the kind of person that the child is becoming."

That's getting pretty close, but it's still not quite there. For Bereiter doesn't mean that an adult who set out to turn a normal child into a madman to exhibit in a freak show would be engaged in education. If the adult who teaches the child (or "structures his environment," or whatever) is engaged in *education,* then that person must be trying to influence the child in ways that the adult believes to be of *benefit* to the child. Ordinarily, this means that the adult tries to influence the child to become the kind of person the adult is or would like to be. Bereiter uses the expression "whole person" throughout his book to indicate that

[15] Carl Bereiter, *Must We Educate?* (Englewood Cliffs, N.J.: Prentice-Hall, Inc., 1972).
[16] Ibid., p. 6.

sort of concern; if you're educating the child, you're trying to give him the values, skills, dispositions, and so on that you believe important to becoming a good *person*. Bereiter's case against education in schools is precisely that: since parents "are the only ones who have a clear-cut right to educate,"[17] it follows that teachers have no right to try to turn children into the kind of whole persons that they (the teachers) believe to be good.

I'm not concerned right here with the merits of Bereiter's moral and political arguments, but rather with what he means by "education." When the various components of his more or less implicit definition are put together, they constitute a start toward what had earlier become the standard analysis of "education"—that given by R. S. Peters.[18] Peters' essay toward an analysis reflects quite accurately, I believe, the actual status of the concept in the English-speaking world. On the one hand, neither the present use of "education" in English nor its etymological history (in Latin or English) permits any precise definition. It's not merely a vague term (one whose domain of application has no precise boundaries); it's not merely an ambiguous term (one that has two or more domains of application). It's not even clear in respect to any use of "education" that there is a central meaning which can be called on to explain the peripheral usages, as, for example, when Bereiter talks about legislating children out of bars as part of *education*.

On the other hand, it is absolutely clear that we need a concept which distinguishes two very different sorts of things: the socialization of the young into a society as it just happens to happen (as a more or less inevitable by-product of the on-going life of a society) and the socialization that is consciously, deliberately contrived to accord with fairly explicit standards of rationality and benevolence. What Peters' analysis both indicates and advances, I believe, is a tendency to restrict the word "education" to the latter. There is, then, a distinctive concept of *education*, but one that has not yet been framed in appropriate semantical and syntactical rules, so as to be clearly and specifically designated as the meaning of the English *word* "education."

What Peters points to in our present usage is very like what Bereiter had started to say. Both recognize at the outset that "education" does not designate any particular activities or practices but rather indicates a kind of purpose or intention with which one might engage in pedagogi-

---

17 Carl Bereiter, "Schools Without Education," *Harvard Educational Review* 42:3 (August 1972), 391.

18 Particularly in Chapter One, "Criteria of 'Education,'" of *Ethics and Education* (Glenview, Ill.: Scott, Foresman & Company, 1967). Also see R. S. Peters, ed., *The Concept of Education* (London: Routledge & Kegan Paul Ltd., 1967), especially essays by Peters, Paul H. Hirst, G. Vesey, and Gilbert Ryle.

cal activities of various sorts, where "pedagogical activities" means those designed to produce learning in another. Peters summarizes a complex treatise of how education can be distinguished from other sorts of pedagogical activity by saying that "the criteria implicit in central cases of 'education' are . . .

(i) that education implies the transmission of what is worthwhile to those who become committed to it;

(ii) that 'education' must involve knowledge and understanding and some kind of cognitive perspective which are not inert;

(iii) that 'education' at least rules out some procedures of transmission, on the grounds that they lack wittingness and voluntariness on the part of the learner."[19]

If we take Peters' definition as I think we should take it, it is directed not toward the use of the word "education" in English but toward the *concept* of education as that concept is slowly penetrating our social consciousness: a concept marking off a distinctive way of inducting the young into society, one which is constrained by certain logical and ethical criteria. I think it fair to say that Peters had already formulated precisely the idea that Bereiter was groping for with his weakly phrased remarks about the "whole person." It might seem, then, that if Peters' definition is accurate, the practice of philosophy of education should declare itself completed. Question: Would we not cease the practice of epistemology if we could formulate a definition that captured our concept of knowledge? Answer: Only if our concept of knowledge were itself free from ambiguities and inconsistencies.

And likewise for Peters' definition of education. It does reflect quite accurately, I believe, the most general beliefs about education held (or coming to be held) by the concerned and reflective segments of our society. But these beliefs are themselves confused and superficial. The grammatical awkwardness in each of the three sentences quoted above is a clue, for Peters writes taut and elegant sentences when his ideas are clear. But here he is reflecting our own ideas back to us, and the result is a muddle.

Consider just one obvious question: What are we to do when conflicts arise from the application of these three very different sets of criteria? Many different conflicts might arise, but one *must* arise: criterion (i) mandates pedagogical intentions that will inevitably require pedagogical actions prohibited by (iii). To speak vulgarly, if you start out committed to transmitting what's worth while to kids in such a way that the *kids* will become committed to it, you're inevitably going to violate their "wittingness and voluntariness." And you'll not succeed in concealing

---

[19] *Ethics and Education*, p. 20.

that conflict by any interspersed twaddle about "knowledge and understanding and cognitive perspective."

To repeat, the muddle lies not in Peters' formulation but in the concept itself. We have come a long way in recognizing (a) that there *is* a concept of education that can be distinguished from socialization, and (b) that (a) poses some pretty severe strains on our institutions of mass schooling. Peters and Bereiter take positions in respect to (b) that are so predictably English and American as to be almost caricatures. Peters assumes that reasonable men and women can make adjustments to their inherited institutions on an *ad hoc* basis and then *somehow* muddle through to an acceptable reform of those institutions. Bereiter assumes that collective action motivated by a commitment to what is worthwhile is (or inevitably leads to) tyranny. That assumption leads Bereiter to claim that the only safe function for a public institution is a narrowly circumscribed technical function: in the case of schools, child care and training in the 3 R's. Within that assumption (which, by the way, is not an unreasonable one in the context of the American historical experience) one can feel sympathy with Bereiter's insistence that the resolution of the conflict between Peters' criteria (i) and (iii) must lie with individual parents. But it's a hard choice. In Bereiter's little book one doesn't sense, as one always does sense in Peters' writing, a background *community* of men and women trying to grope their way to a common resolution of the conflicts inherent in our conception of education. Apart from membership in such a community, parenthood is a corrosive enterprise.

Is it possible to frame a definition of "education" which is both (i) internally precise and consistent and (ii) accurate as a description of the use of the word in serious and informed discourse? The answer is obviously no, if my assessment of our current state of consciousness is correct. But we don't have to stop there: whatever else the concept of education should do, it should capture our very highest and most consistent conceptions of teaching and learning. When we get our ideas about teaching and learning perfectly straight, the concept of education will take care of itself.

A final word on the criteria for evaluating any instance of doing philosophy of education.

(a) Is it done well?
(b) Is it worth doing?

The critical discipline of philosophy is the only way to determine an answer to (a). The arguments are either clear or confused. If clear, they're either valid or fallacious. If valid, they contain premises that are either true or false. And when the confused, fallacious, and false elements have been identified and removed, the remaining conceptual structure either reflects our most comprehensive conception of what teaching and learning ought to be, or it does not. Only to the extent that it does, can the answer to (a) be in the affirmative.

And that still leaves (b), which can be answered only by reference to some larger purpose into which this activity fits. In my view, philosophy of education is worth doing only in relation to building a rational and loving world community. One indispensable aspect of such a world is education for all youngsters. Education—not conditioning, not indoctrination. We make that distinction clear not only to guide our present pedagogical practices but also to illuminate our most fundamental political and ethical commitments: no existing political system can claim our loyalty if its preservation depends on substituting conditioning or indoctrination for education. No political movement can enlist our support except as it is also an educational movement. And no philosophy of education is worth doing except as that activity expresses and develops the sense of a worldwide human community in each of us.

# CHAPTER TWO

# The Generic
# Concept
# of Teaching

**SOCRATES**
**AND THE SLAVE BOY**
It is traditional to begin philosophy of education with Plato's *Meno*. It is also very convenient for the chapters that follow to have a straightforward example of a teaching encounter against which to test various arguments about the nature or definition of teaching. Since Socrates' teaching a geometrical theorem to Meno's slave boy is exemplary in many ways, let us recall that episode to see exactly what it was intended to prove.

Uncharacteristically for a Platonic dialogue, the *Meno* begins with a point-blank question: "Can you tell me, O Socrates, whether men learn virtue by teaching or by practice? Or if neither learned nor inherited, how then is virtue acquired?" Characteristically, Socrates dodges this direct question by feigning ignorance of a point the question presupposes—in this case, an answer to the logically prior question: "What is virtue?" The major arguments in the dialogue derive from Meno's attempts to define virtue and defend his answers against Socrates' challenges.

The nature of those challenges shows that Socrates had, in effect, forced Meno to accept a very stringent criterion: the definition is not adequate unless it states the necessary and sufficient conditions for the application of the term (*Meno*, 73D)! It is not enough, in other words, to explain what the term means by pointing out members of the class to which the term applies. Meno attempted the latter several times in his effort to define virtue; each time Socrates rebuked him for calling out "a swarm of virtues" while Socrates had asked what virtue *is*, "whole and entire."

At that point, some readers feel sympathy for Meno in his struggle; others feel disgust for his snobbish stupidity. But once it is clear what the rules are, it is also clear that Meno had lost the game: he never understood quite what was going on. It is doubtful that Socrates was fully aware that his criterion posed such an overwhelming problem.

After all, it *looks* fairly simple: If we are able to recognize instances of K when we see them, then in principle we ought to be able to state the necessary and sufficient conditions for any X's being a member of K. When Meno is about to withdraw in anger, Socrates encourages him to continue the inquiry by posing a somewhat fanciful explanation for our feeling that we really do *know* what virtue is, even when we cannot *say* what it is: Socrates suggests that we once knew but now have forgotten. But how could that be? Well, our souls are immortal; they learned those things a long time ago. If we will only think clearly (and that means, above all, recognizing how confused we really are even concerning matters on which we have very confident opinions), then we can recollect our previously held knowledge. If that is what inquiry really is, then we do not have to resign in sophistic despair at our apparent ignorance; we can push ahead with reasonable assurance that our efforts to learn will prove successful.

Aye, but what evidence do we have that that fanciful story (that immortal souls have always known all knowable things) is *true*? It's just here that the encounter with the slave boy gets its point. If Socrates can elicit a geometrical theorem from him, without, as he says, *teaching him anything*, then it must follow that he knew that geometrical theorem before. But Meno can guarantee that the slave boy hasn't been taught any geometry in *this* life. Therefore, he must have learned it somewhere else. Then, if what is true of the slave boy is true of men in general (and why shouldn't it be?—he was a purely random selection), and if what is true of knowing a geometrical theorem is true of knowing things such as the definition of virtue (and one can easily see a certain formal similarity), then success in the experiment with the slave boy will provide evidence for Socrates' conjecture that learning is recollecting.

And so the demonstration proceeds. The slave boy confidently asserts that doubling the side of a square will double its area, only to discover that he was wrong. Perhaps, he conjectures, increasing the length of the side by half will double the area. But again no. Now the slave boy must admit his ignorance. Whereupon Socrates draws a diagonal and invites the slave boy to consider the size of the square constructed on it. Sure enough, it turns out to be twice the area of the original square. The slave boy now has a true opinion about the necessary and sufficient conditions for constructing a square twice the size of a given square. Socrates could surely fill in the missing premises so that the boy could supply a rigorous proof and thereby have warrant to claim knowledge of the theorem that a square constructed on the diagonal of a given square is twice the size of the given square (Theorem $\theta$ henceforth). The experiment is successful; its outcome encourages Meno to pursue the inquiry with a trace more honesty, diligence, and humility than he had shown previously.

(In the dialogue, of course, this straightforward argument is placed in counterpoint with the drama of Socrates' interchange with Meno and Anytus, an event which is perhaps apocryphal but even so, in Plato's account, poignantly ironic and allusive throughout. It's hard to say whether the inconclusive ending of the dialogue has more to do with drama or logic; perhaps Plato would not approve so sharp a separation of the two.)[1]

There are several questionable points about this teaching encounter. First, why would Socrates initially claim that he was not teaching but later admit that the sort of thing he was doing could be called teaching? (Cf. *Meno* 84D with 87B.) It is easy enough to understand the historical, circumstantial reasons for Socrates's reluctance to use the word "teaching" ($\delta\iota\delta\acute{\alpha}\xi\epsilon\iota\nu$, whence our word "didactic") in this connection. The social form that all Hellenes would regard as teaching was the interaction between pedagogue and pupil: the pedagogue reciting a line of Homer and the pupil repeating that line after him. What occurred when Socrates brought the slave boy around to a right opinion about Theorem $\theta$ differed sufficiently from the typical encounter of pedagogue and pupil to make one reluctant to use the same word for both activities.

But if the difference between these activities is substantial, so also is their similarity. In the end, Socrates succumbs to common sense and uses the term "teach" (at first a little self-consciously and then quite naturally) to describe all sorts of activities that differ in important respects not only from the typical pedagogue-pupil encounter but also from his own encounter with the slave boy. And that fact sets the first philosophical question: Just what is it about those different sorts of activities

---

1 Jacob Klein, *A Commentary on Plato's Meno* (Chapel Hill: The University of North Carolina Press, 1965).

that makes it natural to describe them all by the same term? Teaching is interesting philosophically not just because there are borderline cases where we aren't sure whether or not to apply the term (*that's* true of "chair") but because it is so difficult to say exactly what it is about the clear cases that makes us sure that the term applies. Thus understanding what teaching is is like understanding what virtue is and unlike understanding what a chair is.

But please notice a second curious thing about this slave-boy episode in the *Meno*. The demonstration was supposed to lend plausibility to an explanation of how learning is possible. The curious thing is that that fanciful account does not explain learning at all. Suppose, *mirabile dictu,* that the "soul is immortal and has been born many times, and has seen all things both here and in the other world" (*Meno, 81C*). From that it does *not* follow that the soul "has learned everything there is" (ibid., W. K. G. Guthrie translation). It may be true by the application of Murphy's Law (given enough time, anything that can happen will happen) that if the soul is immortal, it has somewhere, sometime learned everything it *can* learn. But even with Murphy's Law the account in the *Meno* doesn't explain how the soul can learn anything at all. It seems to have encouraged Socrates and Meno in their inquiry to hold that they were only seeking to recollect what they had learned previously. But in the absence of any conception of how learning is possible, Socrates' story could have been discouraging rather than the reverse. Perhaps the nature of virtue is simply one of those things we could not and did not learn previously; hence it is fruitless to attempt to recollect it now. The success of the slave boy in recollecting what *we* already know provides no assurance that our joint pursuit of the unknown will catch anything worth having.

In the *Republic,* of course, Plato changes this account in some significant ways so that it does, at least formally, satisfy certain conditions for a theory of learning. Persephone's "other world" mentioned casually in the *Meno* becomes the realm of pure ideas; the individual soul, while dwelling in that realm, shares certain properties with pure ideas (immortality, immateriality). There the soul knows ideas directly.

Plato made other uses of the idea that the soul gains knowledge in the "other world." In the so-called Myth of Er in the *Republic* (614–621) the knowledge gained in the other world should encourage us to pursue virtue and shun evil; in the *Phaedo* (75–78) the same idea is used as the basic premise in the argument for human immortality. But in none of these accounts is the explanation of learning any more satisfactory than in the *Meno*. Even if one grants Plato his fanciful story of a world of pure Ideas in which the soul dwells with perfect understanding, we have no clues to explain how the soul comes to grasp, apprehend, incorporate

(?!) any Idea. Learning in this world, as Plato always insisted, is a mental activity mediated by the senses. But in the "other world," where are our senses? Plato would seem to leave us our "eyes" so that we can "see" pure essences when we are pure spirit. But even with "eyes" we would have to learn that *that* pure Idea is the idea of Justice, *that* of Piety, and so on. And there's nothing in Plato's account to explain how *that* learning is possible.

There may be a larger point here. Perhaps no purely rationalist epistemology can account for the sensory, processual, temporal character of learning. And perhaps no purely empiricist epistemology can account for the distinction between learning something true and learning something false. The two ideas are related, of course. If we call what Socrates was doing teaching, we would have to call the slave boy's activity learning. But the slave boy differs from a pupil in the typical pedagogical encounter in just the way that Socrates differs from a typical pedagogue. And Plato's imagery was specifically intended to reveal that difference. What the typical pedagogue taught and pupil learned could be true or false; truth or falsity varied independently of the success of teaching. What Socrates taught the slave boy had to be true, else learning could not occur.

By a slight exercise of the imagination, we may make that contrast quite stark: Suppose Socrates had used his stick to beat the slave boy rather than to draw geometrical figures in the sand. He could have brought it about that on hearing the question: "How can one double the size of a square?" the slave boy would respond: "A square erected on the diagonal of a given square is twice the size of the given square."[2] Under those conditions we would not hesitate to say that Socrates had taught the slave boy something. We would hesitate only a moment before agreeing that the boy had learned something. But can we find a description of "something" which applies both to what Socrates had taught and what the boy had learned? Now we must hesitate for more than a moment. About the episode recounted by Plato, we say that Socrates taught the slave boy Theorem $\theta$, that the slave boy learned Theorem $\theta$, that he understood Theorem $\theta$, that he believed Theorem $\theta$, and (since Theorem $\theta$ is true) that when he had learned a few additional theorems with which he could produce an adequate demonstration of Theorem $\theta$, the slave boy could claim correctly that he *knew* Theorem $\theta$. But if Socrates had beat the boy till he could produce a cor-

2 H. I. Marrou, *A History of Education in Antiquity* (New York: Sheed & Ward, 1956), p. XVI. "The ears of the stripling are on his back. He hears when he is being beaten." Marrou is here quoting an ancient Egyptian inscription; didactic teaching for literacy seems everywhere to have been the same, perhaps because the relation of written symbol to spoken word is inherently arbitrary.

rect recital of Theorem $\theta$ on command, we could not say any of those things. We could say that Socrates had taught the boy to repeat Theorem $\theta$ on command and that the boy had learned to repeat it. It is likely that the boy would also have learned to fear old men, hard sticks, and geometry, but it is not clear that Socrates had taught him those things. It might even be the case that the slave boy had learned—had come to understand and be on the road to knowing—Theorem $\theta$. But nothing about beating a boy on the back leads one to expect that kind of intellectual achievement.

These are our problems, then: to understand, first, how such very different human encounters are gathered under the heading of "teaching" and, second, what makes learning, apparently so simple an idea, a concept about which Plato and his latter-day successors, such as psychologists, have to invent myths. Like Plato, we shall assume that to understand a philosophically significant concept means (perhaps among other things) to understand the necessary and sufficient conditions for the correct application of the term designating that concept.[3] To understand what teaching is is (at least *first*) to understand the use of the verb "teach" in English.

**THE TEACHING CLAIM**

Consider, then, this grammatical paradigm in which we can express both Plato's account of Socrates and the slave boy as well as our less happy re-account of the episode:

|   |   |   |
|---|---|---|
| A teach_____ | B _____ | X |
| (tensed verb) | that | |
| | the | |
| | how to | |
| | to | |
| | when to | |
| | who(m) | |
| | why | |
| | how | |
| | when | |
| | etc. | |

When any sentence generated from that paradigm is asserted, it makes what is to be called a *teaching claim*. We use the word "teach" in many

---

[3] Cf. Richard Robinson: *Definition* (Oxford: The Clarendon Press, 1954), chap. VI.

ways other than to make teaching claims, of course. We say: When experience teaches, only fools fail to learn. That's wisdom, but it isn't a teaching claim. I believe that making teaching claims is the underlying, root use of "teach" from which all other uses are derived; to establish that belief in the logical grammar of natural language(s) is, however, beyond my purpose as well as my power. In any event, understanding the teaching claim is what's important for philosophy of education.

Thus we have two very different teaching claims. Plato's account: Socrates taught the slave boy that Theorem $\theta$. Our re-account: Socrates taught the slave boy to repeat Theorem $\theta$ on command. It's the genius of a natural language that we would never be inclined to confuse the two, never be inclined to think that one implies the other, never look at evidence which confirms the one as confirming the other. The absolute generality of the paradigm is what makes possible such subtle but vital distinctions among teaching claims.

Despite the very wide range of values that can be given to the "_____" in a teaching claim, there are only four basic forms into which all the other values can be analyzed. These are the first four listed in the paradigm above. Thus if A teaches B when and why to kiss, that teaching can be analyzed as teaching B *the* proper time and reasons for kissing. To teach B *the* proper techniques of kissing is to teach him *how to* do it, which is more than teaching him *that* certain techniques are proper and less than teaching him *to* use them.

There are all sorts of contextual implications among teaching claims. Thus if A teaches B *that* Caesar crossed the Rubicon in 49 B.C., it follows that A taught B *what* river (among others) Caesar crossed in 49 B.C., *when* (among other times) Caesar crossed the Rubicon, as well as *who* (among others) crossed the Rubicon in 49 B.C. But a general logic of those implications has not been worked out. It is doubtful that any such logic could capture the nuances of actual usage. Sometimes "teach B to X" implies "teach B how to X" (X = play chess), sometimes not (X = enjoy playing chess; X = come when called).

But these contextual implications also make it impossible to draw any clear lines among these basic forms—what might be called truth-functional teaching (the X), teaching propositions (that X), teaching skills (how to X), and teaching dispositions (to X).[4] In any case, those categories are far too coarse to make the distinctions that we want to make among kinds of teaching. By that simple grammatical test, both the following would be examples of teaching propositions: teaching B that Caesar crossed the Rubicon and teaching B that one ought to return

[4] These distinctions have been adapted from Green's analysis of types of learning. T. F. Green, *The Activities of Teaching* (New York: McGraw-Hill Book Company, 1971), chap. 6.

injury with love. So those simple grammatical categories will not be used here.

The remainder of this chapter is devoted to formulating and testing the conditions that are necessary and sufficient for a teaching claim to be true and to describe a successful teaching encounter. But first, some preliminary remarks about what must be true if a teaching claim is to be (called) intelligible.

**INTELLIGIBILITY**
**CONDITIONS**

Let me stipulate the following two restrictions on the values "A" may take in a teaching claim. First, A must be an entity capable of intending to bring about something in another. Whether so-called teaching machines so qualify, because acting *in loco magistris,* we shall not pause to consider. Whether wolves teach their young to hunt caribou (as recounted in Farley Mowat's wholly engaging albeit not wholly trustworthy *Never Cry Wolf*) is an empirical, not a conceptual, question. And so on.

Second, whatever pedagogical intentions A may have, he must be capable of *acting* on those intentions—that is to say, capable of doing something to and with other entities: talking, striking, showing, holding, guiding or goading, or whatever. Thus St. Thomas's contention that angels may cause knowledge in men directly—without mediation by sense experience—cannot be formulated as an intelligible *teaching* claim, though it is necessarily true if angels possess the properties St. Thomas assigns them.

B (whatever is given the value of "B" in our paradigm) must be an organism capable of self-activated motion. I am told that Japanese experts in bonsai culture speak of teaching trees to grow slowly. Whether this is a literal or purely metaphorical usage only a tree could tell—and trees don't talk nor do they indicate by other actions that their speed of growth is self-activated motion. But clearly we do teach other things to animals lower than man on the phylogenetic scale. It might be possible, however improbable, that someone could teach a parrot to repeat Theorem $\theta$ on command. But one could not teach the parrot *that* Theorem $\theta$. So when I say that B can be any self-moving organism, I mean only if proper restrictions are placed on the variables that follow "B" in the paradigm.

There are occasions when teaching is directed to groups: The coach is teaching the offense how to execute trap right. But he is not teaching any individual how to execute trap right; he's teaching the guard how to pivot, the tackle how to veer, the fullback how to feint, and so on. A team learns how to execute the play; the individual player learns how to execute his particular movement, and, if the team is to win games,

the individual player learns how to adjust his execution of his assign-
ment in accordance with how others are executing theirs. And there is
nothing left over. All teaching acts are analyzable without remainder
into acts of teaching individuals. Thus "B" ranges over names or
specific designators of individuals only.

For the moment, let "X" take any value that sounds English. Thus,
following "that" one must insert a proposition, such as Theorem $\theta$ or
the contradictory of Theorem $\theta$. Following "how to" comes an action
verb. Following "to" comes an action verb or a feeling verb, such as
hate, love, fear. Or a character trait: to *be* honest or deceitful, kind or
cruel. And you can tell by ear whether any set of words following the
other blank-fillers under "that" in the paradigm produces an intelligible
sentence.

**TRUTH CONDITIONS**    So much for intelligibility. Now, what conditions
                        must be satisfied if a teaching claim is to be true?
Let me propose rough statements of three conditions. We will then try
to defend or refine each of these statements until it captures a necessary
condition for the truth of a teaching claim. Finally we will test the entire set for sufficiency.

1. There must be some encounter between A and B; ordinarily that means their
   coming together in time and place (the contact condition).
2. A must intend that B learn _____ X (the intent condition).
3. The interaction between A and B must reveal the _____ X which A intends that B learn (the content condition).

The contact condition need not detain us. Whether A and B may be
said to have engaged in a teaching encounter by means of some electronic medium *may* be a simple empirical question, to be answered by
appeal to the other truth conditions. But long-distance teaching may
be like long-distance telephone conversation: Ma Bell claims only that
it's the next best thing to being there, not that it's another way of being
there.

THE INTENT CONDITION

There are two distinct lines of attack against the necessity of the
second truth condition. One attacks the idea that intention is necessary,
the other that any specific intention is necessary. Let us consider them in
turn.

One might doubt that intention is necessary to the truth of a teaching
claim for the following reason: it seems perfectly natural to say

(S): "De Pew taught me to despise conventional morality, although he didn't
intend to teach me anything at all."

Now (S) has all the traits one could ask of a counterexample. Its first clause is unequivocally a teaching claim. The second clause denies any pedagogical intention in A. There is no contradiction between the first and second clauses. We can easily imagine a scenario in which (S) seems an ordinary way to say something true. Therefore, the intent condition cannot be necessary for the truth of *all* teaching claims. Q.E.D.

There are several possible moves to defend against that argument. One is to try to deflect the counterexample. That move turns out to be fruitless. In order to deflect the counterexample one would have to show that the first clause of (S) can be translated into a sentence or set of sentences not using the word "teach" or any other essentially pedagogical predicate. One might try

(S′): "During my association with De Pew, I came to despise conventional morality, although he didn't intend to teach me anything at all."

The trouble is this: if (S′) conveys the full force of causal efficacy implied by the first clause of (S), then "during my association with him" means more than "coincidentally with our association." For (S) provides an explanation, and (S′) does not provide an explanation of *how* I came to despise something I had hitherto respected; hence (S′) is an inadequate rendering of (S).

Now the failure of (S′) to deflect the counterexample does not prove that there is no (S″) that could deflect (S). But it is hard to imagine any (S″) that could deflect all counterexamples. Our common-sense experience runs the other way: our actions do affect others without our intending them to do so. Our actions may have consequences exactly the opposite of what we intend. The results are sometimes comic, sometimes tragic. But there is no necessity in the connection between the intention of an act and its consequence. And that leads to the conclusion that the truth of a teaching claim is *logically* independent of A's having any pedagogical intention whatever.

What, then, are we to do with the intent condition so as to accommodate the counterexample? We could add to the stated condition "usually" or "ordinarily" or some such qualifier. This move, of course, would deny that intention is a necessary condition for the truth of a teaching claim. It would then be an empirical hypothesis that more often than otherwise we intend to teach when we are teaching. If the proportion of cases like (S) were small enough, perhaps they could be ignored. But consider the difficulties in testing such an empirical hypothesis. We should have to compare a third-person description of an action or series of actions, such as (S), with a first-person account of the agent's intention, such as De Pew's response to the question, "Did you intend to teach this poor fellow to despise conventional morality?" Given an honest denial by De Pew, only a behaviorist could believe that the truth of (S) was unshaken. Sensible folks would look again, and ask De Pew to look again, at the sort of things that led to the affirmation of (S): Just *how* did De Pew teach you? *When* did he teach you? Did he teach you *while* doing certain things or *by* doing certain things? If it turns out that the answers to these and other obvious questions *really* reveal lack of intent on De Pew's part—say it turns out that De Pew consistently throve while he flouted conventional morality and that his case proved the falsity of my previous belief that conventional morality was necessary to material success—and if it turns out that my *only* basis for affirming (S) was that De Pew's example caused me to change my beliefs (which is one sort of learning), then we no longer have an instance of teaching without intention: the first clause of (S) turns out to be false— if not *simply* false, surely a misleading and inappropriate way to say what might be true.

The case might go the other way, of course. Perhaps De Pew patted me on the back at my first slight transgression, later treated me with greater regard as I advanced my career in sin, all the while scoffing at the powerlessness of moral restraints over his own conduct. If De Pew continues to deny his intention to teach when presented with clear evidence that he did all those and similar things, then the honesty of (or, later, the accuracy of the self-awareness behind) his denial comes into doubt. Thus the second clause of (S) turns out to be false or, if you prefer, misleading and inappropriate. Either way, if (S) is taken to be an empirical hypothesis, it turns out to be untestable. Hence (S) cannot be a serious counterexample to the intent condition for a teaching claim.

That point would not be worth pursuing in such detail, had not much of the talk about teaching been devoted to handling the pesky counterexamples. On one hand, if we phrase our second truth condition in simplest form, we would say: "Teaching *implies* intention." And against that formulation the force of (S) is, I take it, conclusive. On the other hand, we do mark off a large class of activities called teaching. And there is surely something more than a contingent connection between any particular act's being a member of that class and its having as one of its characteristics the intention to get someone to learn something. These activities we call teaching are found wherever people are related in any continuing way to one another—in homes, schools, churches, unions, armies, hospitals, factories, farms, bureaus. When we try to say exactly what it is that all these activities have in common such that we call them all teaching, we have to revert to talk about a particular form or mode of encounter which would have no point or purpose apart from an intention to get someone to learn something. Later we shall analyze that form or mode of encounter in detail; for now it is enough that it has that specific (pedagogical) intention as one of its (defining?) characteristics. And that is how we must understand the intent condition for a teaching claim: it is grounded not in a simple fact about the use of "teach" in English but rather in a complex, quasi-institutional fact about a distinctive mode of human encounter: that mode which is shaped or formed by the intention to promote learning.

That points directly to the second line of criticism against the intent condition for a teaching claim. Once the intention is seen to rest in the *modal* characteristics of an encounter, then it seems clearly unjustified to claim that A must *personally* intend that B learn _____ X. Look again at Socrates and the slave boy, says the critic. During that encounter Socrates had various intentions—toward the slave boy, toward Meno, toward Anytus, toward the audience in the background. Can you point to any specific point at which Socrates *intended* the slave boy to learn Theorem $\theta$? And even if you could, as you might, albeit shakily, say at 84D–85B, would you claim that *only* then was he teaching the slave boy that Theorem $\theta$? Wasn't he teaching, for example, at 84A, where his intention was explicitly to "numb" the boy and to reveal to Meno the danger of claiming to know what one doesn't? As far as demonstrating the separability of A's teaching from A's intending that B learn _____ X, doesn't the case of Socrates and the slave boy stand alongside the usual case where the teacher may be teaching and at the same time be intending anything from making a point to just surviving another hour in the classroom?

Now, in the light of these two very strong criticisms, what refinements must be made in the statement of the intent condition for a teaching claim? It is apparent that "A must intend that B learn _____ X" is far too strong. Let us try two conditionals:

2a. If the teaching claim is true, A must accept some measure of responsibility (in the popular jargon, be to some degree accountable) for B's learning or failing to learn _____X.

2b. If the teaching claim is true, A's more specific actions must be explained by appeal to that intention, plus, of course, other relevant beliefs and motives, where "relevant" also has to be defined by reference to that guiding intention.

But notice that if both those conditionals are true, it would be mighty queer for a teaching claim to be true and yet it be false that the idea of B's learning ever crossed A's mind. That idea may never be terribly "salient," as some psychologists might say, in A's consciousness. It may not be there at all while A is actually teaching. But if A never thought at all about B's learning, then the teaching claim becomes suspect. The intent condition as expressed in 2a and 2b makes no direct statement about A's thoughts and goals, but it presupposes that they are sometimes, somewhat like, intending that B learn _____ X. One could state the intent condition with greater precision, but this is sufficient for now.

## THE CONTENT CONDITION

Let us turn to the content condition. Another way to put it is this: whatever one is doing *in* teaching must reveal what it is that one intends *to* teach. This condition is intended to rule out all those other things, from supplication to surgery, which we might do when we want someone else to learn something. Not everything that counts as trying to get someone to learn counts as trying to teach; it depends on what one does in trying. The content condition is simply one way of putting the restriction that separates all teaching—good and bad, effective and ineffective—from those other ways we (try to) get people to learn things.

This condition sounds straightforward enough. If A is teaching B, surely there must be something he's teaching. And equally surely, *what* he's teaching must be disclosed somehow *in* his teaching, else the teaching claim must be false.

But counterexamples do crop up.

Begin with Komisar's Law: there is nothing one could *do* that one could *not* do with a valid pedagogical intent.[5] Whether a given act is to count as teaching depends on the pattern of action to which it belongs and whether that pattern, in turn, satisfied other conditions, such as the intent condition. Now the rub: Why *must* that pattern of interaction disclose what it is that is being taught?

There really is no necessity that it do so, the critic claims. Surely there are times when we teach best by concealing our actual intentions. Students today are said to be resistant to direct instruction, rather like mosquitoes to DDT. In any case, it is often to be preferred that learners discover things for themselves, an outcome we can help produce by cautious, indirect teaching, such that what we're *really* trying to teach emerges only in the consciousness of the learners and never stands out focally in the interaction of teaching-learning. Consider the more clearly pedagogical dialogues of Plato: does the interaction between Socrates and Meno (or Theaetetus or Timaeus or Euthyphro . . .) *always* reveal Socrates' deeper pedagogical intentions? If the revelation of content is allowed to stand as a necessary condition for the truth of a teaching claim, then truly masterful acts of teaching are excluded. Thus the critic rests his case.

Two brief rejoinders: First, there are times, perhaps lots of times,

---

5 B. P. Komisar, "Teaching: Act and Enterprise," in C. J. B. Macmillan and T. W. Nelson, eds., *Concepts of Teaching* (Chicago: Rand McNally & Co., 1968), esp. p. 70.

when we want to get others to learn (or see or understand or . . .) _____ X but we don't or can't teach them _____ X. Sometimes we have to transcend teaching; the argument of Chapter Five is that that is demonstrably true of moral education, and one can easily see reasons for extending the same argument to esthetic education, education in self-awareness, perhaps elsewhere. If a teaching claim is false because its presupposed pedagogical intention overshoots the kind of human interaction which "teaching" describes, that's something important and true about teaching. Socrates wanted Meno to see that virtue is infinitely more desirable than wealth or beauty. It is not misleading to say that Socrates was trying to get Meno to see that. . . . But it sounds queer as hell to say that Socrates was *teaching* Meno that. . . .

Second, the critic is entirely correct. The content condition has to be softened and rounded out. The content of the teaching, the _____ X, must be disclosed directly or indirectly, immediately or after reflection and introspection, and so on. Especially, where there are cultural barriers between teacher and learner, it may take a *very* skilled eye to see the _____ X in a reasonably skilled teaching performance. Still and all, the _____ X must *be* there if the teaching claim is true, and if it's there, it must be *in* the interaction between A and B; it may be hard but it cannot be impossible to discern.

But the real counter to the counterexamples comes from noting that "intending that B learn _____ X" neither describes A's state of mind nor designates some end-in-view which A's actions are designed to bring about. *That* intention, whatever (if any one thing) may be the case with intentions in general, serves rather as the argument form in which to explain or justify all sorts of particular acts into which teaching may be analyzed. Socrates and the slave boy again: if the story as recounted is true, it is true that Socrates was teaching the slave boy that Theorem $\theta$. If Socrates' personal intent were, let us say, to humiliate the slave boy, we would count his actions with that intent an integral part of the teaching encounter only if Socrates (or one explaining Socrates' actions) could show that learning humility the hard way is reasonably construed as a step toward learning that Theorem $\theta$. Otherwise those actions would have to be seen as an *interruption* rather than an integral *part* of the teaching.

At any given moment the intention that another learn may or may not be present to the consciousness of a person teaching; that intention may or may not be the end-in-view toward which particular acts are directed. But that intention is what gives distinctive form or character to the teaching encounter. It is strictly by reference to that intention that we can tell whether any particular action is to count as part of or a digression from the teaching itself. In short, the intention that B learn

_____ X is one of those intentions that figure prominently when we are deliberating about actions—deciding what to do, explaining what we've done, evaluating what happened—and that typically disappear from consciousness when we're actively engaged with the world. The second line of criticism simply construed "intention" too narrowly as merely a psychological state or goal.

**TRUTH AND SUCCESS**   With the third truth condition established as necessary, is the set sufficient for the truth of a teaching claim? When one tries to conceive a counterexample—a case that satisfies those conditions but isn't a teaching encounter—only one sort of case ever seems to come to mind: the one where no learning occurs. Even when we get ingenious and try to think of other sorts of counterexamples—for example, where A and B speak two languages which are identical except for the meaning of "_____ X" in each—*if* learning occurs, in this case, if B learned _____ X in *either* language, the example fails to counter the claim of sufficiency. But can we maintain that the three conditions are sufficient for the truth of a teaching claim without bringing in learning as an independent, perhaps contingently related, truth condition?

On one hand, we want to say yes. For surely teaching—an encounter that satisfies the conditions stated—can fail and still be teaching. More importantly, we can evaluate the truth of a teaching claim made in the present progressive tense: "Ms. G is now teaching her class the principles of set theory," without first determining whether her teaching is successful or unsuccessful. If we now grant the truth of the claim that Ms. G is teaching and later discover that her efforts proved ineffective, we can then say, "Ms. G taught . . . , but she failed to get it across." Or we can say, "She tried to teach . . . but she failed to get it across." Even then, notice, we do not say that she failed to teach, but rather that she failed to get it across. It's very different from saying: "She tried to teach in spite of a severe migraine headache, but she failed." In that case, of course, she failed to teach—to engage in actions revealing the intention that her class learn the principles of set theory. Hence the claim that she was teaching could be rejected on the third truth condition above.

One can work the pump and fail to draw water, perhaps because the well is dry. One can try to work the pump and fail to work the pump, perhaps because one lacks the strength or skill required. Insofar as teaching is like working the pump—and that is rather further than some seem to realize—the three conditions above are sufficient to establish the truth of a claim that teaching has occurred.

On the other hand, we want to say no. For we do use the word "teach" in ways that are more like "drawing water" than like "working the pump." The fact that we do not have two easily spoken phrases for pedagogical efforts and pedagogical accomplishments is itself a potent argument for the position that the truth conditions for a teaching claim cannot be sufficient unless they encompass success conditions. We use the word "teach" for both effort and accomplishment. When they fail to go together, we sense that something is wrong. The difficult part is to make clear precisely what is wrong; for that we look at what makes teaching successful.

**SUCCESS CONDITIONS**     Let us state the success conditions for a teaching claim in a form compatible with the truth conditions listed earlier. If a teaching encounter—an encounter correctly described by a true teaching claim—is successful, then:

1. There must be an adequate degree of causal efficacy in the encounter, such that B does learn what A had intended (the efficacy condition).
2. What A brings about in B (the "_____ X") must be appropriate to the nature of the encounter (the appropriateness condition).

Again, we will test each for necessity and their conjunction for sufficiency.

Two minor points: (1) The expression "success conditions" is an abbreviation, of course. A teaching claim is true if and only if the three conditions discussed above are satisfied. A success claim, we might say, is true if and only if the episode described in a true teaching claim satisfies the two further conditions discussed below. We're not inventing a new logic; we're simply saving words when we speak of success conditions, as distinct from truth conditions, for a teaching claim.

(2) Considering success in teaching, we must lean pretty heavily on the concept of learning, about which we haven't said much up to this point. Let me here note two points which I defend elsewhere.

(a) There is no *particular* process *called* "learning." There are harmless uses of the expression "process of learning," but they are rare. The argument against misusing "process" when speaking of the process of education (Chapter One) applies with even greater force when speaking about the process of learning.

(b) *Not every outcome that counts as success in teaching is best described as learning.* Concerning many or most of the successful outcomes of teaching, the most natural way to speak is to say "B learned _____ X." But what is true in many or most cases is not true of all. By using the term "learning" where it is natural to do so, I do not mean to suggest the contradictory of (b).[6]

## THE EFFICACY CONDITION

Let us look again at the efficacy condition. It requires little comment. In the practice of teaching, of course, a *prior* recognition of this condition is essential. A person who claimed to be teaching _____ X to B but could not say, even in general terms, what would be an adequate degree of causal efficacy to warrant a claim to success would make his claim to be teaching a quite dubious one. But that dubiety arises from the meaning of "intending," not "teaching." In general, we don't understand a person who says that he intends to do Y but cannot tell us how he would know that Y has been done.

This is where the notion of behavioral objectives gets its foothold. If teaching is defined, in part, by an intention to bring something about in another, then he who claims to be teaching should be able to say *something* about what the other must do or be when the intention is accomplished. If one can specify precisely the behavior the student is to exhibit under precisely specified conditions, then (other conditions being satisfied) one has met the criterion of having clear and intelligible intentions. But there are many other ways of meeting this criterion. And other criteria also apply to claims to be teaching. Even so, the extraordinary popularity of "behavioral objectives," especially among people who wouldn't recognize one if they should see it, attests to the common and correct belief that any genuine intention must include some idea about the causal adequacy of action to its purpose.

But all of that concerns the importance of having clear intentions, and that usually requires thinking about the efficacy condition, prior to or in the act of teaching. If it boils down to good advice to teachers—think about what you would regard as successfully achieving your intentions before you start acting on them—we shouldn't cavil. The idea that the intent condition for the truth of a teaching claim *logically* cannot be satisfied without first establishing what events (such as behavior) would satisfy the efficacy condition for teaching success is merely a vestigial remnant of verificationism as a criterion of meaning. *Both* boil down to the same good advice given above. Worse fates have befallen philosophical doctrines.

But what about teaching that simply fails to bring about _____ X

[6] For a defense of nonlearning objectives, see C. J. B. Macmillan *et al.*, "Can and Should Means-End Reasoning Be Used in Teaching?" in Macmillan and Nelson, *Concepts of Teaching*, pp. 134–140.

in B? We can say: "I taught him Theorem $\theta$, but he failed to learn." On the other hand we can say, "I tried to teach him Theorem $\theta$ but . . . ." The force of the two seems exactly the same. I prefer the second because it seems to evince more humility and willingness to change than does the first, and those are desirable traits in general and particularly in teachers. But there is no substantive difference between "I taught him, but . . ." and "I tried to teach him, but . . .": they both come down to the simple fact that teaching (like every human activity, except basic acts, if there are such) is sometimes causally efficacious in producing its intended results and sometimes not. From that it follows that the efficacy condition can have no effect one way or the other on the truth of an already established claim of the form "A teach(es) B _____ X."

This conclusion holds absolutely, but the "already established" qualification is essential. If the truth conditions hold, then A is engaged in teaching actions which can be so described independently of their *actual* outcomes, though not, if the argument above is correct, independently of their *intended* outcomes. Under those conditions, "teaching" is like "working the pump."

But let us consider a borderline case to see where we begin to talk about teaching in other ways. "I taught my son to use good table manners, but he's now twenty-one and he eats like a pig at the trough." [Assume the son is normal in all (other?) respects.] Was the father teaching? Or would we have to insist that in this case "tried to teach" is required, not merely preferable? The case is borderline because we would have to know more about what the father *did*. Suppose we ask and he says: "Why, nothing, of course, other than what I would have done anyway. I just assumed that a child learns by imitation and I gave him a good example to imitate." His explanation is sufficient to warrant the claim that he tried to teach, but lack of causal efficacy is sufficient not only to deny that he succeeded in getting his son to learn good manners but also to deny that what he did could be called *teaching* his son to use good table manners. We would grant, given his erroneous theory of how children learn such things, that he can be said to have *tried* to teach, but in fact his efforts failed on the third truth condition: what he intended to teach was not revealed in his activity of, *simply,* eating.

If the father replies to our question of what he did in a different way, we have to give a different analysis. Suppose he says: "I told him to mind his table manners every time I sent him off to the nursery to eat his meals." But telling without showing is not teaching nor even trying to teach. The contact condition is not satisfied, hence we won't even allow this father's effort to be called *trying to teach* good manners, though it does seem that he tried (unsuccessfully) to get his son to learn good manners.

But suppose the father responds to the question about what he did in this way: "I take it that the first rule of good manners is that one never comment on the manners of another. Following that rule, I conducted my teaching as discreetly as possible, slightly exaggerating certain movements when I saw his eyes were following them, being just a bit more attentive to certain conventions than I would have been had I no pedagogical intentions, and so on." Here is a case of showing without telling; it seems clear that the father was not only trying to teach, he was actually demonstrating good manners toward as well as *to* his son. Was he therefore teaching despite the lack of causal efficacy? We would have to grant that the father was teaching and hope that the son learned something more important than table manners.

Most discussions of teaching stop at this point: the point where it is decided that teaching is or is not an intentional act and that it does or does not imply some success in achieving that intention. But how is one to decide those questions? If the discussion above has succeeded in laying out the issues correctly, it is apparent that there is no simple answer either way. Ordinarily we do use the word "teach" in the way that makes a teaching claim seem to be a claim about an intentional act, but there are exceptions. Ordinarily we can separate the truth of a teaching claim from a claim about success in achieving what the agent intended, but again there are exceptions. The analysis is simple but inconclusive. Isn't there anything more certain about what's involved in a teaching claim? There is, but finishing it becomes more complicated.

## THE APPROPRIATENESS CONDITION

Let us suppose that the common belief is true and say:

R: Caesar crossed the Rubicon in 49 B.C.

Now let us suppose that we have a true sentence from our paradigm—the teaching claim:

1. A teaches B that R.

And let us suppose that there is causal efficacy in A's teaching and that the facts about Roman history are appropriate to this encounter. Then a teaching claim is defensible against all possible objections. (We are still ignoring the *merely* pesky counterexamples, such as that A intended to teach the date as A.D. 32 and inadvertently said "49 B.C." at the pedagogically significant point.)

Let us also suppose that R' is false:

R': Marcus Aurelius crossed the Rubicon in 49 B.C.

Assuming throughout that all the words in these sentences are used in normal ways, we should then believe that there is *something* wrong with

2. A teaches B that R'.

Is there anything wrong with 2? It all depends. Following Komisar's Law, we might say that if 2 describes an action that A might perform, we can always imagine a context in which 2 might be done with a valid pedagogical intent. Perhaps A wants B to acquire some insignificant but false beliefs, in order that B may discover later that they *are* false and thus may strengthen the habit of treating significant beliefs with critical skepticism. In that context there would be nothing wrong about 2 *per se,* although there is something morally repugnant about that way of teaching. The point is that when we claim that there *is* something wrong with 2, we always recognize that our claim might be denied by appeal to a larger purpose to which 2 might contribute.

But let us suppose that no mitigating circumstances intervene. There *is* something wrong with 2. The purpose of the second success condition is to make clear what's wrong with 2: R' is an inappropriate value for X when the facts of Roman history are appropriate to the teaching encounter. In itself, there's nothing at all interesting about such an obvious condition. What is not so obvious is how the appropriateness condition relates to the other conditions such that we can rightly regard it as a *success* condition for teaching, rather than as a separate, normative criterion that we might or might not apply to teaching acts and intentions.

Consider the question: Can 2 fail *only* on the second success condition —that is, fail on that condition without jeopardy to the truth conditions and the first success condition? At first glance it appears that the answer is clearly yes. The truth of 2 does not depend on the truth of R'. Nor does the causal efficacy of the teaching encounter. We can easily imagine a number of different contexts in which 2 might be true, in some of which A believes that R', others where A teaches R' knowing that it is false. Both are everyday occurrences. Just as a teaching claim may be true without satisfying the first success condition, so may it be true and satisfy the efficacy condition without satisfying the further condition of appropriateness.

But a little more reflection leads us to doubt that it is quite so simple. We are alerted to something peculiar by a simple consideration of logic. If 1 is impeccable on all conditions, then the following are true:

3. A taught B that someone crossed the Rubicon in 49 B.C.
4. A taught B who crossed the Rubicon in 49 B.C.
5. A taught B what river Caesar crossed in 49 B.C.
6. A taught B when Caesar crossed the Rubicon.

Now 2 implies 3 and 4 as well as

5'. A taught B what river Marcus Aurelius crossed in 49 B.C.
6'. A taught B when Marcus Aurelius crossed the Rubicon.

Since 3 is true, the implication does not throw 2 into jeopardy. And 4 *may* be ambiguous; if one stretches his use of language sufficiently, he can read 4 to mean merely that A taught B *some* name to put in front of ". . . crossed the Rubicon in 49 B.C." On that reading, 4 could be true even when filled in with the values implied by 2. But 2 also implies 5' and 6', which are clearly false. Therefore 2 is false. One might want to say that in the case of 5' the question of truth or falsity does not arise, since there is no event to which "Marcus Aurelius' crossing a river in 49 B.C." could refer. I still *think* 5' is clearly false. Even so, 6' will do by itself, since the event (that could be) referred to by "Marcus Aurelius' crossing the Rubicon" did occur (many times). And 6' *is* clearly false.

In the face of that argument one may adopt any one of several strategies. One may claim that 2 does not imply 5' or 6'. One may admit the implication but maintain that in the sense implied, 5' and 6' are true. Or one may admit that the appropriateness condition does affect the truth conditions given earlier.

To deny the implication seems fruitless. If 2 does not imply 3 and 4, then we simply do not know what 2 is supposed to mean. If it does imply 3 and 4, then how can a line be drawn to deny that 2 implies 5' and 6'? It won't work.

But are 5' and 6' false? One can, of course, construct sentences that resemble 5' and 6' and are also compatible with the truth of 2. One can say:

5" "A brought B to believe that Marcus Aurelius crossed a river in 49 B.C. and to believe that the name of that river was 'the Rubicon.' " In the sense in which 5' is implied by 2, 5" is equivalent to 5'. On the hypothesis that 2 is true and satisfies the first success condition, 5" is also true, and therefore so is 5'. Likewise, for 6'.

That defense is subject to two rebuttals. First, as I shall argue when discussing learning, sentences such as 5" are not entirely neutral with respect to the truth values of their constituent claims, though they may appear to be. But, second and most obviously, to assert that 5" is equivalent to 5' begs the question at issue. 5" is deliberately designed to conceal what appears to be an assertive risk in teaching claims such as 1 and 2. In 5 and 6, that assertive risk is recognized and its hazards successfully met. To insist, in the face of 5' and 6', that 2 does not involve assertive risk, to offer translations of those implications which conceal that risk, is to be guilty of *petitio principii*.

But now we seem to be at an impasse. It seems straightforward common sense that 2 could well be true even though R′ is false. It also appears inescapable that 2 implies 5′ and 6′, which are false, hence 2 must be false. Does this mean that we have to move the appropriateness condition into the position of being a fourth *truth* condition for any teaching claim? If we took that step, how could we deal with the anomalies resulting? For example, every time we discovered that something we had taught (with adequate causal efficacy) in the past was false, we should then have to deny that we had (really?) taught it.

There is, as you probably anticipated, a way out of this impasse. We find it in a more careful description of the teacher's intentions as required in the second and third truth conditions for a teaching claim. If A tries to teach B that R or R′, we could describe A's intention as trying to get B to learn who crossed what river on what date. This would be a grossly incomplete description of A's intent, if A were anything other than a robot. For A *should* be setting that event in some larger pattern of historical narrative, which, in turn, might be set in a purpose going beyond the mere recital of colorful events. But the incompleteness of the description of A's intention does not mean that the description is false. One could give an intelligent account of Rome's transition from republic to empire without mentioning Caesar's passage across a small stream. But if one intends to teach R, then certainly *that* intention can be described as teaching who crossed what river when.

But what about the intention to teach R′? The first distinction, of course, is whether or not A believes R′ (to be true). If A believes R′, whatever might be his reasons for that belief, then his intention can be described as teaching who crossed what river when. How would he describe his previous teaching after he discovered his error? He would *not* be likely to say that he had tried to teach and failed, but rather that he had taught what he then believed but, unfortunately, had not taught who crossed what river when.

But what if A teaches R′ knowing it to be false? A second distinction: A believes R′ to be an appropriate thing to teach in this encounter. Or, A teaches R′ just for the hell of it. (The latter possibility is by no means pure invention, as anyone who has ever been or known a bored but imaginative history teacher can testify.) Now to say that A believes R′ (though false) to be an appropriate thing to teach means that A's intention can be given an alternative description which still describes a pedagogical encounter. One has to imagine a peculiarly deranged person who would believe it worthwhile for B to learn R′. It's a more common derangement among some teachers to believe that children should come to accept what the teachers know to be falsehoods about their nation, religion, or bodies. Let R″ stand for any such falsehood: "The USA has never engaged in an aggressive war." Or: "Christianity encompasses all that's valid in every religion." Or: "Masturbation will stunt your growth." And so on. Then A's intention in teaching R″ can be described as bringing B to accept something that is, A believes, good for B to believe. A's belief that it is good to teach falsehoods must be grounded in some sort of reason, such as, "The facts about wars of national aggression are too complicated for children of this age to understand. But I want the children to hate aggression and to love their own country. So I try to get them to accept R″."

A must have some sort of reason like that, else he falls into the class of teaching falsehoods just for the hell of it. And those reasons give us an alternative description of his teaching act from which "teaching that R‴" *disappears altogether.* That's when we would allow him to say: "I was not *really* teaching that R″; I was teaching the children to hate aggression and to love their country."

I strongly disapprove of teaching known falsehoods for any reason whatsoever. But conceptually, that case is different from teaching known falsehoods for *no* reason whatsoever, just for the hell of it. In the latter case, if A claims that he taught B that R′, we *are* likely to deny that he taught anything at all. Perhaps he amused himself at the students' expense by making them believe something false. But when he did so, he ceased being a teacher and became something else. We could still provide an alternative description of his intentions, a description from which "taught them that R‴" disappears. That alternative description, however, no longer describes a pedagogical encounter. A bored and imaginative teacher can make a classroom the scene for a different kind of interaction only *because* it is ordinarily used for pedagogical purposes.

The claim, then, is that the appropriateness condition does *not* express a mere value preference, a sort of feeling that it's better to teach truth than falsehood—on the whole. The claim is much stronger: unless the content of the teaching satisfies the appropriateness condition, we simply cannot call the encounter successful; we're even dubious about calling it teaching. Please notice that the argument for this case was deliberately directed toward the instance in which it might seem most plausible to deny it. The rogue who fills his students' minds with lies may well succeed in achieving his intended end. We have to see what "teaching that X" implies before we are assured that that end is not rightly called successful teaching. It's much more obvious in other cases: If the movements I succeed in getting my students to learn will not, could not, help them stay afloat and propel themselves through the water, then no one would be inclined to say that I was teaching them how to swim, much less doing so with success. If the recruit's movements do not protect him from reprimand, I have not (successfully) taught him how (when, where, whom) to salute. It's just that the criteria for appropriateness in so-called verbal learning, "that X," are less obtrusive that leads us to forget that they are still there, still quite real even when so general as, say, that it isn't to count as A's successfully teaching that X unless A believes X, believes it important for B to learn X, has reasons for both those beliefs, proves willing to share those reasons with B. . . . More crudely, it isn't successful *teaching* just because you get the students to learn; it also depends on a lot of other things, including *what* they learn.

The important cases, those that arise in situations of practice, are very different from those we have been considering. In the important cases we do not have a clear-cut choice between teaching truths and teaching falsehoods. We run the risk of error whenever we teach anything at all. But when we say that we are teaching X, we acknowledge an unqualified obligation to change—to *quit* teaching X—in the face of conclusive reasons that X is inappropriate to the encounter we're in.

That obligation, it seems to me, is what distinguishes failure on the efficacy condition from failure on the appropriateness condition. If my teaching fails on the criterion of causal efficacy, I do have an obligation to change my teaching—if I can, if I know a better way to do it, if my supervisors will allow it, and so on. But if I know that the X I am teaching is inappropriate to the encounter, then I must either give up the claim to be teaching or give up teaching X. Imagine an honest teacher under the Nazi regime who was ordered to teach his pupils that the German Army was victorious in WWI while the war was lost by traitors at home. What can we say about his intention to teach such a lie? Here the common-sense notion of "possibly" and the logician's use of the term strangely coincide: unless he were a convinced Nazi himself, he couldn't *possibly* obey the order. For he would not be teaching them what happened in the fall of 1918.

In the practical situation, the various _____ X's, which we can analyze as the content of teaching, flow together as a whole. In practice we do not, logically could not, teach a student that Theorem $\theta$ *simpliciter*. In teaching him Theorem $\theta$, we also teach him reasons for believing Theorem $\theta$ true, how to prove Theorem $\theta$, how to defend his belief in Theorem $\theta$ against deliberately contrived attacks, when to use Theorem $\theta$ in solving other problems in geometry, and so on. Some have argued that this multiplicity of intentions in any actual teaching encounter means that the goal of having students learn goes beyond *any* intention of teaching. There is truth in the claim that the goal of having students learn transcends the intention to teach. But *not* because there are many _____ X's in any actual encounter. When our intentions in teaching are multiple, as they invariably are, that multiplicity can be analyzed into a sequence of teaching B _____ X—that, to, how to, when, . . .— and *each* of the analyzanda is subject to the exact conditions of truth and success given above. The whole is exactly equal to the sum of its parts, however difficult it may be in practice to name all the parts.

# CHAPTER THREE

# Toward
# a Specific Concept
# of Teaching

**A MAP** And yet . . . nothing important can be terminated so apodictically as the previous chapter. Some loose ends must be tidied up before we move on to the central concern of this chapter. The goal is to formulate a useful as well as neat distinction to separate teaching from its counterfeits. To reach that goal we will take a somewhat circuitous route, not because it's logically impossible to get there more directly but because this is the only route I know. Besides, it provides some interesting prospects along the way.

So may we, first, retrace a few steps and deal with two of the more visible questions left over from the preceding chapter. Do the truth conditions therein presented define teaching distinctly, or do they define only a broad class of concepts that incidentally includes teaching? Do the success conditions distinguish the achievement of our intentions in teaching from other intentions we might have in a pedagogical encounter? Those two questions are closely related: neither can be answered satisfactorily until we have nailed down certain key points about learning, and that is the second leg of the journey. Finally we can head directly toward an understanding of what teaching is, where the idea of teaching no longer includes indoctrinating and conditioning but is radically distinct from them.

**THE PEDAGOGICAL PARADIGM**  Any teaching claim, we said in Chapter Two, could be expressed as a sentence formed by providing appropriate values for each of the place-holders in the following paradigm:

$$A \text{ teach(es)} \quad B \quad \underline{\hspace{2cm}} \quad X$$
$$\text{(tensed verb)}$$
$$\text{that}$$
$$\text{the}$$
$$\text{how to}$$
$$\text{to}$$
$$\cdot$$
$$\cdot$$
$$\cdot$$

Now a question naturally arises. Aren't there other verbs which also fit that paradigm? If so, aren't we making a mistake in thinking that our stated conditions actually define "teaching" rather than a broad category of concepts in which teaching is only one member among many?

In fact only two verbs in English, other than "teach," come close to fitting that paradigm. They are "tell" and "show." In a pedagogical context they *are* teaching; in a nonpedagogical context they are distinguishable from teaching by one or more of the conditions stated in the previous chapter. We shall return to showing and telling in the next chapter.

But look for a moment at some of the other terms that might be substituted for "teach" in the paradigm. You might start with ideas rather close to teaching, such as training, instructing, questioning, conditioning. Going a little further, you might try ordering, forcing, begging, asking . . . then signaling, inciting, convincing, persuading. . . . What you discover immediately is that none of those other verbs will take the range of blank-fillers, the _____ X's, that follow so easily yet so richly after "teach." You can train B to X or in X(ing); but you can neither train him *that* X nor train *the* (way to) X. And the same is true of most of the other terms listed. They are ways of getting B to do something, either right now, on-the-spot (for example, inciting B to riot) or else as a disposition (for example, conditioning B to jump whenever a particular tone is sounded). Questioning is different: you can question B on or about X, which is asking him who, when, what, why . . . rather than asking him to X or for X. And so on.

Only convincing seems to resemble teaching in taking "that X" as a natural blank-filler. You can, of course, persuade B that X, but if you follow it up, the X, usually at least, turns out to be that he should *do* some Y. But you can convince B that X, where (grammatically, if not psychologically, speaking) X can take *any* value so long as it's a proposition. (You can, of course, convince B *of* her innocence, but that translates immediately as convincing B *that* she is innocent.) So let us substitute "convince" for "teach" in the paradigm; "A convince(s) (tensed verb) B that X" forms what we may call a convincing claim. What comes next is to test whether it has the same truth and success conditions as a teaching claim.

The three truth conditions for a convincing claim seem to fit rather well. (1) There must be some encounter between A and B. This first condition is somewhat laxer for a convincing than for a teaching claim. We might say: "Reading Tully convinced me of Cataline's guilt." There is no syntactically corresponding use of "teach." We don't feel quite as easy with: "Tully convinced me that Cataline was guilty," while we just *wouldn't* say: "Tully taught me. . . ." But convincing requires *some* sort of encounter, (2) shaped by A's intention to bring it about that B comes to believe that X (again, that is the pedagogically central sense of "learn that X"). That intent (3) must be revealed, however subtly, in the *interaction* between A and B. As with the corresponding condition for a teaching claim, this condition means, among other things, that what A is doing to bring it about that B comes to believe that X *is* to interact in certain ways with B; that is, the interaction cannot be merely a camouflage for some other action intended to change B's beliefs—for example, by physical or chemical means.

These three conditions for a teaching claim are clearly necessary also to the truth of a convincing claim, but are they sufficient? Clearly not. We can say: "I taught him that X, but he never believed that X." But we should not say: "I convinced him that X, but he never believed that X." Or, better, if we do say the latter, we must mean something other than what we are saying. We may mean, perhaps, that he made it appear that he believed while really remaining unconvinced. Or that not-X is so firmly ingrained in his unconscious that no amount of convincing is really going to shake it. Or the like. But if we don't mean something like that, we are saying both that he was convinced and that he was not convinced, which is, in effect, to say nothing at all.

So the first *success* condition for a teaching claim, that of causal efficacy, now becomes a fourth *truth* condition for a convincing claim. And there are no independent success conditions. Which is not to say that a convincing claim can't go wrong, of course. B says to A: "I believe that X; you have succeeded in convincing me." B may be lying; B may not believe X at all. B may be mistaken; B may have believed X a long time ago, and A's efforts may only have caused him, all unbeknownst to himself, to bring an old belief back into consciousness. B may be mistaken in other ways; what actually caused him to change his mind about X may have been some drug he took unwittingly and not A's efforts at all. But those are ways in which the condition of causal efficacy can fail to be satisfied, and remember: for a convincing claim, causal efficacy is a truth condition, not a success condition.

**TEACHING**
**AND CONVINCING**
**DISTINGUISHED**

The situation is quite different for a teaching claim. To show why, let me give a particular value to the "X" of the preceding paragraph. B says to A: "I believe that conventional morality is a crock of shit; you have succeeded in teaching me." That teaching claim can go wrong in all the ways the corresponding convincing claim could go wrong; plus:

(i) Assume that A had intended to teach B to despise conventional morality, that the interaction between A and B had revealed that intention, and that B was neither lying nor mistaken in the ways mentioned above. Still and all, A may not be persuaded that his teaching was successful. A must ask B why he holds that belief, and only some answers from B are indicative of success in teaching. If B says, "That's just the way I feel, thanks to you," then A may laugh or cry, but he has received no confirmation of the teaching claim. Suppose B says: "Thanks to your teaching, I have come to see conventional morality as an ideological facade for economic exploitation." Then A has confirming evidence for success in teaching, even if (perhaps *particularly* if) that was not among the reasons offered by A in teaching B to despise conventional morality. The condition of causal efficacy gets narrower; only some ways of causing B to believe that X will count as success in teaching B that X.

(ii) Make the same assumptions as in (i) and add an impartial observer, C, to the scene. After the interchange between A and B, either interchange, C says to A: "I grant that you succeeded in getting the poor fellow to despise conventional morality, but I don't see how you can call that *teaching*." Could C make that sort of objection to a convincing claim?

The answer is yes and no. It is true, of course, that there are restrictions in manner such that not just *any* way of getting a person to believe something will count as convincing that person. The only thing you can convince a person of by violence is that you are a violent person. (This restriction seems to have been missed by Mr. Henry Kissinger when he encouraged the Christmas bombing of population centers to "convince Hanoi" of certain points. *New York Times,* June 2, 1974, p. E13.) But let us suppose that A succeeded in getting B to believe that X without using violence or the threat of it, nor drugs, surgery, deprivation, hypnosis, nor any combination of them; he succeeded by appeal to B through B's normal senses—by talking and presenting other sensory stimuli from which B was reasonably free to withdraw. Could C *then* say: ". . . but I don't see how you could call that *convincing"*? Not if C knows what "convince" means in English. If B was convinced by A under those conditions, then A was convincing (as well as convincing to) B.

The restrictions in manner that customarily apply to teaching are actually somewhat less stringent than those applicable to convincing. Persons who possess normal sensibilities find it abominable that teaching in schools is regularly accompanied by threats, violence, and deprivation, particularly deprivation of freedom. However, we don't say: ". . . but I don't see how you can call that *teaching"* just because it occurs in that sort of institution. As we all know, such violations of ordinary human decency make it psychologically difficult for teaching to occur. But such restrictions are not among those that make teaching *conceptually* impossible—for example, those which rule out surgery as a way of teaching, even surgery which should actually succeed in changing a person's mind.

But let just *any* restrictions in manner apply to A's bringing B to despise conventional morality. Long after the convincing claim has been thoroughly established, C may still have a case for denying that A's actions are properly called teaching. They may resemble teaching enough that one is inclined to call them that at first sight. But it is always possible, on looking again, to make C's charge. "I grant that you have succeeded in conditioning B to despise conventional morality, but. . . ." Or, ". . . you have succeeded in indoctrinating B to believe that conventional morality is to be despised, but. . . ." Thus there is a feature which distinguishes teaching claims not only from convincing claims but also, though this has yet to be shown, from *all* the other claims we might form by substituting other verbs for "teach" in the basic pedagogical paradigm.

But exactly what is that feature? It is not enough to say that a teaching claim, like any value claim, is subject to the "open question argument."[1] Nor is it enough to say that the truth and success conditions for a teaching claim are more stringent than those for a convincing or persuading or other quasi-pedagogical claim. Rather, it is that we can apply the truth and success conditions for a teaching claim with whatever degree of strictness we choose. And when we choose to be very strict, we sometimes discover that, well, the teaching claim isn't false, quite. It does designate a pedagogical encounter that was not unproductive or unsuccessful, exactly. But somehow the whole episode was wrong; it was a phony, a fake, a counterfeit. It turns out not to have been real teaching but indoctrination or conditioning. That's always possible.

**"COUNTERFEIT"?**    Before we can show precisely how teaching can be distinguished from indoctrination or conditioning, we will have to bring the concept of learning up to the point we have reached in our treatment of teaching. But first a note on terminology. There are several ways in which the term "counterfeit" fits very badly as a characterization of indoctrination or conditioning in their relation to teaching. Historically as well as logically, "counterfeit" doesn't make sense apart from some prior recognition of the legally authorized item— the coin of the realm, as it were. Further, to call an item counterfeit is to say something about the intention of its maker, that he deliberately made it look like the real thing, and that he did so for some further purpose, ordinarily his own enrichment. Finally, to say that an item is a counterfeit is to say not only that it won't be redeemed if recognized for what it is, but also that it is irredeemably defective: no matter how excellent the counterfeit in every other respect, it can never *become* real (except, perhaps, through an act of unmerited Grace by the Sovereign.)

The relation of indoctrination and conditioning to teaching has none of those features. Historically, on the evolutionary scale at any rate, conditioning is the first to appear, followed (we must assume on the basis of all plausible theories of social development) by indoctrination, while teaching is clearly a latecomer. (Remember Socrates' reluctance to use the term διδάξειν for what he was doing, which was very close to *real* teaching.) Logically, we don't (have to) define the other terms as fraudulent imitations of teaching; we don't (have to) impute any specific intention at all to the indoctrinator or conditioner. And if, while intending to teach, a person discovers that he is actually indoctrinating or conditioning someone, then, if he knows how, and so on, he can simply

---

[1] Cf. C. D. Hardie, *Truth and Fallacy in Educational Theory* (New York: Teachers College Press, 1962), pp. 17 ff. The open-question argument comes from G. E. Moore, *Principia Ethica,* 1903, chap. I.

change; the act can be redeemed right up to the moment the bell sounds.

So why use a term that seems to fit so badly? Because "counterfeit" has two other features that *do* fit. First, both counterfeit coins (or bills, stamps, airline tickets . . .) and genuine coins (or . . .) are *coins* (or . . .). They have most of the same properties, while amongst properties in which they differ there is at least one that crucially qualifies all the others. And that, as I shall try to show, is a point central to understanding teaching when it's opposed to indoctrination or conditioning.

Second, counterfeiting subverts the institution that gives point or purpose to the counterfeiting itself. There are societies in which the institution of legal tender does not exist; in such societies there are no counterfeits; coins may be exchanged for other goods by barter if the owner of a coin finds a trading partner who values coins for their roundness, metallic content, or the like. But the institution of legal tender loses its point or purpose unless there is some *regulated* relationship between coins and other things—metal in the coins, or total goods available, or rate of investment in the society, or other. Counterfeiting contravenes that regulated relationship and thereby acts to defeat the point or purpose of the institution of legal tender, even though subverting that institution is not ordinarily the goal of the counterfeiter—that is, unless he is acting to achieve some extraneous military or political purpose.

And that feature of counterfeiting is shared by indoctrination and conditioning, as I shall try to show. Just as the institution of legal tender emerged long before economic theory could explain the basic point and purpose of the institution (and why counterfeiting subverts it), so also we have institutions of schooling though we still lack an adequate understanding of the central activity—teaching-and-learning—which gives point or purpose to that institution. Without understanding, teachers typically engage in a mélange of activities including a great deal of indoctrinating and conditioning; thus they subvert the very institution they intend to serve. That last point must and will be argued; at present I hope it sounds plausible enough to explain the otherwise peculiar use of "counterfeit" here.

**LEARNING AND PHILOSOPHY** Learning has been treated rather badly by philosophers. They drag out the idea when they're working on standard philosophical questions, such as how a person may come to know that he is in pain. But when its work is done, learning is returned to the tool shed in the same rough, unanalyzed state as when removed. Why that should be is hard to understand.

How *do* people learn—come to know—things? That has always been a central question in the epistemological tradition of Western philosophy. But in twentieth-century Anglo-American philosophy, that question has been regarded as academic property, belonging to the empirical, particularly experimental and comparative, study of psychology. So we have standard analyses (and arguments defending analyses) of "B knows _____ X," only the beginnings of "B learns _____ X." A good case can be made for the view that learning was relegated to the psychologists much too hastily. Their efforts to study the phenomenon of learning have been badly hampered (or so, at least, it can be argued) by the fact that no one had bothered to figure out what learning really is. Even if that isn't so, it can easily be shown that the psychologists' attempts to *define* learning (an activity they seem constrained to engage in either as prelude or as conclusion to their empirical studies) have proved totally unrewarding.[2] They produce so-called "working" definitions that may (but usually don't) work to mark off a particular phenomenon for study. Such definitions, however, are worse than useless in advancing our understanding of what learning is. For psychologists' definitions invariably (so far as I can tell) assume that there is some causally determined process by which learning occurs; they disagree on the nature of that process, whether it's basically neurophysiological or (autonomously or epiphenomenally) behavioral. They disagree on whether that process is learning, causes learning, or results from learning. They agree only that those are the important questions.

Whereas, to anticipate what's yet to be shown, those questions about causal processes simply don't arise when our attention turns to learning itself. It makes no more sense to speak of a process of learning than a process of believing, or knowing, or willing, or feeling, or asserting, or referring, or what have you. It's no more reasonable to believe that there is one process of learning than that there is one process which includes composing sonatas, arguing logically, making love, dancing the Texas

2 I have examined a half dozen or more textbooks in the psychology of learning. Each presents its own version of the "change of behavior" definition; the more sophisticated do so with a fairly clear recognition that such definitions do not really say what learning *is*. For example, John Travers, *Learning: Analysis and Application* (New York: David McKay Co., Inc., 1972), pp. 9–10: "Consequently, this book rests upon a definition of learning as a process that results in the modification of behavior. . . . The reader should now understand the magnitude of the problem of definition and should realize that a book on learning can be categorized rather quickly by its definition of learning. This is as it should be, particularly at a time of scanty knowledge about the process itself." Cf. W. L. Mikulas, *Concepts in Learning* (Philadelphia: W. B. Saunders Company, 1974), chap. I, for similar comments. There remains a continuing problem whether conflicting theories of learning present competing explanations (or accounts) of *how and why learning occurs* or alternative definitions of *what learning is*. In my view that problem is insoluble within the framework of behaviorism. See Ernest Hilgard, *Theories of Learning* (New York: Appleton-Century-Crofts, 1956), chap. I.

Star, and riding a unicycle. There is learning how to do all those things, learning to enjoy or to hate doing them, learning when, where, and with whom to do them, learning why one should or shouldn't. . . . *One process?*—in the sense that photosynthesis, however complex and varied, is one process? False. Absurd. Insane.

But to give up the notion that there is a *process* of learning must not force us into the opposite fallacy: the notion that there are as many senses of the term "learn" as there are distinct phrases and clauses that can fill the "_____ X" in an intelligible learning claim. Look again at the range of learning claims that can be constructed from among the different activities mentioned in the preceding paragraph. Though there is no one process going on in all of them, it is not the case that the concept of learning is merely an idle gear, taking its force entirely from the other terms of each context. No, when we say "B learn(s) _____ X," the term "learn" must be presumed to have one meaning, which meaning is to be shown by philosophical analysis—that is, by specifying the necessary and sufficient condition for the truth of a learning claim. If it can be demonstrated that such conditions cannot be specified, of course, then we have grounds for retreating to an argument for multiple senses of the term "learn." All that is standard analysis; the only question is why "learning" has so seldom been accorded its rightful place as an object of philosophical inquiry. I don't know why this is so, but the consequence is that the analysis given here is much less complete than I should like it to be.[3]

**INTELLIGIBILITY
CONDITIONS**

But we can begin to sketch how a philosophical analysis of learning might go. A learning claim is the assertion of a sentence formed on the paradigm: B learn (tensed verb) _____ X. The claim is intelligible only

---

[3] The Macmillan Company and The Free Press published three major encyclopedias during the 1960's. The *Encyclopedia of Philosophy* contains no article on learning and only one substantial reference to the concept, that in Charles Taylor's article on behaviorism, excellent but limited in scope. The *Encyclopedia of Education* is full of articles on and references to learning, but none of the philosophical articles is concerned directly with learning, and the article entitled "Learning Theory" (by Winfred F. Hill) quite consciously omits philosophical concerns. Only the *International Encyclopedia of the Social Sciences* takes learning as a focus of theoretical concern. A dozen major articles are organized under the editorship of Gregory Kimble, while a score or more appear on closely related topics—"Thinking," "Reasoning," and so on. All in all, they contain a wealth of fascinating information about how learning occurs, but none questions the behavioristic definition of Professor Kimble, and all presuppose the mechanistic model that learning is a "dependent variable" under the control of one or two or a great number of "independent variables." Except for Taylor's article, there isn't even a hint in *any* of these works that learning is a philosophically contested concept. My own article on psychological concepts in the *Encyclopedia of Philosophy* is conspicuously deficient in regard to learning.

if the "B Xes" is (i) itself intelligible and (ii) distinct from the learning claim.

"Rosie, my pet earthworm, learned to sing 'Dixie' in F#." That's intelligible if you can understand what it would be for an earthworm to sing. I think I can imagine it with enough detail that the claim satisfies (i), but I'm not sure.

"The universe as a whole is learning to expand more slowly." Can you distinguish that learning claim from the claim that the universe *is* expanding more slowly (than it used to)? I can imagine evidence convincing me that the rate of expansion is decreasing; but can I imagine evidence that would distinguish *that* from the learning claim? I think the claim fails on (ii), but again I'm not sure. The problems in testing for intelligibility become more complicated in "B learns *that* X" (a proposition). We will treat some of those problems in more detail when we consider the central role of beliefs in all learning. For now, the test is: "B learns that X" is intelligible only if "B believes that X" is (i) itself intelligible and (ii) distinguishable from "B learns that X." These conditions, of course, are far from sufficient; but that they are necessary points along the way to some important truth conditions.

## LEARNING AND CHANGING BEHAVIOR

If a learning claim is to make sense, then, there has to be a clear distinction between B Xes and B learns to X. The question is how to pass from one to the other. It's in trying to negotiate that passage that most efforts to define learning run aground. For there appears to be a time dimension in the relation of the two, and that makes one want to look for some process occurring over time as the central point in a definition of learning.

For example, at time $t_1$ B has never swum. At time $t_2$ he swims. Then at $t_1$ he must have had the capacity or potentiality for swimming. By $t_2$ that potentiality has become an actual ability. The learning claim is true, one is tempted to say, if and only if the time-stamped statements are true; that yields the basic formula: learning *is* change of behavior over time.

The basic formula admits so many and such obvious counterexamples that almost no one would want to hold to it as a definition all by itself. It does have, however, a sort of prima facie plausibility that tempts one to try again and again to save it by qualifications. So we say that B learns _____ X is true if and only if B not-Xes at $t_1$, B Xes at $t_2$ *and* certain alternative explanations for the change are ruled out, such as maturation (B being at $t_1$ a larva, at $t_2$ a tadpole) or (B being at $t_1$ a corpse, at $t_2$ the revivified Lazarus) miracles. From that it's a natural step to assimilate in the idea of learning both the change in behavior and also the process which produces the change.

The problem is, then, to formulate a clear and useful definition of learning, starting from the simple and undeniable fact that learning and changing behavior are close relatives. Please excuse the shorthand expressions that follow; they will help, I think, to make it clear how one would go about solving that problem.[4]

Let $\Delta b \dfrac{\quad\quad}{t_1 - t_2} X$ be defined as a change in observable _____ X-type behavior in the time interval between $t_1$ and $t_2$. More precisely, to assert $\Delta b \dfrac{\quad\quad}{t_1 - t_2} X$ of B is to assert the conjunction of two propositions: B not-Xes at $t_1$; B Xes at $t_2$, thus defining learning, literally now, in terms of *terminal* behavior, the behavior observed at the end of the interval.

Let [C] be a sort of *ceteris paribus* qualification, the relevant conditions for the emission of _____ X-type behavior being the same at $t_1$ and $t_2$. Thus, if $\Delta b \dfrac{\quad\quad}{t_1 - t_2} X$ is the change from not-swimming to swimming, then water has to be present at both $t_1$ and $t_2$, the water has to be in the same range of temperature, and so on, and all the other conditions relevant to swimming-type behavior have to be standard.

Let "E" be an *explanation* for $\Delta b \dfrac{\quad\quad}{t_1 - t_2} X$, and let the expression "$\sim(E_1 \lor E_2 \lor \ldots \lor E_n)$" read: "It is not the case that explanation $E_1$ or $E_2$ or . . . or $E_n$ holds, any one of which would falsify or render otiose the learning claim." There are reasons to doubt both that all the $E_i$'s can be specified in advance and that the definition proposed below can escape fatal circularity if all the $E_i$'s are *not* specified in advance. For if they are not specified, $\sim(E_1 \lor E_2 \lor \ldots \lor E_n)$ means simply "No nonlearning explanation supervenes," and thus the definition is hopelessly compromised by circularity. So let us simply grant that all the $E_i$'s are specified. The definition we are working toward is defective in more radical ways, so we may simply give them this point by stipulation.[5]

At last we have the technical apparatus necessary to formulate a behavioral definition of learning. Thus:

---

[4] For a clear example of how such a definition might be constructed, see James L. Kuethe, *The Teaching-Learning Process* (Glenview, Ill.: Scott, Foresman and Company, 1968), pp. 5–11.

[5] This qualification does not solve the problem of overdetermination in the causes of $\Delta b$: Cinderella had worked very hard trying to learn how to be a lady. The occasion for emitting the desired behavior finally arrived: just as she was preparing to make her first ladylike gesture—so delicate yet so bold—she was zapped by her fairy godmother and thus endowed with all the traits she had striven to acquire. Did she learn them? Would we or she ever know?

Formula Q: B(learns _____ X) $=_{df}$ B$\left(\triangle b \dfrac{}{t_1 - t_2} X\right)$ & $\sim(E_1 \vee E_2 \vee \ldots \vee E_n)$ & [C]

Formula Q will do, I think, for our purposes, though many other qualifications, some quite ingenious, have been proposed to help make this type of formula work as a translation of a learning claim. A fairly standard formulation would put the "$\triangle b$ _____ X" clause in the subjunctive conditional, so that Formula Q no longer says anything about behavior directly, but rather defines learning as a change in "tendency to behave." That move, in my opinion, merely raises many new difficulties, such as those in trying to explain what "tendency" in this very general sense amounts to—is it merely a statistical concept or does it designate some psychological dynamic?—while adding no strength against objections (i) and (ii) below.[6] The question now is not whether Formula Q might be improved but whether any such formula is worth improving.

**FORMULA Q APPRAISED AND REJECTED** A principal alleged advantage of Formula Q is that the question: Did B learn _____ X? now becomes mostly, if not strictly, a matter for empirical research. Did the $\triangle b$ ____ X "obtain" under standard conditions? Do the alternative explanations fail to hold? The latter question doesn't seem to be straightforwardly empirical, of course, but in the practice of experimental and comparative psychology it poses no particular difficulties. One simply specifies [C] much more precisely, primarily by conducting research on the kind of $b$ that can be induced under controlled laboratory conditions. In that case, the $\sim(E_1 \vee E_2 \vee \ldots \vee E_n)$ qualifier becomes a simple caveat: make sure you control for maturation, fatigue, and so on before you claim that your $\triangle b$ is learning. And it *is* a fairly straightforward empirical question, if indeed any question can be called straightforwardly empirical, whether the experimental conditions do rule out those alternative explanations. Thus, this way of defining learning makes it subject to scientific study, from which, some folks say, we may confidently expect to gain practical know-how as well as precise theoretical understanding.

[6] Gregory Kimble, "Learning, Introduction," in *International Encyclopedia of the Social Sciences* (New York: The Macmillan Company and The Free Press, 1968): "Learning has been defined as a relatively permanent change in a behavioral tendency, which occurs as a result of reinforced practice." The last expression is supposed to be the equivalent of the "$(E_1 \vee E_2 \vee \ldots \vee E_n)$" qualification in Formula Q. Kimble goes on: "[T]he term 'tendency' allows the definition to cover cases in which the products of learning do not immediately appear in performance. In this way the definition covers the numerous cases in which an individual learns something that may not be put to practical use for years" (ix–114). Does it cover the equally numerous cases in which learning is never put to practical use? What, exactly, is a tendency? Professor Kimble doesn't say.

In fact, of course, those claims for the advantages of experimental science in the study of learning are seldom made these days, though they appear uniformly in textbooks written only a few years ago. Whether on balance the resources poured into the laboratory study of learning have produced more good than harm is a question some future historian may choose to ponder, perhaps as Burckhardt, in *The Age of Constantine the Great,* attempted to assess the effects of more innocent superstitions and their contribution to the decay of Hellenistic civilization. There is a decided difference, however: during the age of Constantine, men and women of all degrees and stations seem actually to have relied on astrology, necromancy, the haruspices, and so on, to provide them both general conceptions of how the world works and practical, day-to-day advice on how to live with it. But I greatly doubt that anyone receives either from psychological studies built on a Formula Q definition of learning.

My reason for so doubting is this: (i) Formula Q, in fact if not in intent, proposes a very fundamental logical shift from the meaning of "learn" in English (and its equivalent in other natural languages), and (ii) the common-sense concept of learning is far more plausible, from a scientific standpoint, than any Formula Q-type definition of learning could ever be.

A full defense of (i) and (ii) is another book, but the outline is quite simple.

(i) When we make a learning claim—assert something about B's learning _____ X—any $\Delta b$ we have in mind is taken to be *evidence for* our claim, *not* in any literal sense *a translation of* that claim. The fundamental, *logical* difference between evidence and translation is easily seen.

1. Evidence statement $\longleftarrow R_E \longrightarrow$ Claim
2. Translation $\longleftarrow R_T \longrightarrow$ Claim

Now $R_E$ holds only if, in principle, the truth of the evidence statement is logically independent of the truth of the claim. Even when $R_E$ is very close, when the evidence is final, conclusive, unquestionable, when (as we say) the evidence *proves* the claim true (and whether there can *be* such evidence for empirical claims is strongly denied by a long and honorable tradition in philosophy of science), even so, it must be logically possible for the evidence to be true and the claim false; otherwise the evidence is merely a restatement of the claim, and we should then have to seek some other evidence that has a relation $R_E$ to the restated claim. That notion of what constitutes evidence is as clear in law courts as it is in manuals of scientific research.

It is equally clear that an accurate translation of a claim logically *must* have the same truth value as the original claim, else there has been an error in translation. Certainly if we translated a learning claim into Urdu, we should know that our translation was wrong if it should turn out that the sentence in Urdu was true and the English sentence false. It is monstrously difficult to say *exactly* what the relation $R_T$ is in any translation, especially from one natural language to another, but this much we *do* know about $R_T$: if it doesn't preserve truth value, it's an error.

Now when we ask for evidence for a learning claim, it is almost always some true statement about behavior that we seek. "What makes you think that B has learned _____ X?" is one way of asking for evidence that B has learned _____ X—that is, for evidence that the planarian has learned to wince, that the slave boy has learned Theorem $\theta$, and so on. In whatever words we ask the question, we normally expect some statement about behavior in return. If the person who initiated the interchange by claiming that B learned _____ X didn't recognize that statements about B's behavior are peculiarly relevant as evidence, we should (eventually) conclude that he didn't mean his original statement to be taken as a learning claim.

In sum, however it is patched up to try to resist counterexamples from common sense, the Formula Q definition differs from the ordinary language definition of learning in this fundamental, logical way: the Formula Q definition would establish an $R_T$ relation of behavioral statement to learning claim; the ordinary language conception of learning presupposes that relation to be $R_E$.

The argument above, unless it is in error in some significant way, is conclusive proof of point (i) above. But it might not *sound* convincing to those not accustomed to think about the difference between the meaning of and evidence for various sorts of claims. Just think of Meno's slave boy. When we say that he learned Theorem $\theta$, don't we *mean* that his behavior changed in the way described by Plato? Don't we also regard that change as something we can appeal to when we want to *support* our claim that he learned? Here the difference between explaining the meaning of what we claim and offering support for our claim is not clear at all. One way to ask someone to give evidence for what he says is to ask him what he means. "What do you *mean*—he learned Theorem $\theta$?" (The dash in the sentence indicates a drop in pitch, an ellipsis of ". . . when you claim that. . . .") And the most appropriate way to answer is to cite evidence in support of the claim—that is, to cite the changes in behavior described by Plato.

Sometimes, then, this logical distinction can't be made out very clearly; at other times the distinction is as clear as crystal. If, on one hand, we should ask a proponent of a $\Delta b$-type definition of learning what he *means* when he claims that he has learned that Formula Q, we wouldn't think that he had answered our question if he went on talking about the changes in his own behavior. On the other hand, if we ask him for *evidence* that he has learned that Formula Q, then his behavior (or a properly warranted set of statements about his behavior) is precisely what would satisfy. In ordinary language there is a difference between claiming to have learned *that* Formula Q and claiming to have learned *to say* "Formula Q" on the presentation of certain stimuli. That is strictly a difference in meaning; it holds even though some evidence— $\Delta b$ statements—which would support the former claim would equally well support the latter. To ask B what he means when he says that he has learned that Formula Q is to ask him, among other things, for reasons to believe that Formula Q is a valid definition. But if Formula Q *is* a valid definition, the only response that B can make is to refer to his own $\Delta b$: we ask for a reasoned argument, and all we can get is a confession. In sum, if one considers how anyone could ever learn that Formula Q, it should appear intuitively obvious that Formula Q, however many additions we add to it, can never capture our common-sense notion of learning.

(ii) But the believer in a Formula Q definition has a second line of defense. Many scientific concepts, such as mass, force, gravity, speed (of light), differ quite markedly from their common-sense origins and counterparts. Why should it be different for learning? After all, our ordinary language conception of learning had already been sealed into relatively fixed relations to ordinary language conceptions of knowing, believing, acting, willing, feeling, and so on, long before the appearance of scientific psychology and the discovery of the laws of learning, classical conditioning, operant conditioning, and the like. Should we not expect those ordinary language concepts to undergo rather fundamental shifts in response to those new scientific discoveries?

In many of the details of our beliefs *about* learning, the answer is yes indeed. There is no hard and fast line between a philosophical inquiry into the concept of learning and a psychological study of how learning occurs. It is probably true that at one time the common-sense notion of learning carried within it the doctrine of "Spare the rod and spoil the child"; that is to say, the *belief* that punishment was a necessary condition for learning may well have been considered part of the *meaning* of "learn." Moral enlightenment and psychological research have, fortunately, worked together to free the concept of learning from that obnoxious belief.

But in one respect, and that an absolutely crucial one, the antiquated common-sense notion is closer to a scientifically informed view of learning than any Formula Q definition can ever become. For all such definitions hinge on a particular understanding of what it is to be scientific, specifically that a science must eschew value judgments. So it is presumed that psychological theories of learning and research studies informed by those theories must rigorously avoid any value component in the definition. Hence the $\Delta b$ in Formula Q must be quite neutral as to value.

Our ordinary language notion of learning, however, as the rest of this chapter will demonstrate, reserves "learning" for those changes (in organisms, not behavior) that serve some intuitively understandable point or purpose, changes that have "direction," as Charles Taylor says.[7] A Formula Q, value-free definition of learning might work satisfactorily within a science of "behavioristics," to use the term and idea proposed by H. H. Price.[8] But such a science must inevitably be a dead end, if our more general scientific understanding of the world is accurate. For we would have to understand learning in a particular organism and the capacity for learning in a species all within a general evolutionary view of the world. And within that view of things, learning always has some definite point or purpose, even when it becomes too trivial to warrant mention. For example, we call what happened to Pavlov's poor dogs learning only because we can recognize a point or purpose in salivating before masticating and thus in salivating when presented with a wholly artificial sign of food. Without that connection, tenuous though it be, to some life-sustaining purpose, we wouldn't even be tempted to call the changes induced in Pavlov's dogs learning. When behavioristics tries to eliminate all value judgments from its inquiry, it also separates itself from an evolutionary view of the world and thus from any consideration as a serious branch of science.

The remarks of the last paragraph do not constitute advocacy of vitalism. The mechanisms of evolution are the same basic physical (including chemical) processes found everywhere in the universe, or so we presuppose in any scientific inquiry. But that this species survives and another becomes extinct is a function of adaptability, speaking roughly —the same rough sense of point or purpose that ordinary language builds into the concept of learning. The ordinary language conception of learning should have been a signpost on the way to an evolutionary view of life, though I know of no evidence that anyone ever saw it so.[9] But

[7] Charles Taylor: *The Explanation of Behavior* (London: Routledge & Kegan Paul Ltd., 1964), chap. IX. Taylor's work has informed many of the arguments of this chapter. It is a welcome counterexample to the charge that contemporary epistemologists have ignored the concept of learning.

[8] "Some Objections to Behaviorism" in Sidney Hook, ed., *Dimensions of Mind* (New York: New York University Press, 1960), p. 78.

[9] One can read that notion into Erasmus Darwin's "Hymn of Life" (1808), but it takes a bit of stretching to do so.

given that we share an evolutionary view of *all* organisms, it seems absurd to exchange our ordinary concept of learning (which has the appropriate directionality built into it) for a Formula Q definition, the *sole* virtue of which would be some utility in a dead-end science.

[As I said before, a full defense of these views (i and ii) would be another book. This sketch is simply to explain the decision to drop Formula Q and to return to the main route.]

**THE CAUSAL CONDITIONS RESTATED**    Let us now try to retrace our steps and escape this cul-de-sac. We are seeking the point of plausibility that tempts psychologists to erect a full-scale definition of learning on the formula that begins with $\Delta b$. When we say that B learned _____ X, we mean that B has changed in some way but not in just any old way. The cause of such change must be found in B's interaction with the world around him—in what B does in certain relations to what is done to B. The consequences of such change must be found in B himself: in B's ideas, beliefs, feelings, inclinations, dispositions, tendencies, or habits.

Thus there *is* a $t_1 - t_2$ implication in a learning claim. The $t_1$ is always expressible in the imperfect, active and passive: B was doing so-and-so while such-and-such was being done to B. (Experience, said John Dewey somewhere, is doing and undergoing. So be it.) If the learning claim itself is in the future tense, the $t_1$ part of it will take the future imperfect: B will have been doing so-and-so while such-and-such will have been happening to B.

The $t_2$ part of a learning claim is always simple indicative. As a consequence of that doing and undergoing, B *is* a (_____ X)er. Transposed to past or future, B was or will be a (_____ X)er. If B learned to hate Fascism, he is a Fascism-hater, unless he died or forgot or changed his mind. If B learned fifteen nonsense syllables, then for at least one shining, triumphant moment, B *was* a fifteen-nonsense-syllables-reciter, even if a half-hour later he could recall none of them. It would be excessively tedious to go through all the tenses and transformations that are involved in this $t_1 - t_2$ aspect of a learning claim. Let me just summarize it in this very rough way.

B learned _____ X is true only if:

at $t_1$    (i) B was (is, will be) doing something while
           (ii) Something was (. . .) happening in or to B
          (iii) such that and as a consequence of which
at $t_2$   (iv) B became (becomes, will become) a (_____ X)er.

This we will call the causal condition. The central philosophical claim

I wish to make right here is that what makes the learning claim what it is is not the specifically observable claims (i) and (ii) nor the dispositional claim (iv) but rather the connection between them—that is: (iii). *That connection must be intuitively plausible to any human being,* once he understands the account, *else the learning claim is false.* That is why learning theories—systematic attempts to account for that connection—must be either common sense or else total nonsense. Any learning claim presupposes a principle of sufficient reason: whatever is asserted in (i) and (ii) must describe an experience sufficient to *cause* B to become a (_____ X)er. If not, B didn't learn it *there.*

Put another way, to explain B's becoming a (_____ X)er as a consequence of *learning* is to make B's disposition or state of mind rationally intelligible to any rational mind. Perhaps that last statement makes it sound as if I am arbitrarily stipulating a definition of learning that applies only to full rational human beings. Quite the contrary! Let B be a specimen of the species planaria, a flatworm, a very simple and primitive little organism. Let B′ be his cousin. B has learned to wince (emit avoidance behavior) when a light is turned on his tank. B′ emits the same behavior, but he didn't learn it. How did it happen? Well, B was given a shock every time the light was turned on. After a while he didn't need the shock; he started to wince directly the light was turned on. *Wouldn't you?* After that response had been firmly established, B was terminated: his mortal remains were centrifuged and served to B′, who ate them with relish. After *that* B′ winced (a little) when the light was turned on, whereas he hadn't previously. Now it's a puzzler how B′ came to be a when-the-light-is-turned-on-wincer; but it is perfectly plain that B′ didn't, although B did, *learn* to.[10]

B, as we say, was conditioned to wince. B′ wasn't. However it may appear to flatworms, to Pavlov's dogs, or to Skinner's pigeons, conditioning is learning *because* the connection between the events at $t_1$ and those at $t_2$ is a totally rational connection. To show that this is so, let me cite another set of experiments designed to show just the opposite. Everyone is probably familiar with the phenomenon known as superstitious behavior in operant conditioning. You start with a group of active and motivated organisms. In the language of operant conditioning (though, unfortunately, not in ordinary discourse) "motivated" has a very precise meaning: an organism is motivated when it has been deprived of some specific element necessary to its well-being—food, water, sex, sensory stimulation, and sleep being examples. Motivated organisms, except for

[10] Sarnoff A. Mednick, *Learning* (Englewood Cliffs, N.J.: Prentice-Hall, Inc., 1964), chap. I. Mr. Mednick regards the experiment with the planarian as a "bit of a miracle," an opinion shared by several other psychologists who have told me of their inability to replicate the second (nonlearning) part of the experiment.

sleepy ones, tend to be active; they also tend to notice when presented with a piece of whatever it is that they're motivated for. Thus, slightly hungry children make excellent organisms for these experiments.

You put the children into identical little cubicles, each of which contains the same set of gadgets connected to a tray that dispenses gumdrops. In each tray appears a gumdrop at the same time, dispensed on a random but fairly frequent schedule. Each child, invisible to the others, will soon work out an individual little ritual of pulling, pushing, touching, turning, and so on. Like a pitcher or batter in baseball (and for the same reason) or a bowler stepping up to his lane, each child will reiterate a series of movements that are, to use the language of operant conditioning, a function of the contingencies of reinforcement. To some of these movements the child will be giving conscious attention, tugging at a lever, watching for results. To others he will be oblivious, rubbing his head, jerking his leg, and so on. Both the consciously directed movements and their unconscious parallels express the same basic rational principle: try to repeat that movement made just as (actually about a half second before) the candy appeared.

The actual behavior observed in such an experiment might well look irrational. But it is, and is rightly called, learned behavior *because* there is a principle of rationality behind it. Post hoc . . . propter hoc is not fallacious reasoning; the fallacy comes only when "ergo" is inserted between them. The experimenters have in fact severed the connection between the child's actions and their consequences for satisfying wants. But in the real world that connection must be presupposed, for it is what makes life possible. The principles of learning that all organisms follow derive from that same natural connection of cause and effect. Those principles, in turn, inevitably but unfortunately make pinball and slot machines immensely profitable.

**THE ORGANISM CONDITION** So whatever may be the case with other ways of explaining behavior, when we say that an organism has *learned* to act in a particular way, the reasons and causes for the behavior are the same. There must be a rational principle connecting the learning experience and the consequent change in the organism, else the learning claim must be rejected. There is only one small point to add before we turn the topic back to the psychologist. Notice the expression: "change in the organism." That expression seems the most natural way to express what happens when learning occurs. But it leads, also naturally, to the question: *where* in the organism does the learning occur? Learning some things must surely have neurological consequences; it has been proposed that the changes in muscular responsiveness that must occur in motor learning constitute the spatial location of the learning.[11] But it's fairly obvious that when we say that the organism has learned something, we don't mean just that some particular change has occurred in the neurological or muscular structure of the organism. If our theoretical understanding of neurophysiology advances to the point that it influences ordinary language, we might come to include the neuromuscular correlates as part of the meaning of learning claims, but we could never mean those *only* in the assertion of a learning claim. If the language should change, as well it might, such that "B learns _____ X" means *only* "There has been a $\Delta Y$ in B" where "$\Delta Y$" is defined entirely as neuromuscular changes (in language referring exclusively to electrochemical exchanges of energy, say), then "B learns _____ X" no longer makes a learning claim. So when we ask where in the organism learning occurs, we cannot take answers referring to neuromuscular changes as complete in themselves.

Where else, then? It may be harmless enough just to say that the learning is in the behavior of the organism. After all, the language of behavior, in ordinary discourse, is fairly accommodating. Even when we are talking about rather internal matters, we do have (actual or potential) behavior in mind also. Thus, when we say that Jones has learned to feel comradeship with his fellow workers, we have in mind the changes in his ways of acting toward those around him as well as that purely psychic state we call a warm feeling. Even if his own gruffness of manner or the repression of superiors should prevent Jones from manifesting his feeling of comradeship openly, we should expect it to show a little, perhaps in a twinkle of the eye or the like. And even if it didn't show at all, we mean that it would show had other forces not prevented it.

The only danger in saying that learning is to be found in the organism's behavior (as opposed to in his nervous system or muscles) is that many behaviorists, being quite mad, will take that to mean that learning *is* $\Delta b$, thus returning us to that cul-de-sac from which we were trying to escape. So let us just say that the learning is to be found in the organism as a whole. If B learns _____ X, then it is not B's neurones or dendrites or his supply of ATP, nor his id, nor ego (super- or alter), nor his personality, nor . . . ; it is *B* who becomes a (_____ X)er. The language of learning is the language of experience—thinking, feeling, and acting.

Let us now return the question of causes of learning to the psychologists, with the following (samples of) needed admonitions:

---

[11] The question of where reinforcement occurs is no longer of serious import among learning theorists. See Howard Rachlin, *Introduction to Modern Behaviorism* (San Francisco: W. H. Freeman and Company Publishers, 1970), pp. 105–113.

You have attempted to be scientists discovering arcane, esoteric processes in learning, like those discovered by physicists in radioactive decay or biologists in photosynthesis. Quite contrary to your intent, you have revealed to us in fact the essential unity of learning in all sentient creatures. Thanks to you, we understand how the planarian learns because it's exactly the same way *we* learn. You have imprisoned innumerable animals, starved them, tortured them, mangled them, and destroyed them. You have been prevented from doing the worst of those things to human beings, but not from deceiving, manipulating, frightening, testing, and confusing thousands of persons whom you call, all too appropriately, subjects.

So stop that infernal pursuit of science and start treating your subject (as well as "subjects") with respect. How does the principle of rationality work itself out in various species? You can induce neurotic and superstitious behavior in damned near any organism you choose, but only because that organism already possesses the capacity for rational learning. Having shown us how that capacity can be corrupted, show us how, under conditions of love, trust, and freedom, it can be most fully actualized.

Let me pause for breath and try to summarize the argument to this point before we move on. In Chapter Two, teaching was defined by two sets of conditions, one set for the truth of a teaching claim, the second for a claim that the teaching was successful. But in the first part of this chapter it was shown that those conditions do not distinguish teaching from its counterfeits—indoctrination and conditioning. Which is exactly as it should be. "Teaching" is the most general pedagogical predicate in English. We can know that Mr. Jones is teaching right now, even if we don't know whether his teaching will be successful, and even if, later, we recognize that what he was doing were better called indoctrination or conditioning. "Teaching" both includes and excludes its counterfeits, somewhat as "money" both includes and excludes *its* counterfeits.

But to show *how* teaching can be distinguished from indoctrination or conditioning we have to get clear exactly what learning is. For we do and should feel intuitively that the main basis for distinguishing teaching from its counterfeits lies in what happens to those to whom the teaching is directed—in the kind or quality of learning promoted. What makes an act teaching in the generic sense is the intent of the teacher and how that intent shapes an encounter. What makes it teaching in the specific sense, where "teaching" now excludes its counterfeits, is how and what kind of learning occurs. And all we have on that question, so far, is a recognition that a learning claim implies a rationally intelligible connection between B's doing-and-undergoing something at a particular time and B's being thereby changed in some specific way for later doings and undergoings. Since that condition for a learning claim applies as well to planaria as to physicists, it cannot be by understanding *that* condition of learning that we can distinguish teaching from its counterfeits. So let us look at learning a little more closely.

**LEARNING AS ACHIEVEMENT**     It has been said on many occasions that learning is an achievement. The argument usually offered for that view is a purely linguistic one, a claim that "learning" stands to its appropriate task word as "winning" to "striving," "finding" to "seeking," "catching" to "stalking," "curing" to "treating," and so on. I wish to examine that linguistic claim, for it is partially true, partially false. Seeing the linguistic argument more precisely will help to make clear the substantive point:

Sometimes learning is an achievement, sometimes not.

If Martha is practicing a particular run on the tuba, then learning to make that run (gracefully, and so on) is ordinarily a sign that she (or whoever set her to practice) has achieved what doing (or setting) the task aimed to achieve. If Marilyn is studying Boolean algebra, then learning Boolean algebra is . . . an appropriate achievement. For studying X, practicing X, taking instruction in X are ways in which one can try to learn X. And if one is really *trying* to learn X, why then learning X is, of course, an achievement. But one can be studying, practicing, taking lessons, and so on without really trying to learn anything but rather as ways of trying to avoid boredom or punishment or to pass a course or to achieve other more serious or trivial purposes, which purposes may or may not include learning.

If one learns something incidentally while trying to do something else, that learning may or may not be an achievement. Consider the pitiful sight of an addicted gambler dutifully shoving his life's savings into a one-armed bandit, one silver dollar at a time. He surely wasn't born acting that way. It wasn't something he just grew into. No, that too is learned behavior. But we should not think that learning such an addiction is an achievement. Nor the anxiety reactions of a neurotic, and the like. So let's examine the notion of an achievement word a little more closely. Just what makes "learn" an achievement word?

Consider these two formulae:

(i) If B is trying to S, then S-ing is what B is trying to do.
(ii) If B is trying to S, then R is what B is trying to achieve.

Now English (or any other natural language, I should guess) contains synonyms such that for the "trying to S" in (i), another term can be substituted without change of meaning or truth value, thus the clear-cut task words "striving" for "trying to win," and so on. Formula (i) is a test for that synonymy because its truth is guaranteed for all verbs that follow standard rules. [And even in the clearest cases, of course, synonymy is subject to challenge: "B is seeking a wife, but finding one is the thing he's least trying to do."(?)]

In (ii), the term for R has to be a noun, not a participle. It isn't winning but *a* win, a victory, that B is striving to achieve. If, while recovering from an injury, B is trying to turn his head, then *a* turning of his head is what B is trying to achieve. What counts as an achievement in life, of course, depends on circumstances; damned near anything *might* count. Grammar follows suit; what counts as an achievement *verb* is one that, in its appropriate gerundive, can take the place of R in (ii).

Now "learn _____ X" and its participle work quite well in formula (i). There are some values for "_____ X" such that it doesn't make much sense to say that B is *trying* to learn them—for example, that some things have names. It does make sense to say that a baby or a chimpanzee or a Helen Keller is learning that some things have names, but how could learning *that* (perhaps *any* learning that X) be something a person *tries* to do? But one can try to learn how to X, learn to X, learn the X; learning those things then becomes what one is trying to do.

But in formula (ii) *a* learning is (almost?) never the name of an achievement. If B is trying to learn _____ X, there is some name which designates what B is trying to achieve: a knowledge of X, a mastery of, an understanding or appreciation or awareness of, an acquaintance with, some skill in, a disposition toward, a feeling of or for, a willingness to, the capacity for or ability to . . . X. If B is trying to learn good manners, then it's good manners, not the learning thereof, that B is trying to *achieve*.

Thus there is reason to doubt that "learn" is *just* like the clearer cases of achievement words. We do designate other achievements by saying "a win," "a find," "a cure," "a catch"; we don't say "a learn." (There *is* a sense in which "learning" is unequivocally an achievement word, as in "She is a person of great learning." But that sort of learning—nowadays alas!—scarcely anyone is trying to achieve.) When "learn" takes the place of "S" in formula (ii), it is usually clear contextually just what would constitute the achievement being sought, but it is seldom (never?) the case that "learn" figures in the name of that achievement. Just because trying to learn is clearly a task, one which may be done in various ways (by studying, practicing, taking instruction, and so on), it doesn't follow that "learn" designates an achievement.

And yet learning does share many features of the typical achievement words. One may seek unsuccessfully, but not find unsuccessfully. One may teach unsuccessfully, but not learn unsuccessfully. Learning is so endemically what we're after in education that it sounds paradoxical or perverse to say that learning is not an achievement, or that learning and achieving come together only by chance, occasionally, as it were. If learning isn't an achievement, what is all our educational effort for?

**TWO "SENSES"**
**OF LEARN?**
The argument for analyzing "learn" as an achievement verb seems to be inconclusive. It shares some features with typical achievement verbs, but not others. There is a natural move to be considered at such a point, and a natural resistance to making that move. Perhaps there are two senses of "learn"—one an achievement sense, the other not. Perhaps the resort to two senses is merely a device for concealing our ignorance of what learning really is.

Let's begin with the negative hypothesis. The word "learn" contains no fundamental equivocation. Learning to read is an achievement, learning to gamble with an addicted compulsion is not an achievement; but they're both learning. Perhaps the difference between an achievement "sense" of learning and a nonachievement "sense" is nothing but the difference between learning worth-while, true, good things and learning useless, false, and evil things. The reason we are inclined to believe that "learn" has a distinctive "sense" of achievement is the simple empirical fact that learning *usually* produces a beneficial change in the organism. It would be strange if things were otherwise: after all, we are products of a long and costly evolutionary struggle; if those changes induced in us by experience—acting and suffering the consequences of our action—were not generally helpful, if those changes did not tend to achieve something of value for the organism, then we should likely have been pushed aside long ago by a smarter species competing for the ecological niche we are privileged to occupy.

The "we" in the sentence just above applies most obviously to Homo sapiens, so-called, but to whom or what else might it refer? Why to *all* the sentient, active organisms and species alive! That's why the way experience induces changes in the planarian is immediately, intuitively intelligible to human beings. In a figurative sense, at least, we are all products of the same learning process, one that began with the origin of the universe itself.

This line of argument I shall call the minimum approach to understanding the nature of learning. It holds, in effect, that a causal definition suffices to capture what "learn" means; that is, to say that B has

learned _____ X is only to *say* that some _____ X-type change in B
was caused by B's doing-and-undergoing in some particular environment.
In context, a learning claim may *imply* more than that, but any such
implication can always be seen to rest on something other than the nature of learning. That further contextual richness makes us regard
learning as an achievement: just because learning usually produces positive, survival-promoting changes in organisms, it doesn't follow that all
changes so produced are positive. We can and do learn useless, false, and
evil things, though, of course, that cannot be the norm, statistically
speaking, for any viable (sic) species. So begins the minimum approach
to an analysis of learning.

**ASSERTIVE RISK**              The maximum approach emphasizes the assertive
                               risks one takes when one makes a learning claim.[12]
There is a sense in which one takes a risk whenever he asserts anything,
for what he says can be false, or misleading, or harmful in its consequences. But the expression "assertive risk" is used here in a more
technical sense: the risk is forfeit if the assertion violates one or more
presuppositions that give point or purpose to the assertion itself.

The defender of the maximum approach holds that any learning
claim (any assertion of the form B learns _____ X) presupposes that
there is *some* value-for-B in the _____ X. To make a learning claim
and at the same time deny any value, in particular any value-for-B, in
the _____ X is to deprive the whole assertion of any point or purpose
in communication. In that sense, to forfeit on the assertive risk is to
render one's assertion meaningless.

This approach is called maximum in that it insists that epistemological and ethical criteria are invoked by any learning claim, and that
failure to satisfy those criteria means that the assertive risk in the learning claim is forfeit. Thus, the proponent of the maximum approach
comes back to the case of our pitifully addicted gambler—hunched, hag-
gard, halo-eyed, feeding silver dollars into the maw of the machine as
fast as his shaking hands will permit—and asks: "How in Hell could
you say he *learned* to act that way? What, exactly, did he *learn* to do?
Granted, he learned *how to* operate the machine, which is no great
achievement. Granted also, he came to be the way he is as a result of
what he did and didn't do and of what the world did and didn't do to
him in return, but to call his present misconduct 'learned behavior' is

---

[12] Analyzing pedagogical concepts from the point of view of the degree of assertive
risk each involves was only one of the major contributions of Paul J. Dietl's "Teaching, Learning, and Knowing," *Educational Philosophy and Theory*, Vol. 5 (New South
Wales University Press, 1973), 1–25.

to make a mockery of the whole idea of learning. There are lots of processes that determine how things turn out in the universe, but surely not all of them are learning."

I recognize that it is tedious to call these two positions "approaches," but it seems the best word. They are not definitions, much less theories of learning. There is the problem of interpreting or analyzing the connection, in a learning claim, between the "learn" and the "_____ X." "Learn" *does* have a causal sense, a change in an organism occurring in or over time. But there is nothing more to be said until one fills in the _____ X. Is it a change in the organism's beliefs, values, disposition, character, ideas, habits, feelings, manners or mannerisms? Which of them are properly called learning? I call these two ways of going about answering such questions "approaches" because you have to decide whether or to what extent epistemological and ethical criteria are tied up into the meaning of "learn" *before* you can say what learning is or what is learned.

Let us look at just a few more learning claims to see how they analyze when approached in these two ways.

1. Joan learned how to swim.
2. Karen is learning "Kubla Khan."
3. Laura learned Theorem $\theta$ yesterday.
4. Marie learned the identity of her father.

Now what we want to do is to qualify these claims to the point that the assertive risk in each is forfeit. Just when does the denial of value in the _____ X render the whole claim false or meaningless? If we add to 1 a long tale about Joan's being a captive of the junta and doomed to be executed before she ever had a chance to use her new skill, we deny that the learning did her any good but don't thereby jeopardize the learning claim. But suppose we add

1'. But the movements Joan makes would never propel her or anyone else through the water.

With enough ingenuity we might envisage a scene in which an honest person asserts 1 and 1' *seriatim*. If 1' is true, then 1 is false, and its falsity is somehow a linguistic error; even native speakers of a language may on occasion misuse it. Perhaps Joan believed the movements she was learning (say from a poorly designed manual) would propel her through the water, and perhaps that is what misled the speaker of 1 and 1' to say what he said. But once he considers just how he is using the word "learn," he will have to concede that the conjunction of 1 and 1' is the wrong way to say whatever it was that he wanted to say.

But exactly *where* does his assertion fail? From the minimum approach, it need not be a misuse of "learn." For 1' is clearly different from the mere negation of 1. We can separate two achievements involved in 1: swimming is an achievement, so is learning, even when it is learning something patently worthless in itself. If 1' is true, then Joan learned to make *certain* movements—to discriminate "correct" movements from others. We have to put "correct" in quotes because the principle of discrimination is not what she thinks it is; but *some* principle is involved, and learning how to X, *is* learning to make such discriminations. What's wrong with 1, assuming 1' is true, is the description of *what* Joan learned.

The contrast between 1 and 1' can be easily distinguished from 2 and

2'. But she'll never be able to get any two words of it right.

Here the antithesis simply cancels out the learning claim. 2' is simply, albeit in other words, the negation of 2. There is no peculiarity in the meaning of "learn" when the assertive risk is forfeit here. One always loses when he both affirms and denies the same claim.

Both 1-1' and 2-2' contrast with 3 and

3'. But Laura believes since yesterday that multiplying the side of a square by 1.5 will yield the side of a square double the original square.

Again there is something wrong with the conjoined assertion of 3 and 3', but there is nothing to indicate that the fault is in the use of "learn." It seems clear that Laura learned something; it is only that "Theorem $\theta$" misnames it. She got something, but she didn't get it right. If "George hit the ball" is asserted, then it must be withdrawn when it is shown that a soap bubble and not a ball was hit. But that does not prove that one forfeits the assertive risk in the use of "hit"; the use of the verb stays constant (or reasonably so) even when the object changes. So also with "learn" in 3-3'.

But now it gets harder to pursue the analysis from the minimum approach. Consider 4 and

4'. But the person Marie identifies as her father is not her father.

If 4' is true, 4 is false. Furthermore, it appears that 4 is false because "learn" is therein misused. There is nothing wrong in affirming:

5. Marie came to believe that Jones is her father.
5'. But Jones is not Marie's father.

Those two can both be true. But there is something wrong with:

6. Marie knows that Jones is her father.
6'. But Jones is not Marie's father.

And 4-4' are more like 6-6' than like 5-5'. The wrongness in 6 (if 6' is true) is in the use of "know." There is an identical wrongness in 4, if

4′ is true. One has not merely misdescribed what Marie learned; rather one has misused the language when he affirms 4 knowing that 4′ is true. There is nearly the same assertive risk in 4 as in 6. Unless the speaker of 4 has good reason to believe 4′ false, he should have said something like 5 instead, where "should have said" can be defended by appeal to the rules of ordinary discourse.

Thus we are into the heart of the case for the strong approach to the analysis of "learn." That case requires that we go back over the same ground. Can the line between 1, 2, 3 on one hand and 4 on the other be drawn as clearly as the previous arguments imply? Cannot the same charge of violating the rules for the use of "learn" be sustained against the speaker of 1 if 1′ is true? More generally, is there not something misleading in saying merely that one normally expects "learn" to be followed by something right or true? Is it not, rather, that the assertive risk in the use of "learn" lies in the fact that "learn" *implies* the truth or rightness of whatever fills the "_____ X" in our paradigm? Thus runs the strong approach to the definition of assertive risk in "learn."

**TWO APPROACHES COMPARED**　The minimum approach has not been defeated merely because it confronts some difficult questions. Its proponent has two lines of argument, mutually supportive. The first line is to claim that 1-4 *are* to be taken together and jointly distinguished from another sort of case altogether. The second line is, therefore, to reinterpret the analysis of 4-4′ so that it marches *pari passu* with the earlier interpretation of 1-1′.

First line: Yes, 1-4 and their antitheses are a package. They are all to be distinguished from:

7. Opal learned that Marcus Aurelius crossed the Rubicon in 49 B.C.
7′. But it is false that Marcus Aurelius crossed the Rubicon in 49 B.C.

If 7′ is true, then there is something wrong with the learning in 7; but what is wrong is not in "learn" nor in the description of what is learned. It is simply that there is very little value in learning something false. The clear line is between a correct description and a false descrip-tion of what is learned. And that line is precisely the line between the cases where a learning claim and its antithesis can both be true, as in 7-7′, and where one of them must be false, as in 1-1′ to 4-4′.

But what is required if 7 is true? A great many things, obviously. "Opal" must be the name of some person who believes, and, under suitable conditions, is able to affirm in one way or another, that Marcus Aurelius crossed the Rubicon in 49 B.C. There are a great many dis-criminations which Opal *must* be able to make if 7 is true; there are other discriminations which, if Opal could not make them, would lead us to doubt 7, if not give it up entirely. Take the discrimination between "historical person" and "fictional character" as descriptive of Marcus Aurelius: Opal's failure to make that discrimination correctly might lead us to deny 7, or it might require that we add a qualification about her lack of understanding of what she had learned. It is only when we are unwilling to recognize the relevant tests for learning that we are actually guilty of misusing the word "learn." Which leads us to the

Second line: No, 4-4′ is not all that different from 1-1′. What makes the strong approach so convincing in the case of 4-4′ is a simple, contingent fact: we do not ordinarily consider the identification of one's father an achievement unless the father is correctly identified. But identification, just by itself, *might* be an achievement. If Marie were a very young child or severely retarded, it would be an achievement if she could learn to identify a person as her father, even though the person so identified were not her father. In that case, of course, given that 4′ is true, 4 is still false, but only because it contains (or would in most contexts imply) a misdescription of what is learned, not a misuse of "learn." Furthermore, the case of the infant or retarded Marie actually reveals the primary sense of "learn" in *all* cases. The only way in which one can establish a violation of the linguistic rules for the use of "learn" in 4 is to conjoin it with a quite different antithesis.

4″. But there are no two men (living or dead or whatever) between whom Marie can discriminate (in any manner whatever) father from not-father.

The proponent of the minimum approach now has the upper hand. He can go on to deliver what seems the *coup de grace* against the strong approach: If "B learns that X" (where X is an intelligible proposition) implies that X is true, we could never say that some persons once learned that the earth is flat, that angels exist, that George Washington threw a silver dollar across the Potomac, and so on. But we do say those things, and we know exactly what we mean when we say them. Or, if learning propositions seems too remote, we can point to learning *to:* we know exactly what is meant if an anthropologist tells us that, in a certain tribe, some men learn how to bring on rain by dancing while other men learn how to attract game by drawing pictures. That's what they *learn,* even though, in fact, rain is unaffected by dancing and game is impervious to the charms of art.

The case for the minimum approach to the definition of "learn" appears so strong that it should win us over completely. But it does not. On the contrary, we find the whole matter more confused than before when we think back over the argument. We can understand why one might be tempted to hold to the doctrine of two achievements—learning as one achievement and what-is-learned's being correct as a second achievement. But the proponent of the strong approach reminds us that these two are not related in just the casual way which the minimum approach would have us believe.

Look again at 7: it does appear that the truth of 7 is independent of the truth of 7′. But if 7′ is true, just what are we saying that Opal has learned? Presumably, we mean more than if we had said: "Opal learned to repeat the sentence: 'Marcus Aurelius crossed the Rubicon in 49 B.C.' on command." Even the proponent of the minimum approach would have her make other "discriminations" which indicate (wouldn't we *have* to say?) her belief that a man named Marcus Aurelius performed a particular act at a particular time. And if that is what Opal believes, wouldn't she have to have *some* reason for her belief? Almost anything will count as a reason: "My teacher told me so." "I seem to remember having read it in a book somewhere." But if Opal could give no reason whatever, irrespective of the quality of the reason, for her belief, we simply would not understand 7. We don't have to know how Opal learned what she did in order to understand 7. But we do have the rule in the back of our minds that, however she learned it, in learning it she also acquired some reason (however minimum) for believing it true. There is that much assertive risk in *any* belief claim.

Now 7 is the sort of example that comes typically from an imagined pedagogical encounter. Such encounters are routinely marred by sloppy reasoning and careless talk by teachers, poor attention and retention by students. Under those conditions, people come to believe some very odd things; just about any false proposition one could make up might be learned, in that sense, by somebody sometime. It follows that "I think I remember having heard it in school" is not a very good reason for any belief. What is more important, however, is why it is a reason at all. It's a reason because the point or purpose in having a school is to promote learning; and learning, the proponent of the strong approach would hold, means more than merely making discriminations according to some rule; it means that the rule itself is a guide to truth in matters of belief, a guide to effective skill in means-ends actions, a guide to personal and social harmony in matters of attitude.

The proponent of the strong approach is on home ground when he gets to 4-4′. This use of "learn" is not typically derived from a pedagogical encounter. It seems quite clear that whatever point there was in using "learn" in 4 is totally lost if 4′ is true. It is instructive that the proponent of the minimum approach had to reinterpret 4 so as to suggest a pedagogical context (shift from "learn the identity of" to "learn to identify") before he could give any plausibility to his account of it.

**THE CASE
OF THE RAIN DANCE
RECONSIDERED**

Following the same rule, the proponent of the strong approach can make equally good sense of the historical and anthropological examples. It is true that we often fail to achieve our desired goals in learning. But that fact does not require us to give up that point or purpose in the meaning of "learn." If the anthropologist chooses to use language which suggests the standpoint of the tribesman rather than the observer, that is his privilege. It doesn't necessarily create misunderstanding. But from the standpoint of the tribesman, learning to bring on rain by dancing is *learning* something *because* the tribesman believes that his dancing causes rain. If he didn't hold that belief, then the term "learn" is misused in the anthropologist's account. Consider:

8. The tribesman learned how to cause rain by dancing.
8′. But the tribesman does not believe that dancing causes rain.

Let us interpret 8′ to mean generally that the tribesman believes that rain is caused by some combination of meteorological conditions, more specifically, that dancing has no effect whatever on rain. If both 8 and 8′ were true, continued questioning of the tribesman would lead to *his* saying: "I am causing rain, but I don't believe that I am"—which is, if not exactly self-contradictory, at least a *very* strange way to talk.

The peculiarity in the conjunction of 8 and 8′ lies strictly in the relation of "learn" and "believe"; it has nothing to do with the truth or falsity of any beliefs about the efficacy of dancing for the production of rain. Suppose the truth of the matter is that the rain dance produces solidarity in the tribe, releasing all the tensions and hostilities that communal living inevitably brings about. Thus

9. The tribesmen produce tribal solidarity by doing the rain dance.
9′. But the tribesmen do not believe that the rain dance produces solidarity.

Let 9′ be interpreted as 8′; the tribesmen hold very specifically that the rain dance has no effect on group solidarity, which, they believe, is produced by another ceremony, one which the anthropologist discounts as functionless, lacking the requisite emotional intensity of the rain dance. Even so, there is no logical nor anthropological oddity in the conjunction of 9 and 9′.[13] But if we change 9 to read "The tribesmen *learn to* produce tribal solidarity . . . ," then its conjunction with 9′ results in the same breakdown of communication as does the conjunction of 8 and 8′.

Can we generalize this example and say that learning how *to* X im-

---

13 On the relation of the anthropologist's point of view to that of the tribesman, see the collection of papers edited by Bryan R. Wilson, *Rationality* (New York: Harper & Row, Publishers, 1970).

plies belief *in* X? Obviously not. Children learn how to say prayers and pledge allegiance (often quite vigorously) without any specific beliefs at all. But we can make an even more important generalization: (learning how to bring about Y by doing X) implies (believing that X produces Y). Learning how to swim implies both learning how to make certain movements *and* coming to believe that making those movements will propel one through the water without drowning. We distinguish between those species that swim instinctively and those that must learn how to swim (mostly) on the belief criterion. The movements a dog makes while swimming he doesn't *learn how to* make; he does the "dog paddle" instinctively, or so it seems. But many full-grown dogs that never swam as pups do seem to have to learn how to swim; terrified at finding themselves in water for the first time, they must *learn that* those movements will keep them safely afloat and get them where they want to go. If it sounds a bit anthropomorphic to speak of a dog's learning *that* so-and-so is the case, so be it. The only fallacy is to treat human learning as if it were *not* anthropomorphic.

**LEARNING TO READ** Speaking more specifically of human learning, we can see that this point has an immediate bearing on the most serious and perplexing practical problem faced in schools —namely, teaching children how to read. The reactionary ideology of many specialists in the teaching of reading leads them to the view that reading is *purely* a skill to be taught and learned by training. Using appropriately military metaphors, these specialists drill their charges in "word-attack skills" and in "strategies of recognition." The question of what one is doing these things *for* never arises, much less, God forbid! the question whether doing these things will indeed produce the end, if any, sought by the learners.

What, in fact, *do* so-called "problem readers" believe that reading is? What relation do *they* see between the particular skills they are asked (or, shameful to say, forced) to master and the purpose that is presumed to lie behind the exercises? Such questions are seldom raised by reading specialists, because research has shown that time-and-effort spent on such matters does not pay off in increased scores on tests. But if one takes the maximum approach to learning, there is an enormous difference between making a particular score on a test and *learning* how to read. The latter implies, and the former does not imply, coming to believe that there is a rule-directed relationship between shapes of ink traced on a page and sounds of spoken language. Never mind that in English those rules are needlessly complicated. Never mind that what is said in writing usually differs in significant ways from what one hears in ordinary spoken discourse. It is nonetheless the connection between shape and sound that gives point and purpose to the activity of reading, such that reading is something that one can *learn* how to do. Unless a person comes to believe that there is such a connection, not just in the abstract but in concrete relation to his own purposes, that person can never learn how to read, even though he may, under expert manipulation, come to score quite high marks on tests. That is how it appears to one who takes the maximum approach; from the minimum approach, of course, there would be no *contradiction* between the following:

10. Wanda has learned how to read English at the fifth-grade level.
10′. Wanda does not believe that there is a connection between shapes on a page and the sounds of spoken English.

Whether the conjunction of 10 and 10′ represents a logical impossibility or a statistical improbability is precisely the difference between the maximum and minimum approaches to the nature of learning.

**TWO APPROACHES**  It is tempting to try to resolve this difference by
**IN SUMMARY**  claiming that the word "learning" has two different meanings (the linguistic cop-out) or that the Essence of Learning is to be found in the simultaneous and reverential perception of One Process from Two Approaches (the theological cop-out). We should start, instead, with what appears as plain as anything: whether we're talking about planaria learning to wince or dogs learning to swim or human beings learning any of the things described (and misdescribed) in 1-1′ through 10-10′, the word "learn" certainly seems to retain the same meaning throughout. Despite the wide range of logically different considerations, 1′ through 10′, which would falsify or nullify the different learning claims, 1 through 10, it is not the case that these differences imply different senses of "learn." Learning does not appear to be an essentially ambiguous concept. This apparent univocality we may designate as Point #1 about learning.

As might be predicted, there is a Point #2, even if, like the second act of many a Broadway play, it is something of a letdown: everything that's important for a *definition* of "learn" has already been said in the causal analysis given in the first part of this chapter. To say that organism B has learned something is to say that one (anyone, any rational mind) understands (immediately, intuitively, without need of connecting generalization) that the particular change in B one is talking about (some change in B's behavior, feelings, beliefs or ideas, attitudes, values, disposition, habits, will, or whatever) is a result of B's experience (is caused by B's acting and suffering/enjoying the consequences of his actions). This definition may lack precision in certain dimensions, but it is precise enough to account for the following distinction:

Q: Why is B walking with a limp?
$A_1$: Because he broke his leg.
$A_2$: Because he's learned to compensate for a broken leg.

$A_1$ presupposes the empirical generalization: broken leg $\longrightarrow$ limp. It requires no particular understanding of B or B's plight. To anyone who knows the generalization, the explanation is as complete as any explanation ever could be. $A_2$, however, requires that one understand that particular limp as achieving some value-for-B: minimizing pain, say, or maximizing efficiency in locomotion despite the incapacitated limb. $A_2$ presupposes the truth and *completeness* of $A_1$; for if B's limp were not caused by a broken leg but by B's efforts to gain sympathy, $A_2$ would be false. Thus $A_2$ implies $A_1$, but $A_1$ does not imply $A_2$. A broken leg can cause B to limp *simpliciter;* or a broken leg can become the occasion for B's learning (how) to limp in some *particular* value-for-B-promoting-sort-of-way.

To advert once again to the addicted gambler, the definition proposed here makes clear exactly what's involved in claiming that the addict's behavior is *learned.* Perhaps surrendering himself to the contingencies of a schedule of intermittent reinforcement *is* something he learned to do, and in so doing, to escape boredom or despair—perhaps some blind stairwell to suicide. The psychologist's insistence on saying that his behavior (all behavior?) is learned *may be* a very wise demand that we see the point or purpose the addiction serves the addict, that we not think that we have correctly understood his compulsive behavior until we see the value-for-the-addict which it serves.[14] Or the psychologist's insistence on calling it "learned behavior" may be nothing more than *his* addiction to neologisms, something *he* learned from a misunderstanding of the nature of scientific inquiry.

Now to Point #3. A learning claim invokes certain epistemological and moral criteria without *exactly* implying that these criteria are satisfied in the particular case. Ordinarily if B learned _____ X and B has not forgotten _____ X, then B *knows* _____ X. Ordinarily, if B learned _____ X, then, even if Xing is otherwise morally reprehensible, *B's* Xing is not subject to the degree of moral condemnation that

[14] A powerful, albeit easily misunderstood, exposition of this view is R. D. Laing, *The Politics of Experience* (Harmondsworth: Penguin Books Ltd., 1967). Laing is not, as some cultists would make him out to be, an advocate of "The Irrational." His point is that quite bizarre forms of thought and action can become intelligible when examined with patient attention to the value-for-B which the behavior must have seemed to possess as B learned so to think and act. Thus, for Laing therapy is best conceived as teaching-and-learning with no fixed roles possible.

attaches to the purely willful, incomprehensible act (or habit) of Xing.

But once again, what is ordinarily the case is not necessarily the case. Bertrand Russell reminds us: "The man who has fed the chicken every day throughout its life at last wrings its neck instead."[15] The poor chicken may be said to have learned that the man's appearance signified the coming of food, but no one would claim that the chicken knew so. Similarly, Adolph Eichmann certainly learned to follow orders no matter what, and that fact changes the nature of the repugnance we feel toward the man and his deeds. It is their *learned* quality that reduces Eichmann's actions from the monstrous to the merely banal.

Q': How then are epistemological and moral criteria related to learning claims? The variety of learning claims presented above and the contrast between the minimum and maximum interpretations of these claims all justify only one conclusion: it is impossible to find an answer to Q' by the analysis of ordinary language. The only answer worthy of serious attention would be a philosophical theory of learning, itself grounded in more general evolutionary theory. It would emphasize the continuity among animal species; that is to say, the theory would relate our conceptions of knowledge and moral worth to empirically validated conceptions of species adaptability. The theory would also make it clear just how the distinctively human capacity for language makes it inevitable that we learn false beliefs; learning falsehoods, in turn, makes it possible to unlearn, which seems to be a uniquely human capacity—one that, sad to say, seems less than fully developed in any of us and totally atrophied among militarists. It is that capacity which makes possible critical self-consciousness; therein lies the foundation for habits of critical reflection which, we hope, may be taught as well as learned. In sum, a theory of learning is or ought to be a branch of philosophical anthropology. Learning is what ties together our nature as dynamic biological organisms and our nature as seekers of truth and justice.

The development of such a theory is clearly the next step in philosophical inquiry. In the meantime, it must be presupposed. The distinction between teaching on one hand and indoctrinating or conditioning on the other can never be made out clearly without appealing to the distinction between what have been called here the maximum and minimum approaches to learning. But what *is* learning, that it can be approached in such different ways? For now, we simply assume that a scientifically adequate theory can be developed, one which accounts both for what is known about the neurophysiological processes involved in learning and for the fact that epistemological and moral criteria are evoked by any learning claim even though the satisfaction of those cri-

15 *The Problems of Philosophy* (Oxford University Press, 1946), first published 1912.

teria is not (always) a necessary condition for the truth of the learning claim. There is still a great deal to be learned about learning.

**TEACHING AND ITS COUNTERFEITS: REPRISE** Teaching is distinguished from other ways of bringing about learning by the kind of learning it brings about. Put most simply, the argument is this: assume the truth of ordinary English sentences constructed on the paradigms for teaching and learning claims.

(i) A teach(es) B _____ X.
(ii) B learn(s) _____ X.

Assume congruent tenses in (i) and (ii) such that (iii) is plausible, and also assume (iii) to be true.

(iii) The event designated by (i) is the cause of the event designated by (ii).

Assume further that (iv) is syntactically possible and semantically plausible.

(iv) B knows _____X.

Assuming the truth of (iii),

(v) If (ii) $\longrightarrow$ (iv), then (i) is teaching in its specific sense—where teaching is conceptually distinct from indoctrination and conditioning.

This way of distinguishing teaching from its counterfeits may seem suspect; it may appear an awfully cheap and easy way to solve a problem that has exercised some of the best minds engaged in philosophy of education in this century.[16] Such suspicion cannot be dismissed lightly. I believe that the simple little argument above really does distinguish teaching from its counterfeits, absolutely and unequivocally. One reason, I think, for its not having been generally recognized as *the* way to make the distinction is quite clear: it's a consequence of the relative neglect of the concept of learning even by those philosophers treating the epistemological questions in philosophy of education most directly.[17] Another, and probably more important, reason is that this way of drawing the distinction leaves very little room where we can be sure that we are teaching and not indoctrinating or conditioning; this argument draws a fairly narrow circle and says: "(Only) within that area can you be sure

[16] The recent literature on indoctrination is remarkable for its seriousness of purpose and the degree of mutual engagement among the contributors. An excellent selection from this literature is I. A. Snook's *Concepts of Indoctrination* (London: Routledge & Kegan Paul Ltd., 1972). Snook is also the author of an extended analysis of the topic, *Indoctrination and Education* (London: Routledge & Kegan Paul Ltd., 1972).

[17] For example, Israel Scheffler, *Conditions of Knowledge: An Introduction to Epistemology and Education* (Glenview, Ill.: Scott, Foresman and Company, 1965).

that what you are doing is teaching and not a counterfeit. If there are instances of teaching outside that circle, their claim to that status has to be established on other grounds." In fact, of course, those "other grounds" come out clearly to be weakened versions of the same argument, with no particularly compelling reasons for relaxing the standards.

But let us review some of the learning claims we have looked at earlier in this chapter to see which of them *do* imply a knowledge claim. Here they are repeated:

1. Joan learned how to swim.
2. Karen is learning *Kubla Khan*.
3. Laura learned Theorem $\theta$ yesterday.
4. Marie learned the identity of her father.
5. (Not a learning claim)
6. (Not a learning claim)
7. Opal learned that Marcus Aurelius crossed the Rubicon in 49 B.C.
8. The tribesman learned how to cause rain by dancing.
9. (Not a learning claim)
10. Wanda learned how to read English at the fifth-grade level.

Now which of those learning claims imply a congruent knowledge claim? Why, all of them, or so one would assume if one encountered them cold, as it were. If 1 is true, there must have been a time interval, however brief, during which Joan *knew* how to swim. If 2 is true, Karen is *coming to know Kubla Khan*. It doesn't matter how much or how little is packed into "learning *Kubla Khan*." It might include only coming to repeat the syllables "In-xa-na-du- . . . ," or it might include a rich comprehension of sound, sense, and imagery as well. No matter; whatever is packed into "learning *Kubla Khan*," exactly the same is packed into "coming to know. . . ."

If 3 is true in whatever sense or degree, then it is also true in the same sense or degree that Laura *knew* Theorem $\theta$. If one takes a rather straitened view of epistemological criteria, one may say that 3 implies only that Laura has a justified true belief about how to double the area of a square. If one holds instead that Laura's *knowing* Theorem $\theta$ requires that she experience a special sort of certainty-feeling, at least enough to overcome her natural timidity so that she raises her hand when the teacher asks "Who knows how to double the area of a square?", then one would have to argue that 3 implies that further condition as well. Likewise with 4; learning and knowing stay in tandem whatever the curves in the road.

Serious problems arise from 7 and 8. Unless Opal has, in fact, revolutionized our understanding of Roman history, and the tribesman our conception of causation in meteorology, then they can't be said to know what 7 and 8 claim they have learned. But notice: unless Opal had come to her false belief because of someone's teaching her exactly that, we wouldn't think of saying that she had *learned* it. If she were herself a historian who had come to that belief by a misconstruction of documentary evidence, we would say simply that she had (erroneously) come to believe that X, not that she had learned that X. The same analysis applies to the tribesman's learning how to cause rain by dancing. If his were an untutored action, not even the most radical anthropologist would be inclined to say that he had *learned* how to cause rain by dancing, unless, *mirabile dictu*, he *did* cause rain by dancing.

Thus we face a tough decision in relating 7 and 8 to our earlier analyses of successful learning. If the distinction between teaching and its counterfeits is made out as in (i)–(v), then Opal must have been indoctrinated or conditioned to believe that Marcus Aurelius crossed the Rubicon in 49 B.C. No matter that her teacher was most conscientious, that there was no intent to deceive or short-circuit her critical faculty. If her belief can truly be said to have been *caused* by that interaction (that is, the interaction informed by her teacher's intention to bring it about that she learn that Marcus Aurelius crossed the Rubicon in 49 B.C.), then that interaction was teaching only in the generic sense; more specifically it was indoctrination or conditioning.

I don't claim that that conclusion sounds entirely plausible by itself. The reason that it sounds implausible is this: The knowledge claim implied by 7 seems to fail only on the truth condition. We are asked to imagine a teaching encounter which is by all standards impeccable; Opal only happened to learn a false belief in that encounter, and for that reason alone we are required to say that that otherwise splendid example of teaching wasn't teaching at all but indoctrination or conditioning. That's *too* tough, you want to say.

*I* want to say that your standards are simply too low. You are still using "teaching" as the Greeks were when Socrates resisted the word as descriptive of his interaction with the slave boy. In the chapter following appears a conception of teaching in its specific sense which can guarantee, at the very minimum, that B not be caused to have false or unjustified beliefs by engaging with A in a teaching-learning interaction.

There is another tough decision made (and perhaps concealed) in (i)–(iv). One might want to say that learning always entails knowing, hence that 7 is self-contradictory. Suppose that we had developed in detail a theory which relates the epistemological and moral criteria in learning claims to an evolutionary view of the value-for-B in learning activities. It *might* be that that theory would have learning $\longrightarrow$ knowing as one of its basic axioms. But I doubt it. I think that the ability to learn false beliefs is a distinct evolutionary advantage in any species; it is clear that that ability increases with advances on any reasonable phylogenetic scale, reaching its high point (on Earth) in Homo sapiens. It is also clear that that ability came to God only late in His development, learned, we might say, as the Son of Man.[18] For all those reasons, I am inclined to presume a theory in which (i)–(iv) are consistent with a full-fledged definition of "learning."

May we then conclude this chapter by proposing the following claim:

(B has learned _____ X) ⟶ (B knows _____ X) or (vel) (B has been
      (successfully) taught _____ X)

When the "vel" comes through as "both," then we know that teaching and not conditioning or indoctrination (or both) has occurred. And that is the only way we can ever be sure that we have the genuine article and not a counterfeit.

It would be easy but tedious to show that this formula captures what's important and true in the more standard analyses of indoctrination—those which concentrate on instructional content, method, and intent. Especially when dealing with ideological or theological doctrines, it seems (to me) simpler to begin one's analysis with a consideration of whether or not the propositions therein can be rationally believed, exactly what sort of reasoning would be required to justify the beliefs, in what sense, if any, they can be true—and then to consider whether they can be taught or whether only indoctrination or conditioning can be effective in getting people to accept them. That sort of analysis would inevitably lead to some drastic changes in our notions of a justifiable curriculum. So be it.[19]

[18] I'm indebted to J. L. Kuethe's insight for this point.

[19] Just that sort of analysis is sketched (or clearly presupposed) in many efforts to justify a curriculum. See Jane Martin, ed., *Readings in the Philosophy of Education: A Study of Curriculum* (Boston: Allyn & Bacon, Inc., 1970).

# CHAPTER FOUR

# The Acts
# of Teaching

**THE SPECIFIC**
**CONCEPT**
**OF TEACHING**

The tasks left for this chapter follow quite predictably from the conclusions of the last. (a) It is impossible to build a definition of "learning" on the model that begins with "change in behavior." Therefore, we have to pursue further the idea that learning is coming to know. And (b) the way in which teaching can be distinguished from its counterfeits—indoctrinating and conditioning—involves an appeal to the same idea of coming to know. In this chapter the effort is to pull (a) and (b) together in such a way that we can see an act of teaching-and-learning which satisfies the epistemological and moral constraints involved in both those ideas.

Is the idea of teaching-and-learning here proposed one that can become the normal, routinely expected pattern of interaction between teachers and learners in school? Or is it merely a utopian vision? I try to show in this chapter that the conception of teaching which follows from a recognition that learning *is* coming to know is exactly what we are already committed to in our common-sense view of the *particular* acts of which teaching is composed. There is a radical political message here, but it is nothing more than a conscious recognition of what's implicit in our everyday beliefs about teaching and learning.

**LEARNING AS ACTION AND AS INCIDENT** Sometimes when we learn something, even when we don't learn exactly what we set out to learn, learning is nevertheless what we *do;* it is an action, more or less deliberate or intentional. A person is asked: "What are you doing right now?" He replies: "I'm learning a new song." Or ". . . what really happened at Sarajevo." And so on.

It might be claimed that in such contexts "I am learning" is only an inflated way of saying "I am studying" or "working on" or, most generally, "*trying* to learn." I propose that we reject that claim. For when there is a clear presumption that by doing X we will get Y, the rules of language permit or encourage us to describe what we're doing as getting Y. To say "I am watering the horses" is not an inflated but rather a perfectly natural way to describe one's action when one is moving the pump handle up and down expecting water to appear. It is equally natural to say "I am learning a new proof" when one is just beginning to puzzle out an unfamiliar set of symbols. Learning can be what one is doing, even when one does a lot of other things, in the process, as it were (but *only* "as it were").

Sometimes learning is something that happens to us; it is an unanticipated, even unnoticed, consequence of doing something else. It *can* be something that we pay attention to, as St. Paul no doubt paid attention to what he just happened to learn on the road to Damascus. Or it can be something that we don't even notice, which is the way most of us learn how to reach a familiar light switch in the dark.

Let us call those two "active" and "incidental" learning respectively, meaning only to distinguish between learning as something a person is *doing* (more or less deliberately) and learning as what happens to a person incidentally to that person's doing something else. The terminology may be unfortunate if it brings up mental pictures of vigorously active people being contrasted with people just allowing things to happen to them. That isn't it at all: incidental learning happens to people who are, perhaps very actively, doing other things; and active learning may be going on while the learner is sitting in what looks like utter passivity. The question is whether, from the point of view of the agent, the point or purpose of what he's doing is to learn something or whether it's something else. Three students are working side by side in the school's engine shop. They make identical movements—look intently at a manual, examine a tool, unscrew a nut. The first is replacing a gasket, the second is learning how to replace a gasket, the third doing both.

How do you know? You ask them.

This distinction between active and incidental learning is totally independent of the earlier argument that no learning is changed (or changing) behavior. The basic idea on which to construct a definition of learning is that learning has to do with coming to know. But we can't make any sense out of "I am knowing X" as an answer to the question: "What are you doing right now?—nor of "I am trying to know X"— unless "X" is the name of a person and "know" means "become acquainted with." Let's leave that aside and deal only with know that, the, how to, and mixtures, such as know when to depress the clutch pedal in shifting gears.

If it is possible for one to try to learn X, and if learning is coming to know, then we should be able to make sense out of "I am trying to come to know X." That usage seems to me awkward but not ungrammatical. A person who was simultaneously learning how to speak English and how to drive an automobile might say: "I am trying to come to know when to depress the clutch pedal in shifting gears." If his mastery of driving were exactly equal to his mastery of English diction, we should expect the gears to mesh successfully, albeit less than smoothly. If he should say, instead, "I am trying to change my clutch pedal depressing behavior in response to auditory, visual, and kinesthetic stimuli," we should despair of his ever learning either driving or English. In short, I do not count it a decisive objection to the conceptual scheme here developing that the active sense of learning translates rather awkwardly as coming to know. Perhaps we just need more practice with "trying to learn."

## THE ANOMALY OF "THAT X"

Anything that can be learned can be learned incidentally. Every skill is ultimately subsumable under some more inclusive skill. One can learn how to ride a bicycle incidentally in the course of learning how to ride a motorcycle. One could learn the techniques of brain surgery incidentally in the course of doing cancer research, or whatever. One has to be actively doing something before one can learn something else incidentally, and it would be strange as hell if one learned incidentally that the $\log_{10}$ value of $e$ is .43429448 . . . while playing mah-jongg in Rittenhouse Square. That would be awfully hard to explain but quite easy to say. Insofar as there really could be an empirical science of learning, it would be an investigation of how an organism can learn how much of X incidentally, in the course of doing Y. Needless to add, there is no such science at the moment.

But can one make sense of the idea of coming to know *that* X as active learning? It isn't easy to say. One can easily imagine situations in which the natural and informative way to tell what's going on is to say "I am learning that X." A historian has been studying some just-revealed documents. He says: "I am learning that the Austrians received ample warning." He wouldn't say *that* in response to the question: "What are you *doing* right now?" Rather, if he did, he would not answer the question. But he might well say that in answer to: "What do you make of the new evidence?"

The significance of that little point will appear later. But it does indicate a limit to active learning. It makes sense to say that one is trying to replace a gasket or trying to learn how to replace a gasket or trying to do both at the same time. But does it make sense to say that one is trying to learn that so-and-so is the case? A person might say: "I am trying to learn that one ought to return injury with love." But what he means, one must suppose, is that he's trying to acquire the habit or disposition of returning injury with love; he's trying to learn *to act* that way, not *that* so-and-so is the case. What would be the point or purpose of trying to learn what one already believes? Or, to compound the absurdity, of trying to learn (come to know) some proposition one does *not* believe? There's a point in trying to learn *whether* so-and-so is the case, but not to learn *that* it is.

We can know, then, that if B learns that X at a particular time $t_1$, then at $t_1$ B was *doing* something else, possibly learning (to, how to) something else. Whereas if B learned to X, or how to X, or the X (or any other _____ X) at $t_1$, it *could* be the case that learning _____ X was what B was doing at $t_1$. That's a small point, but it points toward an important limit on the doctrine of learning by doing. Insofar as pedagogical intent is directed toward propositional learning—getting someone to learn *that* X ("X" being a place-filler for a proposition)—that intent cannot be satisfied by promoting active learning: learning that X logically cannot be what one is doing. The moral to be drawn from that logical point is not necessarily to give up the attempt to promote learning by doing; the moral may be (I believe it is) to give up the notion that one ought *ever* set out a list of propositions to be taught. One can set out such a list as the intended outcome of indoctrination; but teaching, as we are getting closer to it, is something else.

**ACTIVE AND INCIDENTAL LEARNING RELATED**

It's an enlightening perspective on the history of pedagogical theory to note the way in which various thinkers have seen the relationship between active and incidental learning. Every significant philosopher of education (by definition?) has recognized the overwhelming importance of incidental learning in establishing those fundamental traits of character which make further, active learning possible. I think one can distinguish two streams flowing through our tradition of educational thought. One stream, from Plato through Freud, seems to regard the really central (incidental) learning of character traits as coming very early in life and as being irreversible. Another tradition flows from Aristotle through Dewey; in that tradition maturity is defined as that stage of life when one becomes responsible for one's own incidental learning and thus responsible for one's own character. For character is defined not by fixed traits but by patterns of habits. And habits do not control our destiny, they only incline us to act in certain ways. We come to have the habits that comprise our character as a consequence of what we do in the world, of what happens to us as a consequence of our doings, and, most importantly, of how we come to understand the connection between what we do and what happens as a result. For our actions and our understanding each of us is responsible personally; that responsibility cannot be laid off on the incidental learning of one's childhood.

As far as I can tell, Rousseau was the first educational theorist who went beyond a somewhat ritualistic acknowledgment of the importance of incidental learning to a carefully thought out conception of *how* incidental learning could be controlled by conscious pedagogical intent. The conditions necessary for such control, as Rousseau saw clearly, are enormously difficult to establish. They include not only shielding a child from pernicious examples and habits—a matter already given thorough treatment by classical and medieval thinkers—but also making sure that a "natural" system of rewards and punishments is allowed to work itself into control of the child's growth. Rousseau seems to have believed that only incidental learning should occur to the child prior to the age of reason (vaguely associated with sexual maturity), but he also had an almost unlimited faith in what could be taught to a child by conscious and planned control of his incidental learning. Given the conditions described with such immediacy by Rousseau, described as though seen from inside Émile, that faith seems plausible. What Émile finally learned, however, was to be utterly dependent on the world around him (and thus on J. J., who manipulated that world) for his own sense of self. We never see Émile actively learning to become the person *he* chooses to be.

John Dewey's analysis is unquestionably an advance over Rousseau's, both practically and conceptually. Rather than making the distinction between incidental and active learning correspond to a (mythical) line between two stages in the life of a person, Dewey saw that both kinds of learning are indispensable moments in every significant experience. The initial occasion for learning must arise (for most people most of the time) incidentally—that is, in the process of doing something else. But as activity is blocked and the recalcitrant situation penetrates the agent's consciousness, learning comes to be itself what the agent is doing. Doing *that* requires not only clarifying and seeking consistency among one's beliefs; for Dewey it also means getting out into the material world, literally moving *things* about, to see whether they behave as one's clarified beliefs had led one to expect that they would. To test one's beliefs by trying them out objectively (in the world of objects) is no doubt excellent advice in general, though it sounds a bit strained when made a condition for knowing mathematics and formal logic.[1]

There may be some hedging at points in Dewey's voluminous writings, but the general tenor is clear: the complete act of thought, including its complementary moments of active and incidental learning, has the same form (and thus the same formal criteria of adequacy) for the two year old and the eighty-two year old, for the philosopher as well as for the plumber, for the dishwasher, the artist, the scientist, for Everyman and Everywoman. It follows, so Dewey believes, that the duty of education is to enable each individual to achieve a maximum competence in learning and in acting on what he or she has come to know. The accumulated wisdom of the human race—which is found in our enormous heritage of culturally collected experience rather than in our narrowly circumscribed pool of genes—is what we can and must pass on to individuals in order that their competence be freed from the limits of what they can experience directly. But the only way we can pass on that heritage meaningfully is by helping each child to *use* some relevant portion of it in his efforts to control what happens in life. Freedom to follow one's own purposes thus becomes a necessary condition of education for Dewey—or for anyone else who bothers to think straight on the question.

Dewey's views are so unquestionably true and right that we cannot lose hope for their ultimate effect on educational institutions. But on the question I am trying to answer, Dewey said little that was clear and convincing. To put our question in Dewey's terms: What role, if any, does *teaching* play in the complete act of thought? Here we must call again for the distinction between incidental and active learning. In those phases of the educative experience in which learning is incidental, teaching is creating for every child a wholesome and free learning environment—an environment that presents a harmonious balance of challenge and security to every child. And that task belongs, as Dewey saw quite clearly, to the entire society, not just to the school as such. It is a task that has been shamefully neglected by most societies: we had rather

1 John Dewey, *Logic: The Theory of Inquiry* (New York: Henry Holt and Co., 1938), pp. 394–395.

"teach" our children by cruel and irrational repression to stay out of the streets than to transform our streets into avenues that children may explore and through which they may expand their world. The signal importance of incidental learning in every human life sets an educational task of high seriousness for every society; it is in recognition of that seriousness that high-minded educators often say: "We do not teach; instead we attempt to create an environment in which children can learn." The sentiment is noble, but the thought is incomplete.

**ANALOGY**
**TO BUYING-SELLING**

For there is also a phase of active learning in the educative experience. It is in relation to active learning that teaching, distinct now from indoctrination or conditioning, gets its foothold. It is here that the oft-cited analogy between teaching and learning, on one hand, and buying and selling, on the other, gets its plausibility. Dewey linked the analogy closely to the active sense of learning:

> There is the same exact equation between teaching and learning that there is between selling and buying. The only way to increase the learning of pupils is to augment the quantity and quality of real teaching. Since learning is something that the pupil has to do himself and for himself, the initiative lies with the learner. The teacher is a guide and director; he steers the boat, but the energy that propels it must come from those who are learning.[2]

In this passage, as in much of Dewey's writings, one finds strangely incompatible figures of speech. If the "equation" mentioned in the first quoted sentence were really "exact," we should expect that "buying" could be substituted for "learning" and "selling" for "teaching" in the second sentence—with a result somewhat different from the Dale Carnegie-ish sound that in fact comes if we make those substitutions. Where *does* the "initiative" lie in buying and selling? Is the relation of seller and buyer *or* teacher and learner like that of guide, director, or steersman to those guided, directed, or steered? The answer in each case is somewhat, sometimes, but not close enough nor often enough to make the analogies at all illuminating.

If Dewey had but stayed with his "equation" rather than wandering off in many other directions at once, he could well have prevented the lengthy and confused arguments that have followed from it.[3] The significance of Dewey's analogy lies not in an answer to the question

2 John Dewey, *How We Think* (Boston: D. C. Heath & Company, 1933). The original edition was published in 1910.
3 This line of argument has been summarized at various points, perhaps most thoroughly in K. W. Schuler, *A Philosophical Analysis of the Conceptual Relationship Between Teaching and Learning* (unpublished Ed. D. dissertation, Temple University, 1972), chap. 1.

whether "teaching" implies "learning" or, alternatively, whether teaching causes learning. It lies rather in a recognition of the fact that teaching-and-learning, like buying-and-selling, is one of the great modal forms of social interaction without which human life would be impossible. In a commercial transaction, the human interchange takes its form from the (possible) exchange of economically valuable goods. It's difficult to give so brief a formula that captures the modal symmetry in the pedagogical interaction, a fact that has led some thinkers to despair of the authenticity of the teaching encounter.[4] But that conclusion is, I believe, premature. For if we examine the analogy between the two encounters more closely, we find clues that point toward a clean distinction between (authentic) teaching and its counterfeits (phoney teaching?). So let's look more closely at buying-and-selling on one hand and teaching-and-learning on the other.

One could easily formulate truth conditions for a selling claim that are formally similar to the conditions proposed in Chapter Two as necessary to the truth of a teaching claim. "A sells (some) X to B" implies "B buys X from A"; together they point to an encounter between A and B, guided by A's intention to get the highest price for X, B's intention to get X for the lowest price, which conflicting intentions are resolved by agreement. The exact amount agreed on may be the outcome of a lengthy interaction between A and B, it may be a fair price reflecting communal standards, as in the Middle Ages, or it may be a figure set by a computer to maximize the profits of a corporation. But it's a sale only if the exchange signifies an agreement.

The more interesting points of analogy emerge when we try to formulate success conditions for a commercial exchange similar to the success conditions for a teaching claim. The encounter of buyer and seller may end in an exchange of goods and money, but it isn't successfully (finally) consummated unless the agreement was arrived at without (excessive) force or fraud, intimidation or coercion, threat, duress, misrepresentation. Even so, no line can be drawn in advance to determine whether or not a given interaction is successful buying-and-selling. A gunman who takes an expensive watch from his victim cannot claim it was a sale just because he leaves a dime behind. But what about a gunman who leaves in exchange for the watch an amount of money that everyone, including the victim, would acknowledge as a fair price? That may count as a sale —"He forced me to sell him my watch"—but it isn't a final sale. The victim can revoke the contract, and we should all support his demand to have his watch returned. (Even if the gunman leaves a bonus to com-

---

[4] For example, B. P. Komisar, "Is Teaching Phoney?" *Teachers College Record,* 70:5 (February 1969), 407–411. Also Maxine Greene, *Teacher As Stranger: Educational Philosophy for the Modern Age* (Belmont, Calif.: Wadsworth Publishing Company, 1973).

pensate his victim's unwillingness, the transaction is still expropriation.)

But if the gunman uses his weapon solely to gain attention and then offers to buy the watch at a price that changes the erstwhile victim to a willing seller, would the completed transaction then be regarded as a (final) sale? It all depends, we should say, on the details of the interaction. Was the offer made in good faith? (An offer you can't refuse is no *offer* at all.) Was the acceptance genuine, or did some vestige of extraneous power enter into it? Was there opportunity—time and attention available—for a counteroffer to be made and considered? And so on. The point is this: buying-and-selling is not an irreducible simple transaction. We can analyze it into simpler elements; indeed, we are forced to do so when a borderline case arises and we must decide whether it was *really* buying-and-selling or some counterfeit of that mode of encounter.

Formally similar principles apply when we want to decide whether a pedagogical encounter is really teaching or a counterfeit thereof. We reconsider *au fond* the nexus between teaching and learning. It is not that teaching *causes* learning nor that "teaching" *implies* "learning." It is rather that a distinctive kind of *inter*action is occurring, one in which the individual actions can be labeled, in the most general terms, as teaching on one hand and learning on the other. Those labels are correct only if the more specific (and true) descriptions of individual agents' actions are the intellectual acts described below. Only then is what Dewey calls an "equation" (and Kilpatrick a "proportion"—"teaching : learning :: selling : buying")[5] truly "exact." For it's buying-and-selling only if the more specific descriptions are offering, bidding, asking, accepting, rejecting, and so on—and only if these acts are done *bona fide* voluntarily, wittingly, and so on, under conditions that (tend to) insure freedom, personal security, undistracted attention to the business at hand, and so forth. Now we have to look at the specific acts that must occur and the specific conditions that must be satisfied if the *inter*action called "teaching-and-learning" is to occur. They all come out to be exceedingly like the necessary conditions for buying-and-selling, but would you have expected any other outcome?

**A REVISED**      Grammar again provides a clue. In Chapter Two
**PARADIGM**      we followed a useful and common paradigm for a
teaching claim: A teach(es) B _____ X. For "teach" in that generic paradigm we may insert any other pedagogical predicate in the English language. Some of those predicates—drill, train,

5 William Heard Kilpatrick, *Foundations of Method* (New York: The Macmillan Company, 1926), p. 268.

condition, instruct, counsel, motivate, indoctrinate, coach, maybe others
—sound very schoollike; we saw that that same general paradigm also
accommodates a much wider class of predicates—convince, persuade,
entice, encourage, force, incite, tempt, and *many* others—each of which
suggests a particular *way* in which one agent may affect the character or,
more directly, the behavior of another. None of these other predicates
takes the range of blank-fillers ("_____ Xes") that "teach" takes, and
"teach" always suggests an element of rationality that none of the other
predicates carries with it on its face. (You incite B to riot, *simpliciter*.
But if you teach B to riot, you teach him how to riot, when to riot,
where to riot—righ-ot?) Even so, "teach" is clearly at home among those
other causal verbs that fit into the generic paradigm.

But "teach" also fits a very different paradigm and has a clear logical
connection to a wholly different set of pedagogical verbs. So:

A teach(es)     (*)     to B.

Some of the other verbs that fit easily and exactly into *that* paradigm
are included among those which Komisar has named, albeit with a certain reluctance, "intellectual acts."[6]

demonstrate
explain
indicate
introduce
justify
prove
report

To those mentioned by Komisar we may add a couple of others:

announce
describe
narrate
present

And there must be still more, but the list is long enough to sustain
a few comments. One just *wouldn't* put all and only those verbs into a
common list if one were making the list on something other than a
grammatical basis. Komisar and Green put many other terms in their
lists, for they were taking their cues more from what they saw as a

6 B. P. Komisar, "Teaching: Act and Enterprise," in C. J. B. Macmillan and T. W.
Nelson, eds., *Concepts of Teaching* (Chicago: Rand McNally & Company, 1968), pp.
75–76. "I wish there were another term, less toxic to colleagues, to designate these
acts. But *cognitive act* is no sweeter, *communicative act* and *interaction* are too un-
chaste, and, with regard to the latter, jejune, and *logical act* gives a false connotation.
. . . ." T. F. Green does use the last expression, despite its connotation, for a smaller
but largely overlapping set of terms, in *The Activities of Teaching* (New York: Mc-
Graw Hill Book Company, 1971), p. 4.

similarity of acts than from similarity in grammar. It is hard to take grammatical cues as seriously, but only as seriously, as they deserve.[7] But if we stay with only those predicates that are *like* Komisar's in meaning and also fit precisely within the specific paradigm, we notice something a little peculiar: these are all Latin-based verbs. Are there no Anglo-Saxon pedagogical verbs? Indeed there are: showing and telling. In fact, "show" and "tell," like "teach" and (so far as I've been able to discover) unlike any other pedagogical predicates, fit *both* paradigms. Here is a grammatical clue that simply can't be ignored. It points toward the possibility that "teaching" cannot ever be distinguished from its counterfeits, indeed that the designation of indoctrination and conditioning as "counterfeits" is merely an attempt to denigrate certain actions by the emotional tone of words instead of dealing with the issues in explicit argument; for when you analyze it far enough "teaching" (in the generic paradigm) *is* "teaching" (in the specific paradigm): it all comes down to the same simple thing—showing and telling something to someone.

**DIGRESSION ON SHOWING AND TELLING**　　But if we are to accept that last proposition as the conclusion to our case, we must do so with a clear recognition of its counterrevolutionary implications. For the direction of the argument in this chapter is toward a radical distinction such that when teaching is separated out from all the other pedagogical activities which are its counterfeits, a teaching claim *implies* both that there is genuine inter*action* between A and B and also that the focus of that interaction, the matter being communicated, is true and right for the occasion. But "show" and "tell" clearly do *not* have such implications. You show a picture to someone: that does imply that what you show him is really a picture, but not at all that it is a picture of what it purports to be. A phony picture can be shown as easily as a genuine picture. You tell a story to someone: in my youth, that would have been taken first off to

---

[7] The fact that "teach" can appear in two different paradigms has been noted (perhaps many times) before this. Here are two examples. (1) "Teaching John is very different from teaching French—compare teaching John French. . . . It is not clear that the classical direct and indirect object distinction does full justice to such cases." (2) "Thus we *may* say 'George taught the Pythagorean theorem to his class.' But we *must* say: 'George taught his class that the square on the hypotenuse. . . .' The purely grammatical distinction between dative and accusative cases is useless as a clue to the logic of the paradigm." (1) is from E. J. Lemmon, "If I Know, Do I Know That I Know?" in A. Stroll, ed., *Epistemology: New Essays in the Theory of Knowledge* (New York: Harper & Row, Publishers, 1967), p. 56 and p. 81 n. (2) is from my "Individualized Instruction" in L. G. Thomas, ed., *Philosophical Redirection of Educational Research, NSSE Yearbook,* 1972, Pt. 1, p. 179 n. The latter was written (I swear, and those familiar with the length of time it takes yearbooks to appear will find it easy to believe) before I learned of Lemmon's essay.

mean that you told the person a lie. Today it's merely neutral; it certainly does not imply that the story is true. Nor will putting the two together work any better: you show-and-tell an illustrated story to someone, such as a 1914 film of Belgian children being marched off to German soap factories. . . .

Nor is there more than a bare minimum of activity on B's part implied in the claim that A tells  (*)  to B or that A shows  (*)  to B. If you tell something to B just after he expires for the last time or when he is fast asleep or even when his attention is firmly riveted elsewhere, then you tried to tell it to him, but failed. Likewise with "show." The acts of showing and telling cannot be performed successfully without some minimum attention, an "uptake" as Komisar aptly names it,[8] on the part of B, the viewer-auditor. But it *is* a minimum uptake that's required. It certainly does not require that A and B be actively and cooperatively engaged in a joint enterprise. If a minimum of attention is given by B, his intention may be anything; he certainly need not be engaged in active learning, much less actively learning exactly what A is showing or telling him.[9]

So if we are to find a reciprocal set of actions in which teaching and learning are related to each other as buying and selling are related in an economic transaction, it won't be by just adding up a series of A shows —B looks at and A tells—B listens to. The interaction in schools that is called teaching-and-learning is typically just that sort of series. Considering the mass scale on which it's done, there's no doubt that it results in a lot of people's learning a lot of things they wouldn't otherwise have learned. But it is also true that, under the most favorable description of the human interactions that, in fact, occur in schools, there is no way in which a clean distinction can be made between teaching and its counterfeits. They are all alike in being a series of showings that are (sometimes) looked at and tellings that are (sometimes) listened to. If you analyze far enough, everything comes out to be the same thing— whatever it is you analyze. When you get teaching down to showing-and-telling, you've gone too far.

The point of this digression, like the question what is an impeachable offense under the Constitution, is purely academic. In fact, a large-scale political movement is under way and, at the time of this writing, gaining momentum. The object of this movement, known variously as Performance- or Competency-Based Teacher Education, is to analyze teaching into the specific performances or (ugh!) competencies of which it is

---

[8] Komisar, "Teaching: Act and Enterprise," p. 81.

[9] The relation between intention and attention is pretty complex, I suspect. We probably couldn't make (or, anyhow, learn to make) the minimum discriminations which "uptake" requires were our intentions not directed toward some goal in the vicinity of the proffered showing-and-telling. Cf. G. E. M. Anscombe, *Intention* (Oxford: Basil Blackwell & Mott Ltd., 1957), sec. 36.

composed, then to train prospective teachers in those specific performances or . . . , and finally to certify as teachers those persons who have mastered the specific performances or. . . . Put forward politically as an alternative to the present practice of admitting into the ranks of employable teachers all and only those persons who have received satisfactory grades in certain courses (including on rare occasions those I have had the pleasure of teaching), the PBTE movement has much to recommend it. Its adoption would at last ensure that a teacher's certificate certified *something*, even if only that its holder was able to show and tell. If the present malaise in our schools is, in fact, caused by the absence of those skills in our contemporary, TV-nurtured generation of teachers, then we surely ought to adopt *some* program which will make certain that they learn how to show and tell. Success in that endeavor, however, does nothing to ensure that prospective teachers understand, much less honor, the distinction between teaching and its counterfeits; showing and telling are found in equal measure in all pedagogical activities. Given the consciously adopted and vigorously defended stance of behaviorism taken by most proponents of PBTE, it is not surprising that the distinction between teaching and its counterfeits is given short shrift in their proposals: that distinction cannot be made out from a behaviorist point of view. That is to say, to adopt a program based on a self-consciously behaviorist point of view is to legislate a particular answer to the philosophically debated question: How does teaching differ from indoctrination and conditioning?—namely: It doesn't. Civilized politics abhors such legislation, but that raises an issue which we must pass by in silence lest it detain us too long.

In any event, the merit of PBTE depends on the prior assumption, namely, that presently trained teachers are limited in competence by their inability to show and tell things to students. That assumption may have a significant element of truth in it. If so, we would do well to concentrate more attention on training prospective teachers in those skills. We should also recognize that a behaviorist interpretation of what it is to exercise a skill, or to train another to exercise a skill, is totally misleading. Further argument on that point appears later in this chapter.

**THE SPECIFIC-TEACHING CLAIM**

The problem here is to avoid the dangers of reductionism without passing up the opportunity to explain by analysis. The fact that "show" and "tell" uniquely fit both the generic and specific paradigms of "teach" is surely more than coincidence. That grammatical fact, however, does not require the reductionist interpretation that teaching is nothing but showing-and-telling. But it does require that our analysis provide an account of how teaching is related to the simpler notions of showing and telling, a point to be kept in mind as we now return to the specific paradigm for "teach." In the discussion that follows, I shall use the expressions "specific sense of 'teach' " and "generic sense . . ." to mean a use of the term "teach" expressible most easily or naturally in one or the other grammatical paradigm. I don't pretend to have any proof that "teach" is systematically ambiguous or otherwise divided into different senses; I intend only a shorthand way of talking about these two paradigms when I talk about "senses."

Following the familiar form, we may speak of a teaching claim in the specific sense, or a specific-teaching claim, as an assertion derived from the specific paradigm. The form is similar to the generic paradigm; the ear of a speaker of idiomatic English can be counted on to discriminate between an intelligible and unintelligible teaching claim in both senses of "teach."

There are a couple of additional intelligibility conditions that I should like to impose on a specific-teaching claim.

(a) Notice that in the specific paradigm the content variable has been expressed with a symbol different from that used in the generic paradigm. I think that the difference in the logical grammar of the two expressions—the "_____ X" in the generic paradigm and the "$(*)$" in the specific paradigm—makes it convenient, if not imperative, to have these different symbols. The "_____ X" in the generic paradigm is grammatically (like?) a predicate complement. You teach (which may mean to indoctrinate or condition or all three) *B,* and the "_____ X" tells what you intended to get him to learn, what he had to give some attention to, and so on. "I taught him for six months" may not convey much information, but it is a sentence. But "I taught *to* him for six months" *says* nothing. A specific-teaching claim must have its "$(*)$" attached, else it doesn't mean anything at all.

Notice that this particular difference in the paradigm both explains and refutes the once-popular slogan: "We teach children, not subjects."[10] In effect, the supposedly progressive sentiment of that slogan is precisely the opposite. The sloganeer is committed to conceiving his actions within the generic paradigm, where it is impossible to distinguish teaching from its counterfeits. "We condition children, not behaviors." Splendid! Your grammar is excellent. "We indoctrinate children, not unjustified beliefs." *Natürlich!* There might have been some point in the slogan had it stated: "We teach young citizens, not subjects." But that point would have been revolutionary, which is something the sloganeers of progressivism definitely were *not.*

---

[10] Cf. Paul Hirst's rejection of this slogan on other grounds, in "What Is Teaching?" in R. S. Peters, ed., *The Philosophy of Education* (Fair Lawn, N.J.: Oxford University Press, 1973), p. 172.

(b) In the generic paradigm, B could be any organism capable of (incidental) learning and A any organism capable of intending that another learn (incidentally). In the specific paradigm the range of the variables is much more restricted. For reasons that come out later, "B" must be the name of (or equivalent indexical designating) a human being or other creature capable of active learning, more specifically, capable of *consciously* doing X in order to learn (or understand or appreciate) Y. "A" must designate a creature who (i) knows that there are creatures capable of consciously doing X in order to learn Y, (ii) is capable of recognizing that a particular person, B, before him is an (a possible) instance of such a creature, and (iii) is capable of consciously doing Z in order to help B do-X-in-order-to-learn-Y.

Actually, I don't wish to argue that those restrictions (on the values over which "A" and "B" may range) are *necessary* for intelligibility of specific-teaching claims in ordinary language. But it seems clear to me that our ordinary language intuitions do tend in that direction. When we speak of other animals' teaching their young—"The lioness is teaching her cubs how to hunt"—we ordinarily use the generic paradigm; if we translate that sort of claim into the specific paradigm—"She's teaching the niceties of stalking to her cubs"—we become consciously and deliberately anthropomorphic. But the argument below doesn't hinge on that intuition. The only occasions on which we would ever be concerned to distinguish teaching from its counterfeits would be occasions in which the values for "A" and "B" would satisfy those restrictions; hence nothing of substance is prejudged by putting in those restrictions as conditions of intelligibility for a specific teaching claim.

So here are the two paradigms:

| THE GENERIC PARADIGM | | | THE SPECIFIC PARADIGM |
|---|---|---|---|
| A teach(es) B | _____ X. | | A teach(es) (*) to B. |
| trains | that | | demonstrates |
| drills | how to | | explains |
| instructs | the | | indicates |
| coaches | to | | introduces |
| conducts | (and combinations: | | justifies |
| . | when to | | proves |
| . | whom to | | reports |
| indoctrinates | where to | | signals |
| conditions | who | | . |
| . | why | | . |
| . | . | | shows |
| shows | . ) | | tells |
| tells | | | |

Both lists are open, of course. As summarized here, they contain only verbs that have a pedagogical ring to them. We have already considered some other verbs that fit the generic paradigm (incite, lead, force, convince, persuade, and so on), and we also find something revealing when we consider the nonpedagogical verbs that fit the specific paradigm, such as "sell." ("Sell" may be found in the generic paradigm when we wish to indicate an unusual degree of fraud or manipulation in the transaction: "He sure sold me a bill of goods!"—which *doesn't* mean that he sold a bill of goods to me.) But these two lists overlap only in the final analysis—at the level of showing and telling. Which leads us inescapably to the hypothesis that the distinction between teaching and its counterfeits is very closely related to the difference between these two sets of verbs. Gird up your loins!

**A LECTING CLAIM**          For we now set out to test that hypothesis. If Komisar can overcome his scruples and call the whole class of verbs "intellectual acts," we may as well follow suit. For the sake of convenience only, let us shorten "intellectual act" to its syllable of primary accent—"lect"—and use the term as an ordinary English verb, standard conjugation. Then the first step in testing our hypothesis is to determine whether there are truth conditions for any lecting claim and, if so, what those conditions are. A lecting claim is any assertion derived from the following paradigm

A lect(s) ___(*)___ to B,

where "A" and "B" are restricted to the values they may take in a specific teaching claim and "lect" is replaced by any one of the pedagogical-sounding verbs which fit that paradigm.

We may begin with an encounter condition for the truth of a lecting claim. If a genuine intellectual encounter between A and B can be mediated by pure spirit, electromagnetic waves, or other vibrations of the ether, then the encounter condition need not imply space-time contiguity. But the occultists and novices at sci-fi writing should be warned that other conditions for the truth of a lecting claim are such that not just any "medium" that can effect "contact" between A and B will suffice to satisfy the encounter condition in a lecting claim.

We can start with the obvious: if a lecting claim is true, then A has to show-and-tell something to B. But what makes it lecting is not *mere* showing-and-telling but rather two sets of very special conditions, which are hard to satisfy if the contact between A and B lacks space-time contiguity. These special conditions I call lucidity and pellucidity, with appropriate apologies for borrowing the first and renovating the second.

**LUCIDITY**           Philosophy of education is indebted to Professor
**IN LECTING**         Komisar for many services, and these include call-
                       ing our attention to the feature he calls "logical
lucidity" in intellectual acts.[11] His definition of "logical lucidity" is
the following:

> [I]ntellectual acts are logically lucid in that the act is done not only with the
> intention of securing a certain "uptake" (an awareness of some point), but also
> so as (a) to divulge to the student what the intention is and (b) to achieve his
> awareness by identifying the reasons given as the intelligible grounds for the
> point the students are to become aware of.[12]

It is well to keep in mind that Professor Komisar uses "uptake" and
"awareness" very broadly as the general terms for whatever outcomes
are intended within an act of teaching. This usage has the advantage
of keeping his treatment of teaching free from the difficulties and ambiguities in "learning," a concept to which Professor Komisar has turned
his attention elsewhere.[13]

The claim I wish to investigate right now is whether lecting *entails*
lucidity—whether lucidity (we may omit "logical," though it is to be
understood) is a necessary condition for lecting. This may or may not
be Professor Komisar's view. My lack of certitude on that point stems
not primarily from any particular passage (in the sentence quoted, does
"in that" mean "for," "only if," "whenever," "since," . . . ?), for Professor Komisar goes on to discuss the matter at some length. The difficulty lies in his desire to see intellectual acts elevated to their proper
status as central to *all* teaching, a desire which he sees, rightly, as un-
achievable within the "enterprise" of teaching—that is, within schools
as presently constituted. Professor Komisar believes that it is somehow
*necessary* that schools—their purposes and procedures—remain opaque to
students:

> It is hoped, of course, that . . . there can be isomorphism between the reasons
> for X being the case and the grounds teachers present to students for taking X
> as so. But this is not typical, else what would education be for? . . . [As] the
> institution of education becomes more scientific, more rationalized, then the
> dissimilarity between the logical lucidity of the act and the logical obscurity of
> the enterprise will be more pronounced.[14]

The reason advanced by Professor Komisar for accepting this (to me)

[11] Komisar, "Teaching: Act and Enterprise," as cited above. Komisar's indebtedness to
earlier works by Grice and Strawson is there acknowledged.
[12] *Ibid.*, pp. 79–80.
[13] B. P. Komisar, "More on the Concept of Learning," in Komisar and Macmillan,
eds., *Psychological Concepts in Education* (Chicago: Rand McNally & Company, 1967);
cf. text above, pp. 72–82.
[14] Komisar, "Teaching: Act and Enterprise," pp. 82, 84.

dreadful conclusion is similar to that advanced by Professor Peters for the view that education must appear irrational to students: children are rather like barbarians without the gates who must be initiated into forms of thought and behavior before they can understand any rational explanations whatever.[15] With that belief fixed, Professor Komisar is left with the alternatives of holding either that intellectual acts are not (necessarily) lucid or else that the teaching act is not (necessarily) an intellectual act. The latter is surely more plausible, for teaching claims derived from the generic paradigm of "teach" do *not* imply lucidity. So let us separate several questions: Does lecting imply lucidity? Does teaching imply lecting? Does education imply teaching? Does schooling imply education? And so on. Those who hold that there *must* be an element of irrationality—coercion or fraud—in the induction of youth into a culture can find plenty of other places to deny the sequence of implications. The little hypothesis we test now need not commit one to any political view on those other questions.

Professor Komisar's definition can now be framed as a logical entailment which we will call hereafter, L.

L: A lects    (*)    to B $\longrightarrow$

> L1: B knows that A is Xing Y to B with the intent that B come to know (or understand or appreciate) whatever it is (ordinarily a fact or skill) that    "(*)"    names.

> L2: B believes both
> > L2i That the meaning of Y (which A is Xing) is intelligibly connected with lecting    (*)    and
> > L2ii That *that* (L2i) is (included in) the grounds for A's Xing Y to B.

"Xing" is the variable for showing-and-telling something or, to use Professor Komisar's language, any one of the "sundry doings, showings, and sayings"[16] of things, some (combination) of which A *must* perform in lecting, and "Y" is the something done, shown, said or told. If B's ground for becoming aware of (or that)    (*)    is just that A is Xing Y, the act is not lucid. If, however, B sees the meaning of the Y that A is Xing as a *reason* for "uptake" [for taking up—that is, for accepting    (*)    as lected], then criterion L2i is satisfied. If, in addition, B believes that A is Xing Y in order to lect    (*)    to B—that is, if B believes that *that* is A's ground (motive?) for Xing (Y to B)—then criterion L2ii is satisfied.

Now these entailments of L work *very* neatly with at least *some* lect-

---

[15] R. S. Peters, *Ethics and Education* (Glenview,, Ill.: Scott, Foresman & Company, 1967), pp. 172, 217.

[16] Komisar, "Teaching: Act and Enterprise," p. 77.

ing verbs. To use Professor Martin's recurrent example, A (a mechanic) explains to B (his helper) why the engine seized up. A says: "It's because of an oil leak."[17] The act is lucid only if B knows that A intends (in Xing Y—in *saying:* "It's because of an oil leak") that B come to understand why the engine seized up. If B believes (it could happen) that A says: "It's because of an oil leak" only to give B an explanation (possibly but not necessarily the explanation) to pass on to an irate customer, then the act is not lucid, nor is it, quite obviously, explaining to B why the engine seized up. Further, it isn't lucid unless B believes that an oil leak bears an intelligible relation to an engine's seizure *and* that that relation is (among) B's grounds for saying: "It's because of an oil leak." Among A's other grounds for saying "It's because of an oil leak" would be A's belief that B understands English, and so on.

The act, notice, can be lucid but not a case of A's explaining to B why the engine seized up. If all the above conditions hold but B *knows* that there wasn't any oil leak, the engine's seizure is still opaque to him, and he has the additional problem of understanding why A said (or implied) something false while intending to explain. Perhaps, to take another case where the implication is not reversible, all the above conditions hold and there was an oil leak, but, in the event, it had nothing to do with the engine's seizure, which, instead, was caused by a saboteur's putting sugar in the fuel. Then the act of explaining fails for lack of truth but not for lack of lucidity.

Notice that I have assumed, in L1, that in Professor Komisar's sense of "divulge" the divulgee comes to *know* (have warranted true belief about) what the divulger is divulging, whereas criterion L2 is stated in terms of B's beliefs. For some degenerate cases of lecting, the knowledge criterion in L1 may be too strong. Teachers might so routinize their acts of lecting that in fact they had no intention at all in performing them, in which case B can't *know what* A intends in Xing Y. But even in that case, if A is lecting __(*)__ to B, B has to know that A has no intention counter to or obstructive of B's coming to know (or understand or appreciate) __(*)__ . Let us ignore the degenerate case.

For other lecting verbs, however, the belief condition in L2i is not strong enough. If A is proving the Pythagorean theorem to B, and at the moment is showing that two triangles have equal areas, then B must *know* what connection that particular Xing, showing, has to what went before (and also, though in a more general way, to what is coming after); if not, A's grounds for showing it cannot be identical with B's grounds

---

17 Jane R. Martin, *Explaining, Understanding and Teaching* (Boston: Allyn & Bacon, Inc., 1967), chap. VI.

for accepting it *as proven*. When "demonstrate" is used synonymously with "prove," the same restriction applies. But being too weak does not invalidate the hypothesis that L2i is a necessary condition for lecting. If B has to *know* that there is an intelligible connection between the Y that A is Xing and the __(*)__ that he's proving, then B must *believe* that there is such a connection. So far, the hypothesis holds.

**A CRUCIAL TEST**       No test of a hypothesis such as L is literally crucial,
**OF L**                 but the meaning and limits of the hypothesis are
                         revealed rather strikingly if we ask whether the
conditions of L were satisfied when Socrates taught Meno's slave boy that Theorem $\theta$. Let us look at four questions (numbered to indicate their relation to L), all of which would have to be answered affirmatively if L were true and that episode could be described in a true lecting claim:

1 (i) In asking the boy questions, in pointing to figures in the sand, in the sundry other things he did and said, did Socrates intend that the boy come to know (or understand or appreciate) Theorem $\theta$?
1(ii) Did the slave boy know that *that* was Socrates' intention?
2 (i) Did the slave boy believe that there was an intelligible connection between what Socrates was doing (showing-and-telling) and Theorem $\theta$?
2(ii) Did the slave boy believe that *that* was Socrates' ground for doing the things he did?

Well, I should think that only 1(i) could be given an affirmative answer, and that not unequivocally. Even if one allows a lot of leeway for tacit knowing and for implicit beliefs, it is still impossible to claim that the slave boy knew what Socrates had in mind *before* the episode was completed. The tone of the boy's response might be read to indicate that he knew that Socrates intended him no harm; that whatever were Socrates' intentions, they were benevolent. But that won't justify a yes answer to 1(ii).

The slave boy may well have believed, 2(i), that there was *some* intelligible connection between what Socrates was doing (or asking him to do) and what Socrates had in mind. But since the slave boy didn't *know* what Socrates had in mind while the episode was going on, he couldn't have any belief at all about the relation of Socrates' actions to Theorem $\theta$, much less any belief about the *grounds* for Socrates' doing and saying the things he did, 2(ii).

Thus it appears that the teaching episode involving Socrates, the slave boy, and Theorem $\theta$ is a counterexample to the hypothesis that lecting implies lucidity. It appears (to use the lecting verb that one would find most plausible for the occasion) that *either* "Socrates demonstrated Theorem $\theta$ to the slave boy" (call it D) must be false *or* "lecting implies lucidity" (L) must be false. Or:

$$\sim(D \& L)$$
$$\text{ergo,} \quad D \longrightarrow \sim L$$

But is D true? It is a plausible description of the episode, but is it a true description? We just can't tell from reading the dialogue. The slave boy is dismissed without a word once he acknowledges that he now believes Theorem $\theta$ to be true (*Meno,* 85B). His acknowledgment does not prove that D is true. What is it about the dialogue that makes D such a plausible description of the episode? I think that it's because all the elements for lucidity *were* present, only the slave boy could not know and believe what L requires (that he know and believe) until after the episode was completed. But the slave boy disappears from history before we had a chance to ask him: "What was Socrates intending when he asked you to look at the figure he had drawn?" "What's the connection between Theorem $\theta$ and the plainly observable fact that a square having a side of 2 has an area of 4?" And so on. We really don't *know* that D is true until we hear the slave boy's answer to those and similar questions derived from L. When we have satisfied ourselves that D is true, we will find, I think, that D and L *are* logically compatible.

My argument for the ultimate compatibility of D and L hinges on a premise that is grounded in everyday experience: the human mind *can* take elements appearing in one temporal sequence and put them into another sequence that has an intelligible, logical or narrative, order. We think D a plausible description of the episode because we assume that the slave boy will "naturally" reconstruct the episode until the whole thing is clear to him—and when that happens, the conditions required by L will be satisfied as well. To generalize: the conditions for lucidity do not specify any temporal order of events. An artist teacher may well do things in a sequence designed more to achieve dramatic interest than immediate logical coherence in teaching, just as an artist-raconteur may re-order his telling of a story with flashbacks, hidden clues, and the like. These techniques work only within the limits of the learner's or hearer's capacity to do the mental exercise of putting things in their "normal" (intelligible) order. The artist had better know that there *is* (at least *one*) intelligible order in the elements to be presented in the teaching or story before he starts messing them about. And he had better be prepared to accept that learners may discover new orders that are quite as intelligible as any he had foreseen.

But to return, if L has successfully survived the challenge of Socrates' demonstrating Theorem $\theta$ to the slave boy, we may take it as reasonably confirmed. But before we move on to a discussion of pellucidity, a pause to consider a curious and general feature of the language of human interaction.

**DIGRESSION TO COUNTER A NATURAL BUT FALLACIOUS OBJECTION**

If lecting implies lucidity, is it ever possible to know that a lecting claim is true? There is a natural tendency to have doubts about such matters, and those doubts will not diminish when we start looking at the more complex implications of pellucidity. A philosophical theory of human action begins with the same problem: when we say that a person is doing something, we seem to ascribe to him various motives, intentions, beliefs, desires, and so on. But in fact we are quite dubious about what is going on in that person's mind, even when we're quite sure that his actions are to be correctly described by a certain predicate. When we are talking about some predicate of *inter*action, I, a member of a class which includes but is not limited to lecting verbs, our dubiety is greatly increased, for we frequently conclude that we cannot say that A is Iing without ascribing to B some particular act(s) of thinking, feeling, or willing. Yet we are hesitant to accept that conclusion, for we believe that we *know*, under easily specified conditions, that A is Iing, even though we may lack grounds to sustain the belief, much less the claim to *know*, that B is engaged in the corresponding mental activity.

This argument has been advanced to sustain the denial that interaction predicates can imply what they seem to imply—for example, the denial that teaching can imply learning: surely we can describe a situation such that we can claim to know that A is teaching, though the description of that situation contains no grounds for any particular belief about B's mental activities. That argument arises in class quite predictably when students ask themselves how they could verify a teaching claim in the face of the proposal that a teaching claim implies a learning claim.

But it is easy to show that that argument is fallacious, the standard move being to point out that, given $p \longrightarrow q$, it doesn't follow that because a person knows that $p$, that person knows or believes that $q$. Let "$p$" = "$7 + 5 = 12$." Let "$q$" = "There are two prime numbers such that their sum equals thrice the square of their difference, and 1 is not a prime number." A person could know that $p$, but (even though in fact $p \longrightarrow q$) he might not even understand what $q$ means, hence could not know or have grounds for believing that $q$. (This is to ignore the "flow'r in the crannied wall" sense of "have grounds for belief"; in that Tennysonian sense we all have grounds, if we would only reflect on them properly, for believing every true proposition that could be formulated.

To ignore that sense of "have grounds for belief" is not to deny that it contains an element of truth.)

That standard move will not do the whole job, however, for it admits the rebuttal: no person is likely to claim that A is teaching B unless that person knows both what "B is learning from A" means and what independent tests may be applied for the truth of the latter. Thus the rebuttal grants the general denial that "A person knows that $p$" and "$p \longrightarrow q$" together imply anything about that person's cognitive stance toward $q$; but the rebuttal says that we are talking about the case where the person knows what "B is learning from A" means, knows what conditions must be satisfied if *that* claim is true, and could still know that A is teaching B without knowing that B is learning from A. Thus, in effect, the rebuttal asks us to consider three propositions, where AP = a person:

1) AP claims truly to know that A is teaching B.
2) AP claims truly to know that "A teaches B" $\longrightarrow$ "B learns from A."
3) AP claims truly not to know that B is learning from A.

Now, the rebuttal continues, this is an inconsistent set. Anyone finding himself in the position of AP must relinquish one of those claims. Can we not easily imagine a situation in which any rational person would regard it as logically preferable to give up 2), having the truth of 1) and 3) staring him in the face, as it were? Won't that same conclusion follow whenever we encounter a set of claims in which we know that A is Iing (to) B but do not, in fact, know that B is doing what (it is said that) I entails B must be doing? Hence, are not all such claims of entailment false? End of rebuttal.

The counter to the rebuttal is obvious. The charge that 1), 2), and 3) are inconsistent is a simple mistake in epistemic logic. They would be inconsistent if 3) were replaced by

3′) AP claims truly to know that B is *not* learning from A. (AP knows that it is false that B is learning from A.)

But without 3′), the set is logically consistent. It would, indeed, be odd if *AP* should say that, despite 1) and 2), AP has no grounds *at all* for believing that B is learning from A. And it would be inconsistent of anyone else to assert 1) and 2) but deny that B is learning from A. Still and all, people do say odd things; they assert and deny inconsistently. *That's* true, but it cannot make every statement having the form of 2) fallacious.

I do not pretend to have solved all the epistemological problems inherent in the complex nature of lecting claims; this standard argument eliminates only one objection, but the one eliminated would have stopped their analysis before it got started. I chose the example not because I believe 2) is true (see Chapter Two, where the implication is explicitly rejected), but because it's so much simpler than the implications of pellucidity, where A must know and believe a lot of things about what B knows and believes . . . if a lecting claim is to be sustained. I presented the epistemological argument to offset any tendency, itself natural, to take a third-party stance and say: "Well, I can know that A is lecting   (*)   to B without knowing that all those things are going on in B's mind." Well, so you can. But don't think that *that* proves anything about the logical relations we're trying to trace out.

**A VALUABLE CLUE IN A WRONG ACCOUNT**
The central idea in lecting is explaining. That idea has received a lot of attention from philosophers, particularly philosophers of science seeking an analysis of the logical criteria for a valid *explanation:* a set of propositions in which one part—the explanandum—(Latin for what is being explained) stands in a definite relation to another part—the explanans (what's doing the explaining). Just what must be the properties of that relation if the explanation is valid? *That* question must be distinguished from the question we are more directly concerned with: just what conditions must be satisfied if it is true that A explain(s)   (*)   to B? This latter question has received intensive analysis by Bromberger and, later, by Martin.[18] The feature of acts of lecting that I call "pellucidity" is mostly a generalization from Bromberger's analysis of explaining, as modified by Martin. But before we can generalize, we must correct; for they start with certain assumptions that yield a hopelessly parochial account of what explaining is. To explain:

Let "A" and "B" remain our two principal characters, for they are so designated by Bromberger and Martin. Let "W" fill in for   "(*)"   in the paradigm for lecting, "W" being a place filler for an indirect question, a noun clause designating what it is that A explains to B—for example, why the engine seized up. The point of the *analysis* is to show what must be true of each member in the triadic relationship if it is true that *A* explains *W* to *B*. (Let us call the assertion of a sentence formed on that model an explaining claim, restricting such claims, as before, to statements asserted about actual episodes, with time-and-place designators attached or implied.) The resulting analysis is quite a complicated affair, requiring not only a careful adherence to the rules of ordinary usage but also judicious decisions where ordinary usage isn't

18 Sylvain Bromberger, "An Approach to Explanation," in R. J. Butler, ed., *Analytic Philosophy*, 2d Series (Oxford: Basil Blackwell & Mott Ltd., 1965), pp. 72–105. J. R. Martin, *Explaining, Understanding and Teaching*, esp. chap. VI.

quite decided—for example, whether an explaining claim can be counted true if followed by "but A got it wrong." (Bromberger calls that a "loose usage"[19] and restricts his analysis accordingly.)

Following Bromberger and Martin, we may call A the tutor and B the tutee. At the beginning of the episode, the tutee, B, must be in a particular state of ignorance or misunderstanding, a "predicament" of somehow not knowing how to begin to find an answer to W, or else knowing a lot of possible answers without knowing how to eliminate all but one, or some other state which resembles or combines one or the other of those, a state which Martin calls generally a rational or cognitive predicament. At the beginning of the episode, the tutor, A, must know or assume or believe lots of things if the explaining claim is to be counted true; that is, A must believe or assume that the tutee is in the appropriate predicament with respect to W, believe or assume that he—A, the tutor—knows some answer to W which, if presented to B, will remove the bases for B's predicament, and so on. And W must be an indirect form of a question or set of questions, Q, where Q is or can be made to be well-formed (admitting of one right answer to each specific constituent question, Q', and so on).

Then, during the explaining episode, the tutor, A, "presents the facts"[20] or "states the right answer"[21] or provides whatever other material the tutor believes necessary to remove the bases of the tutee's predicament. The episode is concluded when all the facts, answers, subsidiary questions, and other helpful material have been presented to the tutee by the tutor.

My truncated account is obviously a travesty of the complex analyses of Bromberger and Martin. In particular it is deficient in treating the two accounts as mere variations on a single theme, for Martin distinguishes (much more clearly than Bromberger) between A's explaining W and A's explaining W to B, the former being a question of whether an inquiry or a research activity has come up with a correct and intelligible answer to W, the latter a question of "didactics" (Bromberger) or "pedagogy" (Martin)—whether A in fact presented the necessary materials *to B*.

And yet for the present purpose my account is trustworthy and they can be considered equivalent; for they both treat B as a purely passive entity in the transaction, an empty vessel into which A pours whatever is needed to bring the level up to where it's supposed to be, on some *totally* unspecified criterion. The episode begins with B in a state of

[19] Bromberger, "An Approach to Explanation," p. 79.
[20] *Ibid.*, p. 86 *et passim.*
[21] Martin, *Explaining, Understanding and Teaching*, p. 129.

want or lack—of understanding, knowledge, facts, truth, or whatever. It closes with B's having received, in some form or other, what is *deemed by A* to satisfy the state of want that B was in. That way of putting it, indeed the whole tenor of both accounts, takes what goes on in schools to be the *model* of what it is for one person to explain something to someone else. "Tutor and tutee" indeed! In the world outside of school, when one person asks another to explain something, one doesn't ordinarily take it for granted that a tutor-tutee relationship is thereby established. Do you?

Why would Bromberger and Martin assume that a schoollike relationship is *the* model in which to think about the truth of explaining claims? Well, like most of us they are teachers who have spent a large proportion of their lives being students; the tutor-tutee relationship is probably for both of them a homey way to think about things. But there is a point in philosophical method as well as purely biographical reasons behind the choice of the school setting here: one wants the analysis to be as clean as possible; the *minimum* set of necessary conditions that are jointly sufficient is always the desideratum. Well, if what is to be analyzed is "A explains W to B," then it seems that the minimum assumptions about B would yield a "tutee"—a person whose only contribution to the enterprise is what is wanting in his head. And the only place you're going to find someone willing to play "tutee" is in schools, especially schools where people take that role under threat of police enforcement if they don't. Thus the model of explaining in schools would seem to provide the minimum set of necessary conditions for any analysis of the concept.

Once it's recognized what Bromberger and Martin have done in their effort (entirely commendable, as such) to find the minimum set of necessary conditions for the truth of an explaining claim, it is (or should be) quite evident that theirs is a terribly wrong as well as parochial view of what's actually going on when A is explaining W to B. An actual episode of explaining would never get started under the conditions set in the Bromberger-Martin account. It is, indeed, necessary to an episode of explaining that B be in a state of rational predicament, but *that's* no more than the condition that B be a human being. Each of us—you, me, the fellow chattering next door—is such that there are an infinite number of Q's with respect to which we are in a rational predicament, as Bromberger and Martin define "predicament"—which is a disingenuous use of a technical definition. For "predicament" carries with it the ordinary language idea of being in a state that one (consciously) wishes to get out of, whereas the only way we can get out of the Bromberger-Martin predicament is to die or become God. So the condition of being in a rational predicament, as technically defined, is really no condition at all; it only appears to be because of the ordinary language notion that is surreptitiously dragged in.

If we follow that ordinary language notion, which is what really gets explaining under way, we see that the point of the activity is *not* that B happens to be in a state of want with respect to answers to W, but rather that *B wants to know W*. From that fact, everything else follows. If "B wants to X" is analyzed (as I believe it should be) as a dispositional claim, then the explaining episode begins when that disposition becomes activity. B wants to know W; B believes that A knows W; if A is saying things that seem to answer W, B listens; if A is not saying those things, B asks A about W and then listens; if what A says answers W for B, the explaining is over; if what A says does not answer W for B, B asks further questions until it does, or B gives up on A, or B decides he doesn't really want to know W, or B's mind wanders off to something else, or. . . .

It would take another book to analyze the truth conditions for an explaining claim if we thus started correctly and tried to provide an account that has the subtlety and precision of the Bromberger-Martin account. My effort here is more modest but also more ambitious: I don't attempt anything like the depth to which Martin explores the intended outcome of explaining—the truth conditions for "B understands W"[22]— but I try to generalize the valid insights in the Bromberger-Martin account as a further set of truth conditions for *all* lecting claims.

**PELLUCIDITY**
**IN LECTING**

Thus we may consider a second hypothesis to put alongside L (the lucidity conditions for lecting). The second hypothesis is that lecting entails pellucidity.

P:      A lect(s) ___(*)___ to B ⟶
Pli:    B wants to know (or understand or appreciate) ___(*)___ .
Plii:   B believes that A knows both
        (a) What B must do or undergo in order to come to know (or . . .) ___(*)___ , and
        (b) That B wants to know ___(*)___ .
Pliii:  B believes that A is Xing Y to B with the intent of helping B to come to know (or . . .) ___(*)___ .
Pliv:   B attends the Y that A is Xing because Pliii.
Plv:    B believes that A knows that (Pliii & Pliv).
P2i:    A believes that B wants to know (or understand or appreciate) ___(*)___ .
P2ii:   A believes that Xing Y to B will help B to come to know (or . . .) ___(*)___ .

---

22 *Ibid.,* Parts III and IV.

P2iii: A Xes Y to B with the intent of helping B to come to know (or . . .)
(∗) .

P2iv: $\overline{\text{A believes that (Pliii \& Pliv).}}$

Separating out all these different intentional and epistemic claims makes pellucidity sound extraordinarily complicated. Which, in a way, it is. But that is to judge things as simple or complicated from a cosmic perspective. From a human perspective, pellucidity is routinely simple. The mechanic's helper wants to know why the engine seized up, P1i. He believes the mechanic can explain it, so he asks: "Why did the engine seize up?" Thus P1ii(a) and (b) are satisfied, as is, assuming that the mechanic understood the question and believed it sincere, P2i. The mechanic believes that the helper knows, in general, what causes engines to seize up; what will help him to know why it happened to this particular engine is to have the precipitating cause pointed out to him, thus P2ii. So the mechanic says: "There was an oil leak," thus P2iii. The mechanic's utterance is taken by the helper to be an answer to his question, and he pays attention to it because he believes it to be an answer to his question. Thus P1iii and P1iv are satisfied. The helper signals his attention by keeping quiet while the mechanic is speaking, by cocking his ear or eyes or eyebrows or whatever custom dictates to be the appropriate signal so as to *make* P1v true.

The mechanic may add "OK?" in order to test his beliefs about the helper's state of previous understanding (P2ii) as well as his beliefs about the helper's attention to his answer (P2iv). But the "OK?" is usually unnecessary; a nod from the helper confirms both beliefs simultaneously, a shake indicates the possible start of a second round of lecting—explaining, demonstrating, justifying, and so on—, or it may not. But if it does, all these conditions will be reinstituted around a new ___(∗)___. The episode requires about five seconds to complete, however long it takes to explicate all that's going on.

> *That, to the height of this great argument,*
> *I may assert Eternal Providence*
> *And justify the ways of God to men.*

Was Milton's a pellucid act? Did men want to understand the reasoning behind His ways? Did men believe that Milton knew what men must do or undergo in order to see the justification for His ways? Well, Milton must have believed that he knew men's desires and beliefs, at least those particular desires and beliefs, else he would not have conceived his poem as an act of lecting. If Milton's beliefs about his hearers' desires and beliefs were true, then his poem was indeed an act of justifying the ways of God to men, an instance of lecting, and also pellucid. If Milton was wrong, then he failed to justify the ways of God *to men.* If the act fails on the criterion of pellucidity, it fails as, or to be, an act of lecting, however noble the work of art that is its residue.

<table>
<tr><td>

**LUCIDITY**
**AND PELLUCIDITY**
**COMPARED**

</td><td>

Hypothesis P has not yet been tested. Lurking in the wings is D ("Socrates demonstrated Theorem $\theta$ to the slave boy"); it seems plausible that D is true and inconsistent with P. Before D is allowed on

</td></tr>
</table>

stage, however, let us recall L and compare it with P.

L1 is both simpler and stronger than P1i–P1v. The latter conjunction of conditions does not entail L1, nor does L1 entail any one of the conjuncts, P1i–P1v. The P1 conditions are all conditions of belief, desire, and intention, whereas L1 asserts a *knowledge* condition for B's participation in the act of lecting. But L1 and the P1 conjunction are consistent: B could *know* that A is acting with the intent of getting B to know whatever it is that    (\*)    names while only *believing* that A is acting with the intent of helping B to know    (\*)  . That is to say, for L1 and P1 to be consistent, it must be possible for B to know (have *true* justified belief) what L1 requires but believe (which implies the possibility of mistake) what P1, especially P1iii, requires. That could happen in at least two ways.

(a) B could know that A is acting with a generally pedagogical intention of L1 but be mistaken in the belief that    "(\*)"    names what, in fact, B wants to know (or understand or appreciate). The word "motivate" is used to designate those acts intended to instill such mistaken beliefs in B. Thus B may be motivated to believe that he wants to know some things labeled "how the people of India live." He discovers that the Y which A Xes to him (for example, the instruction "Answer all the questions at the end of Chapter Four" which the teacher issues to him) has no connection at all with what he believed he wanted to know. Thus he acquires the lifelong conviction that he really cares nothing about how the people of India live.

(b) Assuming that the    "(\*)"    in L1 is really what B wants to learn, it is still possible for B to know that A is trying to bring it about that B learn    (\*)    and be mistaken in the belief that A is trying to *help* B to learn    (\*)  . Instead, A may conceive his effort as that of *getting* B to know (or . . .)    (\*)  . The expression "get B to understand" is employed throughout Martin's Chapter VI as stating A's intention in explaining something to B.[23] We ordinarily speak of trying to *get* people to do what they don't (particularly) want to do. To get B to do something means to bring it about that B does it, even though doing it con-

---

[23] *Ibid.*

flicts with B's inclinations, habits, and (at least surface) tendencies. We contrast "forcing B to X" with "getting B to X of his own free will." A prisoner can be forced to eat by the exertion of physical power, if the counselor or chaplain can't *get* him to break his hunger strike voluntarily. But those two—"force him to X" and "get him to X"—are clearly on the same side of a line that separates both of them from "help him to X."

Thus B can know that A intends his (A's) actions to bring it about that B come to know Z and yet be mistaken in the belief that A intends to help B learn Z, even when exactly the same thing is substituted for "Z" in its two appearances. B wants to learn how to read. B knows that A intends to bring it about that B comes to know how to read; A comes labeled as "Teacher of Reading." B believes, but this time mistakenly, that A intends to help B do what B wants to do. For A intends to *get* B to read; that's what A has been trained to do, unfortunately.

Thus L1 and P1 can both be true without excluding the possibility that the beliefs posited in P1 are false. And it should be obvious by inspection that the conditions of L1 and P1 entail no redundancy or mutual implications.

**A THIRD "REALITY" CONDITION TO ADD TO L AND P?** The more important point of comparison is between L2 and all of P. L2 presents a bare minimum of a *logical* criterion for some interaction to be an act of lecting; L2 does not require that there *be* an intelligible connection between A's Xing Y and what is being lected, but rather that B believe that such a connection exists. Even so, that is the nearest thing to a truth condition internal to either L or P. The question must be faced: can we consider all the belief and intention conditions specified in L and P, particularly the latter, *meaningful* without specifying that at some precisely designated points the beliefs must be true, the intentions accomplished? The point reiterates the second success condition for a teaching claim in the generic paradigm presented in Chapter Two: at least what goes on in the interaction must *be* connected with X, whatever it is that A is trying to teach B, else we can't call the interaction A's teaching B _____ X. But our analysis of a lecting claim, so far, doesn't provide for any such criterion.

Two responses:

(a) Whereas the analysis of the generic paradigm claimed to have presented the minimum set of necessary conditions which would be jointly sufficient for a teaching claim to be true and successful, the analysis of L and P as individually necessary for the truth of a lecting claim has not been accompanied by the claim that P and L are jointly

sufficient for a lecting claim. A lecting claim designates a triadic relationship—A lects _(*)_ to B. It is absurd to think that we can guarantee the conditions for the truth of such a claim by positing conditions
that are true of A and of B without mentioning what must be true
of _(*)_ . Just to take a trivial example, if the lecting claim is "A is
demonstrating R-flying to B," where "R-flying" means propelling oneself
through the air by rotating one's thumbs, then we know that something
is wrong with the claim even if all the conditions of P and L were
satisfied. One cannot prove what's false, demonstrate what's impossible,
explain what's inexplicable, justify what's unjustifiable, describe what's
indescribable, and the like. But if a single criterion can be applied to
the "(*)" in any lecting claim—a criterion that translates appropriately, depending on whether the claim is one of proving, demonstrating, describing, justifying, . . . , as "not false," "not impossible,"
"not unjustifiable," . . . —then that criterion is so general as to be useless. Stated, it would come out to be something like "and whatever is
designated by '(*)' in the lecting claim must not possess any property
that renders nugatory the good toward which the act of lecting is directed." That criterion is, of course, presupposed, no more significant
after being stated than before.

(b) In any event, the absence of independent, "objective" conditions
within P and L does not leave a lecting claim a merely subjective event.
If the conditions specified in P and L are satisfied, some events are taking place in the real world, and at least two people are in intersubjec-
tive agreement on the crucial description of those events. That much P
and L guarantee. Of course, there is always the possibility that A and B
are in a state of symbiotic psychosis such that B's question "Why $\phi$?" is
taken by A to mean that B wants to know why $\psi$, and he, A, then Xes
Y to B, intending some intelligible connection to $\psi$, which B takes as
Xing Y', which he, B, takes as having an intelligible connection to $\phi$,
etc. However difficult it is to conceive systematic delusion in an individual, it's exponentially more difficult to conceive an interaction exempli-
fying a collective delusion such that P and L are satisfied but no lecting
is really going on.

So we are left with the status of P and L as follows: they are not
jointly sufficient for the truth of a lecting claim, but what third set of
conditions has to be added if the set is to be jointly sufficient is (probably) a set of hypothetical disjuncts ["If '(*)' is filled by the name of
something to be proved, that something isn't false," and so on], a set
which cannot be completed unless the list of lecting verbs is complete,
which, in principle, it cannot be.

But now P and L part company. An argument, of sorts, was given for
the view that L states a set of necessary conditions for the truth of a

lecting claim. The argument, you will recall, took the following form. It seemed initially that D was true even though the conditions of lucidity as stated by L were not satisfied. If D is a true lecting claim and L1 and L2 are not satisfied, then L must be false. But the argument countered by showing that a closer look at why we took D to be true gave us grounds for saying that L *was* satisfied. The case hinges on the belief that unless closer examination convinced us that L *was* satisfied, we would give up our initial presumption that D was true. We couldn't prove that would be the case with every apparent counterexample that might be brought against L, but it made the view plausible.

**P TESTED BY D**     That move, however, is not available in our attempt to defend P. The case for D ("Socrates demonstrated Theorem $\theta$ to the slave boy") as a counterexample to P seems irrefutable: D is clearly a lecting claim. Given the encounter described by Plato, D seems clearly true. But there is no way in which one can turn the story around, fill in the flashbacks, as it were, so that the conditions required by P are satisfied. If D is true and P1 and P2 false, then P must be false.   Q.E.D.

Is there *no* way to tell the story such that P1 and P2 are true? Look at how one would have to change it around. Slave Boy is walking the streets of Athens, intent on his own business, when he spies Socrates and Meno engaged in serious discourse. "By the gods!" exclaims Slave Boy under his breath, "there stands the very fellow who can help me." With punctilious attention to the rules of courtesy, Slave Boy approaches Meno and Socrates, clears his throat discreetly, and says, "Gentlemen, please forgive this intrusion on your privacy, but I am in great need of instruction at this very moment. May I have your leave to explain? I have a horse and a square paddock exactly the right size for his needs. But today I am bringing home a second horse for which an equal area would be required. How can I measure the side of a new square exactly twice the area of the square I now have?"

SOCRATES: "Please join us, O Slave Boy. You come at a welcome time. We should be happy to answer your question, but may we ask you to do us a favor in return? We have entertained a curious hypothesis about the nature of teaching and learning. Would you kindly consent to answer a series of questions as candidly as you can? If you will, I promise that you will learn not only how to measure the side of your new paddock but also a simple method for doubling any square."

SLAVE BOY: "Ah yes, the customary price for receiving instruction includes having to learn more than one needs for the moment, and I'm quite happy to pay that price. But I beg you to remember the poor horse trader who even now awaits me."

And so the dialogue proceeds very much as from 82c onward. With this beginning and only an occasional change in wording, D satisfies L as well as P; whereas within the *Meno,* as Plato wrote it, the circumstances that made D true are inconsistent with P and entail L only when rationally reconstructed in the slave boy's mind.

What's the essential difference between the two accounts? Slaves aren't encountered walking about intent on their own business. Slaves attend their masters and attend to their masters' business. If it please a master that his slave receive instruction, the slave tries to give attention to the instruction presented or at least tries to give the appearance of giving attention. In short, the difference is that Meno's slave boy was a *slave;* in the reconstructed account he is a free person with desires and intentions all his own. And that difference is exactly the difference between D's entailing and D's not-entailing P1 and P2—the difference between D's being and not being a counterexample to P. As it stands, D is a counterexample; therefore P is false. But if we change the antecedent such that P becomes P′

P′: Under conditions that guarantee B's freedom and guarantee respect for B's purposes, A lect(s) ___(∗)___ to B $\longrightarrow$ P1 & P2

then a different conclusion obtains. Under those conditions (those found in our reconstructed account of the episode) D is no counterexample at all; it is instead as clear a case of pellucidity as one can find.

I do not know how to prove that P′ is true, but I do not believe that any counterexample could be sustained against it. Here is the reasoning behind my belief. Any lecting claim implies at least "uptake," some minimum but intentionally directed attention on the part of B. Under conditions that guarantee B's freedom, why would B pay (even the minimum price of) attention to A, unless the conjunction P1 were true? Ah, you reply, P1 is far too strong. Perhaps B is only mildly curious, perhaps B is simply bored and would rather pay attention to A's lecting than seek a more stimulating activity elsewhere. In sum, perhaps B attends A's lecting without (particularly) wanting or believing anything, but does so in complete freedom to do otherwise.

Ah, yes, I reply, but those circumstances are precisely those which do *not* guarantee respect for B's purposes. If B is engaged in some activity, say, attending A's lecting, without any desire or reason to do so, that *means* that B's purposes are not respected. (However the notion of "purpose" is to be analyzed, it must hinge on the complementary notions of having desires and reasons for acting.) Perhaps the lack of respect for B's purposes is found primarily, even exclusively, in B himself.

That certainly can happen. Respect for one's own purposes is something one must learn, and our society seems determined that those who learn it shall remain few. Even so, for A to lect ___(\*)___ to B while showing respect for B's purposes surely requires that A's intentions and beliefs must conform to the conjunction P2. That conjunction is rather a minimum definition of what it is to lect ___(\*)___ to B while guaranteeing respect for B's purposes.

The problem here, assuming the argument just above to be plausible, is not that P' is, or may be, false; the problem is deeper. Does the retreat from P to the qualified P' mean that the attempt to distinguish teaching from its counterfeits has tacitly been abandoned? It might seem so, for the line of defense against counterexamples to P' may appear to have left P' true by definition, no longer making any material statement about the realities of people's teaching and learning from each other. In short, the problem is that P' may be true only if it's vacuous. I'm not sure that *that* problem is or can be solved without building a complete theory linking all the pedagogical, psychological, and epistemological predicates we've been working with. But I think that the total argument of these three chapters may be taken as at least an initial defense against the charge that P' is vacuous. Let us recapitulate:

In any teaching claim where "teach" can be replaced by a lecting verb, we can be sure that if the claim is true, it is teaching and not one of its counterfeits that is going on. Grammar guarantees us that, but only if the lecting verb is used candidly and sincerely. If A is "explaining" ___(\*)___ to B, that may be a cover for indoctrinating. But if A is explaining ___(\*)___ to B, then no indoctrination or conditioning is going on. But how are we to make sure that the lecting verb is used candidly and sincerely? Why, by seeing whether L and P are satisfied.

Now, does the act of teaching as lecting satisfy the distinction between teaching and its counterfeits as given in Chapter Three? There, please recall, the distinction was made as follows:

(i) A teaches B _____ X.
(ii) B learns _____ X.
(iii) The event designated by (i) is the cause of the event designated by (ii).
(iv) B knows _____ X.
(v) Assuming (iii) is true, if (ii) $\longrightarrow$ (iv), then the event designated by (i) is teaching in its specific sense, conceptually distinct from indoctrination or conditioning.

There is no way in which this conception of teaching can guarantee the truth condition in (iv). But that is relatively unimportant, for no responsible conception of teaching can guarantee that. What teaching as lecting *can* guarantee, and, so far as I know, no other conception can, is that the justification (in Dewey's word, the "warrant") condition in

(iv) is satisfied. The key, of course, is that lecting requires active learning on the part of B. The circle is thus complete; teaching *is* to learning as buying is to selling. Without L and P, that equation will never balance.

Could we have schools where only teaching occurs? Could we do without indoctrination or conditioning? Why not? The burden of proof lies clearly with those who claim that the logical and moral criteria we ordinarily apply to human actions can be suspended when we talk about the actions of adults dealing with youngsters who are coerced into that encounter. That seems a very strange view in general, particularly strange when we consider moral education, a topic deserving far more space than is possible in the next chapter.

# CHAPTER FIVE

# Moral Education: The Morality of Teaching vs. the Teaching of Morality

---

**THE MORALITY OF LECTING**    The obvious surface ambiguity in the expression "moral education" has been exploited in the sub-title of this chapter; there are also much deeper ambiguities in our beliefs about moral education, and we shall have to dig them out one at a time. What we ultimately have to get clear on in this chapter is whether, in principle, moral education can be a moral enterprise. But first there is the question whether *any* education can be a moral enterprise. The negative answer introduced and strongly defended by Bereiter (Chapter One) is by no means merely idiosyncratic. Bereiter's case rests on the perfectly reasonable premises (i) that education inescapably involves indoctrinating and conditioning children and (ii) that teachers have no right to indoctrinate or condition their neighbors' children. I believe that (ii) is undeniable to anyone who can spare the time and effort to think seriously about it. [I believe (ii) because I believe that it follows from an even stronger true premise: that no one has the right to indoctrinate or condition any children whomsoever, his own *or* another's. But that stronger premise isn't the matter at issue right here.]

Thus if the morality of any educational enterprise is to be established, it will be necessary to deny (i). And the arguments needed to make that denial are now ready to hand. Consider some teaching claim

K: A teaches __(*)__ to B.

If K can be analyzed into a series of true lecting claims, each of which satisfies L and P, then the teaching encounter designated by K is guaranteed to be free of indoctrination or conditioning. Assume that at least one instance of K can be analyzed into lecting satisfying L and P. (Anyone who doubts that there is an instance of K satisfying those conditions can easily *make* one true the next time a [fellow-] student asks a sincere question—a question which reflects a genuine desire to know why, whether, how the . . . and so on.) It follows that *if an educational enterprise consisted exclusively of instances of lecting,* that enterprise would be free of indoctrination and conditioning: hence that enterprise would escape the moral charges which Bereiter aims, with great accuracy, I believe, against the existing enterprise.

The question still remains whether an educational enterprise can be morally sustained with any less severe restriction on manner of teaching. For, as we shall see, the conditional italicized just above is impossible to satisfy. But there is another aspect to the morality of teaching that must be called up and held in mind throughout the remainder of the argument. In its negative sense (as being free of indoctrination and conditioning) lecting clears the enterprise of teaching from the charge of immorality. But even more important is its positive sense: the intellectual acts of demonstrating, proving, explaining, narrating, and so forth are of positive moral value in and of and for themselves. Those are the acts, if any such acts there be, by which human understanding grows from partiality to mutuality. The intellectual act requires each participant to reveal his grounds for belief, to become an impartial judge among competing beliefs, applying ever more explicit criteria to all beliefs he confronts, including his own. These acts, then, extend the distribution of *warranted* beliefs among mankind, while they perfect the rational faculties of those engaged.

The expression "rational faculties" must not be taken to mean some metaphorical "muscles in the mind"; it means, rather, those habits of collective reasoning that make civilized life possible. Although our Western tradition since Aristotle has tended to conceive the contemplative life as one lived in solitude and its virtues as essentially private, there is a still older tradition in which stand the Socratic dialogues. In that tradition, contemplation is a shared, cooperative form of social life. It is one of candor and concentration in the joint pursuit of true answers to the most important questions we can find it within us to ask.

Conspiracy, literally, is a sovereign virtue; it becomes crime in the eyes of authority only because its outcome is inherently unpredictable.

Any instance of K, then, that can be analyzed into a series of lectings represents a net increment of positive moral value to A, to B, and to the universe as a whole. Thus, *if education consisted only of such instances of K,* we would not only not transgress our right to act in educating children, we would indeed be serving a positive moral value in so acting.

**A TEMPTING HYPOTHESIS**     The statement just above is still qualified by that damned sticky conditional, but it suggests a principle by which we might transcend Bereiter's charge against education. Let us try formulating that principle as

M: For any instance of K, if K consists only of lectings satisfying L and P, then the encounter designated by K is of positive moral value.

But is M true? Do we really believe that teaching-and-learning can always work its beneficence no matter who the persons or what the content? Let us try a little thought experiment, one requiring us to imagine (with increasing difficulty) two features of a situation. Imagine, first, a training course in which agents of the CIA are teaching their Latin American counterparts the latest techniques of torturing prisoners. Let K be

$K_L$: Agents of the CIA are teaching the techniques of torture to their Latin American counterparts.

Imagine, second, that the CIA instructors are firmly resolved to avoid indoctrinating or conditioning their trainees, that they are devoted to teaching, in the specific sense of the term, and skilled in lecting that satisfies L and P. In sum, put $K_L$ into M, imagine the antecedent true, and see what follows.

Given those assumptions, must not the question of how to torture inevitably lead to the question of when and whom to torture, hence to the question whether it is ever right to torture? Assuming always that the conditions envisaged in M are satisfied—that no one is ever asked to accept any belief not fully warranted for him, that no point is to be considered explained until it is understood, proved until believed with total conviction, demonstrated until seen or "seen," and so on—then must we not imagine the training course to end with the agents' destroying their infernal machines and the Latin American counterparts' opening their prisons?

It doesn't seem to work out that way, unfortunately. Perhaps it's that truth is divisible, that the truth about how to torture efficiently *is* separable from the question whether one ought to torture; or perhaps it's just that teaching-and-learning has never been given a chance to work its beneficial influence across the full range of human beliefs. However it is, our little thought experiment shows that we are on safer ground if we weaken M and express it as

M': M is true except when the content of instruction [what's inserted for "(*)" in K] is itself a manifestly immoral activity.

**LESSONS**          Given M', we have a very easy way to escape the charge that Bereiter leveled against education. We can decree that instruction in schools be limited to lecting under conditions in which L and P are satisfied, and order that schoolmasters shall not allow the teaching of manifestly immoral content. But there are serious difficulties with that solution. Even if one grants the rather dubious assumption that educational administrators are collectively capable of distinguishing the moral from the immoral, there is still the question of pedagogical utility. We distinguish instances of lecting that count as teaching from instances of lecting that don't (because they occur in clearly nonteaching encounters) by the presence, in the teaching encounter, of another sort of pedagogical activity, one which we've ignored to this point. But now we must broaden the base of our discussion.

Recall the instance of explaining which we followed in some detail in the last chapter. The mechanic's helper asks, "Why did the engine seize up?" The mechanic answers, "There was an oil leak." A perfect case of lecting, easy enough to fill out in detail so that it satisfies L and P. But the success of this instance of lecting presupposes the helper's knowing an awful lot of things that she could not have learned by participating in episodes of lecting only. (If "could not" sounds too strong, read it to mean "in all probability would not.") If the helper understands the connection between an oil leak and an engine seizure, she must know a good deal about the etiology of engine seizures in general; and in order to know *that,* the helper must understand the normal operation of engines. And *that* means, in the normal course of things, that someone must have taught her about engines in pedagogical contexts which include a great deal more than lecting. The helper would ordinarily have studied pictures and diagrams, read explanatory texts, followed lectures, taken apart and assembled model engines, and so on. And those activities of the helper would ordinarily be carried on in interaction with a teacher who supervises, corrects, directs, prescribes, orders, and the like. In short, the pedagogical context ordinarily includes not only the lecting *form* of interaction—A shows-and-tells about

X *to* B—but also, perhaps predominantly, the prescriptive form—A tells
B *to* X. Since *that* sort of interaction seems uneliminable from pedagogy,
isn't it also inevitable that teaching will be contaminated by indoctrination and conditioning?

We have to think this through before giving an answer. Consider this
proposal for educational reform offered by John Milton.

> We do amiss to spend seven or eight years merely in scraping together as much
> Latin and Greek as might be learned easily and delightfully in one year. If,
> after some preparatory grounds of speech by their certain forms got into
> memory, they were led to the *praxis* thereof in some chosen short book *lessoned
> thoroughly to them,* which would bring the whole language quickly into their
> power. This I take to be the most natural and most profitable way of learning
> languages.[1]

The point here is not whether Milton's proposal is a good one for
getting Latin and Greek into the heads of recalcitrant boys. The point
is what kind of pedagogical interaction is going on when someone lessons something to someone else. Grammatically, "lesson" seems to con-
jugate as a lecting verb. But "A lessons ___(*)___ to B" doesn't seem to
designate an encounter that could *ever* satisfy L and P. Pupils are
dragooned into classrooms in order that someone may *lesson* something
to them. And what is lessoned to them? Ordinarily it's obedience to a
system of rules, which rules are, as far as the pupils are concerned,
totally without foundation in reason. The "preparatory grounds of
speech" Milton speaks of are, to the pupils, simply rules that *must* be
memorized and obeyed. The source of the "must"—the schoolmaster's
cane—is ever present to the eye of the pupil.

It had been recognized long before Milton (and constantly thereafter)
that lessoning is an ineffective way of teaching languages—or anything
else for that matter. But the more perspicacious educators saw beyond
the manifest to the latent function of a social enterprise such as lessoning. Immanuel Kant's name has been attached to the clearest possible
statement of that latent-function analysis:

> Unruliness consists in independence of law. By discipline men are placed in
> subjection to the laws of mankind, and brought to feel their constraint. This,
> however, must be accomplished early. Children, for instance, are first sent to
> school, not so much with the object of their learning something, but rather that
> they may become used to sitting still and doing exactly as they are told.[2]

[1] Quoted in "Testimonials" to the Interlinear Translations of the Classics, e.g. *The
Anabasis of Xenophon* (New York: David McKay Co., Inc., n.d.), p. v. The emphasis
and grammar are reproduced as quoted, but I cannot vouch for their accuracy in
respect to the three-century-old original.

[2] Immanuel Kant, *Education* (Ann Arbor: University of Michigan Press, 1960), p. 3.
[A photo-reprint, with no identification, of A. Clinton's (1900) translation of F. T.
Rink's (1803) rendition of Kant's lecture notes.]

I should think it apparent that no schooling which has any significant share of "lessoning" among its normal pedagogical practices can escape Bereiter's charge of indoctrination. There is a clear doctrinal content to the latent teaching that's going on. It brings children to believe either that their own powers of reason and intelligence are totally inadequate to grasp the grounds for the rules they must learn to obey, or else that it is in the nature of things that they must learn to obey rules for which there simply are no reasons. It may not be a criterion of enlightenment among parents to reject the teaching of either of those beliefs to one's children. But surely it is a mark of enlightenment, other things being equal. Hence Bereiter must be right in claiming that such parents have a right to protect their children from lessoning.

**LESSONING IN OUR SCHOOLS**    In our own more enlightened times we have discarded the Latin grammar and the schoolmaster's cane (mostly), but we have maintained the underlying principle in those practices: children must be taught to obey rules that are, or at least to the children must appear, totally without grounding in reason. The rules by which the sounds of the English tongue are represented in conventional visual pattern—the rules that make it possible for us to read—serve this function admirably. They are complicated, filled with *ad hoc* exceptions incomprehensible to all save the trained philologist. The ultimate basis for those rules, of course, is historical accident; but they are (indeed, given the pedagogy of lessoning, they have to be) taught to children as if transcribed from the brow of Athena herself. Children who, for one reason or another, fail to read as well as someone thinks they should read, are given "remedial" treatment in schools, or, if they live in a large city, poor readers can be sent to a "reading clinic" (!).

The insanity of the "Reading" enterprise is concealed within the ideology of societal concern for the welfare of the underprivileged: somehow "technology" (or some other euphemism for an exploitative class system) has made the ability to read "up to grade level" a precondition for receiving an equitable share of the world's goods. This sedulously propagated myth creates an almost intolerable moral conflict for sensitive and concerned teachers of children, a conflict that exhibits all the features of the so-called "double bind" in interpersonal relations.[3] On one hand, teachers of young children are saddled with the task of

[3] Gregory Bateson, Don D. Jackson, Jay Haley, and John Weakland, "Toward a Theory of Schizophrenia," *Behavioral Science*, 1:2 (1956), 251–264. "[The] human being is like any self-correcting system which has lost its governor; it spirals into never-ending but always systematic distortions" (p. 256).

getting each child to read with a degree of proficiency such that he or she will not be penalized in later life. But this task is literally impossible to accomplish. For it is *relative* proficiency in reading (together with a lot of other things highly correlated with proficiency in reading) that, in direct or indirect ways, determines access to the world's goods. And the rule relating teaching and relative proficiency (in *anything*) is this: the more effective the teaching, the greater the variation in performance.[4] Thus, the more the teacher tries to protect the future of the individual child, the more effective is the teacher in perpetuating the system of exploitation. On the other hand, *not* to accept that impossible obligation and strive to fulfill it is to let the full weight of the exploitative system fall directly on those individual children whom one might have helped to escape its worst effects.

To raise that moral conflict to consciousness is not to solve it, by any means. But it may be a necessary first step.[5] The second step is to give up altogether the belief that "lessoning" has any place within a morally acceptable enterprise of education.

**"EXERCISING"**     Does this mean that there are no morally tolerable patterns of pedagogy in which one person can supervise the directed lessoning activities of a second? Of course not! "There do exist," Gilbert Ryle reminds us, "rowing coaches, swimming instructors, golf professionals, laboratory demonstrators, and college tutors, who all teach people to do things chiefly by exercising them in the doing of these things. . . . (F)lying, Latin prose composition, algebra and embroidery can be taught by critically supervised exercises."[6] And so can damned near anything one might *want* to learn, including the reading proficiency that, despite all efforts to cram it into their heads, many children never succeed in acquiring.

The pedagogical form called "exercising" hasn't been subject to detailed philosophical analysis and won't be here. Its significant difference from "lessoning" is clear enough in the examples. These are activities

---

[4] "Individualized Instruction: A Projection" in L. G. Thomas, ed., *Philosophical Redirection of Educational Research*, 71st Yearbook, NSSE, Pt. I (Chicago: University of Chicago Press, 1972), pp. 168–173.

[5] Perhaps an even prior step is to analyze more carefully just what one is coming to know when one learns to read. See John B. Connely: "Reading as a Semantic and Epistemological Problem: Implications of Certain Basic Assumptions about the Nature of Reading," in J. E. Jelinik, *Philosophy of Education 1973–1974* (Proceedings of the Far Western Philosophy of Education Society, December 1973, Arizona State University, pp. 188–189.

[6] Gilbert Ryle: "Can Virtue Be Taught?" in R. F. Dearden, P. H. Hirst, and R. S. Peters, eds., *Education and the Development of Reason* (London: Routledge & Kegan Paul Ltd., 1972), p. 438.

in which a person engages because he wants to, from which he is free to withdraw whenever his interests or inclinations change or when he loses confidence in the effectiveness of his "exerciser" in helping him learn what he wants to learn.

The exercise is, then, a voluntary pedagogical association, controlled at one level by the learner's intentions and beliefs while directed at the more immediate level by the teacher's suggestions and instructions. This is not to say that "A exercises B in X" entails voluntariness on B's part. But neither does it exclude voluntariness. The same indeterminacy holds when certain other verbs are set in the place of "exercise." "A trains B in X" neither entails nor excludes B's voluntary engagement, nor does "A drills B in X." It's not ordinarily said that A practices B in X, but the usage is explicitly sanctioned by the OED. And the same principle applies: the question whether B is doing X voluntarily is independent of the question whether or not B is being practiced in X by A, independent also of whether B is practicing X on his own. And other verbs are more or less substitutable in the paradigm "A exercises B in X," such as "rehearses," "coaches," and perhaps more.

If the exercise verbs neither entail nor exclude voluntariness on the part of B, neither do they presuppose a pedagogical context in which indoctrination or conditioning are dominant features. The innocence of exercising holds even though there are values of "X"—for example, the manual of arms and the arabesque—such that, if A exercises B in X, we naturally expect indoctrination and conditioning to be present also. But the moral obloquy attaching to the latter derives entirely from the institutions in which the exercising occurs, not from the exercising itself. Exercising as done by the drill sergeant or the *maître de ballet* becomes morally repugnant because of the way we organize military servitude and ballet companies, not because there is anything wrong with A's exercising B in X.

Lest one be tempted to account for the moral neutrality of exercising by saying that it holds only for skill training, let us recall a central idea from Chapter Three: learning a skill is seldom, if ever, a simple matter of having one's motor behavior brought into line with a certain rule. It is grossly misleading to think of helping a person to learn a skill as a matter of evoking a particular response from that person on presentation of a particular stimulus. That way of thinking about skill training dominates the ideology of American schools, probably reflecting our myopic preoccupation with "lessoning" children to read when the children had rather be doing something else.

But the activities mentioned by Ryle are of a different order altogether. There *are* clearly intelligible reasons underlying the rules one learns to follow in rowing, swimming, putting, setting up an experiment, and writing a consistent paragraph. That's why learners can be exercised in doing those things as opposed to having those things lessoned to them.

For example: as opposed to the practices of only fifty years ago, teaching people how to swim today (when done by a competent instructor) is a beautiful example of intellectual interchange. There are certain fundamental beliefs one simply has to get right if one is ever to learn to swim properly. For example, one swims submerged *in* the water rather than on top of it. One can inhale in a single gulp all the air one needs for several seconds of vigorous movement. Most generally, learning to swim means (among other things, of course) coming to know that thinking makes a difference in what one does. A nonswimmer finds himself immersed in a strange element. He learns how to control his initial impulse to panic. He learns to move in accordance with beliefs for which there is rational grounding. Expert instruction in swimming is mostly a lecting-form of interaction, helping the learner to become conscious and critical of his in-the-water thinking. "Skill-training" makes it sound very different from what it really is.

We can now return to the main line of argument. Lecting is a morally valuable activity. Exercising is neutral, but it combines quite naturally with lecting when A is helping B to learn what B *wants* to learn. Thus we *could* have an educational institution that is free of the moral charges Bereiter levels against the American schools. For anything in the curriculum could be something someone wanted to learn. Hence it could be taught by lecting and exercising under conditions satisfying L and P. In that way, the question of the morality of teaching could be solved, once and for all. Well?

**WHY NOT, INDEED?** Why don't we restrict our teaching in schools to lecting satisfying L and P, supplemented by exercising learners in ways that do not violate their freedom? That broad question would have to be examined historically: after all, there were schools long before there was any clear distinction between teaching and its counterfeits. And the question would have to be examined politically: before all, the modern school is an instrument of the national state and, like any other political instrument, supported by those who control the resources of the nation only so long as it is deemed by them to serve their interests. It is difficult to see that the political interest of the ruling classes would be served by finer moral discriminations among kinds of teaching promoted in schools.

But I wish to consider a question of principle rather than politics. What arguments can be advanced to show it to be *necessary* that the education of the young include an admixture of indoctrination and conditioning? That question, in turn, can be broken down into two other questions of empirical fact.

(i) Consider only the items in the curriculum which could be construed as aimed at positive knowledge—at bringing it about that students learn, come to know, that X, how to Y, the Z, or combinations of those: assuming that everything in the way of positive knowledge which is taught in schools *could* be taught in such a way as to satisfy L and P, *would* that teaching-and-learning actually occur if all coercion were removed from schooling and every youngster's freedom and rationality respected at all times? We have no reason to assume a yes answer to that question. Despite the inefficiency of schooling, a certain proportion of youngsters do learn how to read, how to write, how to spell (sort of), how to multiply common fractions, how to operate a typewriter, and so forth and so on. Would that proportion remain the same (or perhaps even rise) if those activities were taught only to those who asked to be taught? That's *very* doubtful, but it's the sort of question that requires evidence rather than speculation.

(ii) If the answer to (i) is negative, what difference, if any, would it make in the quality of our social life? Again, that's a question the answer to which requires a sociological theory grounded in empirical research, and I know of no such theory to which we can appeal with any confidence.

The plain fact is that we don't *know* what would happen if the coercive and manipulative aspects of schooling were eliminated, and we're not about to find out. For doing so would require institutional changes of a magnitude that simply won't occur without a vast change in our whole political structure, including (but not limited to) the dissolution of an enormously powerful coalition of teachers unions, administrator-bureaucrats, college professors, and the like. A political shift on that scale won't occur merely to satisfy our desire for an innocent social experiment. So questions (i) and (ii) are unanswerable, practically speaking. We operate within a political context that makes sense only if the answer to (i) were an unequivocal No! and the answer to (ii) were Disaster! We have little reason to believe those answers accurate and no chance to test them.

Thus our effort to exercise our imagination on a question of principle seems to have been thwarted by politics. We recognize with Kant that the main purpose of schooling in eighteenth-century Prussia was to get children to do exactly as they were told. We recognize with our social scientists that the main purpose of schooling in twentieth-century America is to "socialize" children—to get them to act in accordance with rules that are (or to the children must appear) totally ungrounded in reason. But our question remains: is it necessary to build that inherent immorality into our *idea* of education?

**TEACHING AND LEARNING AMONG THE SOO**  We are, it appears, at a standstill in our efforts to understand the principles that limit pedagogical possibility in our own society. So let's invent another society and call it the Soo. Let's set a single condition as fixed: among the Soo is found one and only one form of teaching—lecting satisfying L and P, together with exercising under conditions that protect the learner's freedom and rationality. What we will want to find out is how moral education is handled among the Soo. We shall find that the invention of that society enables us to solve the major, traditional problems in the theory of moral education. Going through the country of the Soo may appear to be a detour, but it's really the shortest way home.

Not that it's easy. Inventing possible societies requires disciplined as well as imaginative thinking. You must begin with the viewpoint of an anthropologist, your mind freed from parochial prejudices, your vision directed by an empirically grounded and tightly articulated theory. The limits of human potentiality will emerge as the boundary separating theoretically possible and impossible social structures and practices of socialization.

Assume that we have established our theoretical position. Given the limitations on teaching we have set for the Soo, we have to invent a *sociologically* possible system of roles and statuses, together with a *psychologically* possible sequence of stages in personal growth and development to fit the progression of social roles. Even further we shall have to imagine a (*physically* possible) material environment in which the social structure of the Soo, with its attendant individual behaviors, provides a (*biologically* possible) continuity of human life from one generation to the next.[7]

Now I leave it to you to fill in the details of Soo society in any way that your theories allow and your imagination happens to run. You may allow them as high or low level of technical and cultural complexity as you desire and believe compatible with the one proviso already stated: the only deliberate effort to modify beliefs found among the Soo is lect-

[7] The idea of social necessities as grounded in the limitations of physical and biological possibilities is summarized quite convincingly by Dorothy Emmet, *Rules, Roles and Relations* (New York: St. Martin's Press, 1966), esp. Chaps. V and VI. A full-scale effort to imagine a possible society, one which in the event was never actualized, is Solon T. Kimball and J. E. McClellan, *Education and the New America* (New York: Random House, Inc., 1962).

ing satisfying L and P, together with exercising in which freedom and rationality are respected absolutely.

At this point, if not earlier, a nagging doubt will have begun to arise. Doesn't the restriction on teaching among the Soo violate the initial assumption that the Soo were a *possible* society? Is it possible to provide for continuity in Soo (or any other) culture without providing for an admixture of indoctrination and conditioning in that most crucial encounter (crucial from the standpoint of cultural transmission), the interaction between adult and child? It seems easy enough to invent a society in which beliefs about the material world are communicated from one generation to another by purely rational interchange. But a society, we tend to think, maintains its existence only by virtue of common sentiments, those basic emotional responses that a child acquires long before he is (or, at any rate, long before adults believe that he is) capable of any sort of rational persuasion. Those fundamental attitudes, those affective tendencies, are essential to moral education; in that domain indoctrination and conditioning are essential. So runs conventional wisdom. Let's see.

**"CONDITIONING"**     In the sense that psychologists use the term, "conditioning" designates a process in the full, honest, technical use of the term "process." Conditioning is omnipresent in the animal kingdom; it may even have analogues in certain species of plants. Evolution would be inconceivable without conditioning; the claim of *Homo sapiens* to the top rung on the evolutionary ladder is the claim to have abstracted and generalized the same fundamental principles of intelligence found in the conditioning of the lowly, primitive planaria. Conditioning establishes our psychical fraternity and sorority with every species that swims, runs, crawls, slithers, or flies.

The function of conditioning is much better understood than its mechanism. Functionally, conditioning is the process that changes the probability of an organism's response to a perceived environment. Overall, the direction of that change is toward increasing the probability of a response favoring the organism's survival within that environment. The physical mechanisms by which the consequences of one response modify the probability of a subsequent response are not well understood, even for the simplest organisms, but recently developed and very sophisticated research techniques give promise of showing the molecular basis for the changes that conditioning produces (with possibly different mechanisms) in different animal species.[8]

8 Cf. J. Konorski, *Integrative Activity of the Brain* (Chicago: University of Chicago Press, 1967). Also Rosenzweig, Bennett, and Diamond, "Brain Changes in Response to

So we may rest assured that conditioning is not absent from Soo society. If you imagine bowling and baseball in Soo society, you must also imagine the superstitious behavior, the mannerisms, tics, and so on that conditioning inevitably produces in bowlers and batters. But now comes the difficult part. Our restriction on the teaching activities of the Soo concerned their communication of belief from one Soo to another. *Can* beliefs be conditioned? Can beliefs *not* be conditioned? More specifically, what connection is there between the following two claims?

1. A teaches B that X, and
2. A conditions B to Y.

At this juncture, some alternative interpretations of conditioning may be discerned. The lunatic fringe of behaviorism would hold that 1 entails 2, quantified as:

3. For any belief X, there is at least one observable behavior Y, such that if, at time $t_1$, A teaches B that X, then, at $t_1$, A conditions B to Y.

Now 3 must fail on either one of the only two possibilities open. Let "X" be given some particular value, say, "$\sqrt{2} \neq a/b$," where $a$ and $b$ are relatively prime, positive integers. Then either the description of a specific observable behavior can be given for Y, or no specific behavior can be so designated. If the latter, then 3 registers "Vacuous" on the test of significance. If the former, then 3 registers "False" on the test of truth. So 3 fails.

Let us try to resurrect the element of truth in the behaviorists' claim. *Why* did 3 fail the truth test? Well, what gives plausibility to the connection between 1 and 2 is really

4. At $t_1$ B believes that X.

What *is* true is that 1 entails 4! It doesn't follow, however, that any particular observable behavior is consequent on the belief that X—for example, that $\sqrt{2} \neq a/b$. Even if, solely for the sake of the argument, we grant that a great many *intentional* conditions are satisfied—such as the nonbehavioral conditions that B wants to affirm his beliefs candidly, that B and his interlocutor share conventions such that one particular behavior is to count as affirming that $\sqrt{2} \neq a/b$, that B rightly understands the question "Do you believe that $\sqrt{2} = a/b?$" and so on—it could still be the case that 1 is true, 4 is true, but 5 is false.

5. B exhibits behavior Y at $t_1$,

where "Y" is the behavior of affirming that $\sqrt{2} \neq a/b$. Perhaps B's at-

Experience," in *The Nature and Nurture of Behavior* (San Francisco: W. H. Freeman and Company Publishers, 1974), pp. 117–124 (from *Scientific American,* February 1972).

tention is distracted by a butterfly and he simply makes no response at all. Or perhaps neither we nor B can explain why he didn't exhibit behavior Y, but nonetheless he didn't. Even with all the stated conditions satisfied, there's no contradiction in the supposition that Y doesn't appear.

The attempt to patch up the case, by eliminating all possible conditions—intentional or otherwise—that might make the entailment fail, in effect makes 5 part of the analysis of 4. Consider

6. There is a class of observable behaviors Z, such that if *all* the intentional and nonintentional conditions for an attentive and candid response by B are satisfied at $t_1$, then the probability that B will fail to exhibit a Z-behavior at $t_1$ approaches zero.

Let "Z" take the value "affirming that X"; then 4 entails 6. But 1 entails 4. Therefore, 1 entails 6. And that includes what's true in the behaviorists' fondness for 3. It leaves open the philosophically contested questions —for example, whether for any X, Z is finite. This view retains the sensible notion that behavior is *evidence* for learning and believing, but no part of the *meaning* of "learn" or "believe."

The more interesting connection between 1 and 2, however, is to be found in the hypothesis that 2 entails 1, as quantified:

7. For every behavior Y, there is at least one belief X, such that if A conditions B to Y at $t_1$, then A teaches B that X at $t_1$.

Consider the classical experiment in which John B. Watson conditioned Albert, an innocent nine-month-old child, to cry in fear when presented with a furry rabbit or, in time, any other object resembling a furry rabbit. (That seems a paradigm case of a conditioning claim, not only because it came so early and is so readily stated in the form of 2, but also because of the distaste it arouses. But Watson did succeed in deconditioning Albert with, we hope, no scars from those stressful experiences.[9]) What are we to say about the corresponding teaching claim derived from 1: Watson taught Albert that rabbits are frightful objects? And the claim derived from 4: Albert believed at $t_1$ that rabbits are frightful objects?

I don't see how the teaching and belief claims can be denied. Are we to say that nine-month-old children are incapable of holding beliefs? Then what about nine-*year*-old children? Just because Albert acquired

---

[9] This experiment, which is reported in most textbooks on learning, appeared in the *Journal of Experimental Psychology*, III (1920), 1–14. Watson's own popularized account, with photographs, is found in his *Psychological Care of Infant and Child* (New York: W. W. Norton & Company, Inc., 1928). His defense against the charge of cruelty in these experiments is clear enough: "They will be worth all they cost if through them we can find a method which will help us remove fear." Has the experience of the past fifty years satisfied that conditional?

that belief without passing through some process of conscious reflection doesn't mean that he didn't learn it, nor that Watson's responsibility for his learning it isn't to be registered in the corresponding teaching claim.

It is this element of personal responsibility which ties the two together, the same element which experimental psychologists so constantly but voicelessly deny. If we expressed the conditioning claim in the way that contemporary behaviorists (those who've gone beyond freedom and dignity) would find most suitable, we should say that it was the simultaneous presentation of the visual stimulus—furry rabbit—and the auditory stimulus—a loud banging of a hammer on an iron bar right behind the infant's head—which conditioned the fear response in Albert. In parallel fashion, we might say that it was that experience (repeated several times, if you can imagine it!) which brought Albert to believe that furry objects are frightful.

How, then, on the assumption that 7 is true, are we to insure that no beliefs are to be conditioned in Soo children? Well, we're not, of course. All we can require is that no adult deliberately set out to bring about some general disposition to behavior Y, when there is some belief X, such that conditioning the child to Y presumptively established the truth of the claim that the child has come to believe X. In other words, the Soo must forbid experimental psychologists access to children, and Soo parents must watch themselves very carefully to avoid the use of conditioning techniques prior to the age that children can acquire beliefs consciously and critically. To repeat, this does not mean that the Soo child will not have been conditioned to believe *lots* of things, such as that certain sounds and smells betoken food, the touch of fire pain, a parent's arms the "oceanic feeling" of warmth and security. But no Soo parent factitiously contrives to establish those beliefs in children. Infants come to believe those things as a consequence of being what infants are —both agents and objects in a world of other agents and objects.

**CONDITIONING BELIEFS**

That restriction on the Soo poses no conceptual problem; your imagination must simply stretch to cover a material environment that infants may explore freely without being killed off in proportions too high to permit collective survival. But now a more serious problem emerges. For thinking, reflecting, or "entertaining" ideas is *itself* subject to conditioning! Little experimental evidence bears on that claim, but to deny it would also seem to deny the general evolutionary point of view within which alone the phenomenon of conditioning is intelligible. That a cigarette smoker's beliefs about the effects of smoking are separable from his conditioned response to the sight and feel and *thought* of the cigarette is

inconceivable. To entertain the thought of smoking *is* to elicit a conditioned response.

Think of this phenomenon as much as possible in evolutionary terms.
The "fixing" of beliefs is then seen to be a function of how different
beliefs *feel* when entertained in thought. There is no evolutionary advantage for the human species in the fact that a hungry person tends to
have a lot of images of food in his head; there is great evolutionary
value in the *feeling* of rightness attaching to the image of food-to-be-had-
in-the-valley when, in fact, food is to be had there. It isn't the mere
image, it's the belief which organizes other thoughts and movements into
food-getting action. And that belief is pulled to the center of the hungry
person's consciousness by the same force which pulls the hungry rat's
foot to the lever in a Skinner box.

Is it asking the superhuman of the Soo to ask that they learn how to
examine by explicit, conscious reflection those beliefs they have acquired
by (mostly unconscious) conditioning? Even more, that they learn to
exercise that volition—that they learn to want to examine their beliefs
critically and do so, even when it may be painful? Neither the Soo nor
any other human being can bring about a change in his beliefs merely
by willing to do so. As William James put it:

> There are at all times *some* ideas from which we shy away like frightened horses
> the moment we get a glimpse of their forbidding profile upon the threshold of
> our thought.

But James goes on in the next breath to define the limits of our power to
escape unpleasant ideas:

> *The only resistance which our will can possibly experience is the resistance
> which such an idea offers to being attended to at all.* To attend to it is the
> volitional act, and the only inward volitional act which we ever perform.[10]
> [Emphasis in original]

If the critical examination of conditioned beliefs is a matter of skill and
volition, then it should be possible to teach that skill by lecting and to
transform that volition into stable habit by exercise. The critical test of
such skills and habits comes not in matter of food gathering: we can
count on our evolutionary heritage to erase the belief in food-in-the-
valley from our minds if the valley prove barren. The test comes in
beliefs about other minds. To the lover, the belief that the beloved loves
in return is so reinforcing that it sweeps aside all evidence to the contrary, unless replaced by the terribly aversive belief that the beloved
loves not, which belief, however implausible, the foolish lover *has* to dis-

10 Wm. James, *The Principles of Psychology* (New York: Henry Holt & Co., 1890),
vol. II, p. 567.

prove even though doing so means that he must suspect all evidence of affection.

So also with teachers and learners, among the Soo as well as among ourselves. When A explains __(*)__ to B, the belief that B understands __(*)__ is well nigh irresistible to A. And to B, A's smile of approval is so reinforcing that it transforms the uncomprehending B's "I see!" from a conscious falsehood to a sincere expression of a false belief about his own mental state. What happens to B's lingering doubts in the face of A's triumphant "Q.E.D."? The classical experiments of Solomon Asch showing the effect of group pressure on judgment are duplicated in thousands of unrecorded experiments every day when learners come to accept beliefs unmerited by evidence or reasons and teachers grieve over their own misjudgment of student achievement.[11] The power of mutual understanding as a reinforcer leads us all too often to accept the simulacrum for the achievement.

What, then, are the Soo to do? They are mandated to engage in no teaching except for lecting that satisfies L and P. But, being human, the Soo are liable to false beliefs conditioned by the powerful reinforcers that always operate in the psychically intimate atmosphere of lecting. Well, if it is important to recognize the power of conditioning in the life of the mind, particularly in the interaction of minds, it is equally important not to mistake power for omnipotence. We *can* override conditioning fairly easily, if we become aware of its effects before they produce deep-grained habits. We all develop techniques for clearing the mind, often along with clearing the throat. "Now, let's see, hrumph, do I really understand this proof? . . . these instructions? . . . his excuses? . . . her argument?" We don't take the learner's "I see!" as conclusive evidence that he understands, not just because, in our system, unfortunately, it's in his interest to make us believe that he understands when he doesn't, but also because the contingencies of reinforcement are likely to make *him* believe that he understands more than he does. Our techniques for checking out our mutual understanding are of dubious value, for all too often they make not-understanding punishable. But our tests and papers and such do enable us to make a pretty good estimate of mutual understanding, and surely you can work out more efficient and humane techniques for the Soo.

If conditioning is an inescapable fact of animal existence, including human interaction, we must be cautious in phrasing our prohibition against its deliberate use among the Soo. Let us say that any pedagogical encounter most easily and naturally described by 2 is forbidden, unless

[11] S. E. Asch, "Effects of Group Pressure Upon the Modification and Distortion of Judgment," in Swanson, Newcombe, and Hartley, eds., *Readings in Social Psychology* (New York: Holt, Rinehart and Winston, Inc., 1952), pp. 2–11.

(a) the corresponding teaching claim, 1, is also true, and (b) in the episode designated by 1, A and B have collaborated in testing X against the highest canons of rationality possible, given B's age and experience. These restrictions prohibit

8. A conditions B to believe that X,

where A intends to bring it about that B believe that X without subjecting X to the highest canons of rational judgment possible to the interaction between A and B. With that proviso, let us allow psychologists back into Soo society so that they can help A to understand the phenomenon of conditioning and thus be on guard against using it unconsciously.

**INDOCTRINATION DEFINED MULTIDIMENSIONALLY**

Conditioning is a root fact of biological existence, but indoctrination is not. Rather, "indoctrination" is just one of those terms by which we pick out certain features of pedagogical interaction. One cannot imagine a human society from which the phenomenon of conditioning is absent, but one doesn't have to imagine societies in which no distinction is made between "education" and "indoctrination." Among most societies for most of human history that distinction simply wouldn't be intelligible. For the distinction between "indoctrination" and "education" presupposes the prior distinction between canons of thought and substantive beliefs subject to criticism by those canons. By insisting on the absolutely crucial nature of that distinction in every area of human belief, Socrates had an unsettling effect on the Athenian society of his time and eventually got himself executed for subverting the morals of youth. The distinction between canons of thought and substantive belief is one that the human species can do without. But once it appears, it cannot be forgotten nor, in the long run, repressed.

It is in relation to that presupposed distinction that I have contrasted the specific sense of teaching with indoctrination. I have used the latter term, up to this point, as a catch-all for failure on the logical and moral criteria for teaching. For that usage I must apologize to my colleagues in philosophy of education, who have succeeded in refining the use of "indoctrination" as a fairly specific way in which teaching in the generic sense can fail to satisfy the criteria for teaching in the specific sense. For some purposes it is imperative that indoctrination be distinguished from conning, charming, beguiling, "brainwashing," browbeating, advertising, propagandizing, and other ways in which A can get B to believe that X without full rational reflection. But we may treat them as equivalent to the extent that they share the central features of indoctrination. At the cost of ignoring the subtleties that make the concept interesting, we may summarize those central features in four categories:

(i) *Content.* The analysis of indoctrination must begin with the notion of doctrine, leading in turn to "docere," Latin *to teach.* Doctrines aren't beliefs you might just happen to learn from experience; they have to be taught; indeed, they typically come in systems organized specifically for effective instruction. Marxism, Maoism, and Roman Catholicism come most readily to mind as such systems of doctrines, but in respect of being systematized for instruction they do not differ from geometry and grammar, both of which received their present systematic form in classical Hellas, precisely in order that they might be taught more effectively.

Doctrinal systems differ from grammars, geometries, and scientific theories, however, in two very important ways. First, a doctrine, as Antony Flew puts it, is "a belief which, if not false, is at least not known to be true."[12] That, as Flew explains, is a minimum characterization of the truth value of a doctrine. More importantly, the doctrinal system does not clearly and cleanly distinguish between substantive beliefs and next-order criteria for belief, whereas grammars, geometries, and scientific theories (at least those that have been subjected to rational reconstruction) *can* be shown to reveal that distinction clearly and cleanly. Doctrinal systems are not formulated so that the basic canons for the truth of beliefs of that sort are first separable from and then applicable to the beliefs in that system. And until that kind of analysis and test has been made, there can be no justification for the claim that a doctrinal system is known to be true.

Second, a system of doctrines is intended to guide one's life, and in ways quite different from geometries, grammars, and scientific theories. The latter we may call upon to help answer specific questions we encounter while trying to achieve our purposes. But a doctrinal system's main function is to teach us what our purposes are. It serves its function by showing a relation between the purposes it offers and the most general features of the world we live in. This last point is what gives doctrinal systems their power in directing human affairs. Who would not wish his or her individual purposes to be consonant with the way things really *are?* No human life which lacks that sense of relatedness to reality can be found good in the living of it, to borrow C. I. Lewis's happy phrase. Doctrinal systems purport to give their believers an unshakable grip on ultimate reality, and at a bargain-counter price: it's yours for the voluntary suspension of doubt.

---

12 A. G. N. Flew, "Indoctrination and Doctrines," in I. A. Snook, ed., *Concepts of Indoctrination* (London: Routledge & Kegan Paul Ltd., 1972), pp. 67–92.

(ii) *Intent*. When A indoctrinates B in X, A wants to get B to believe that X in the way that a true believer believes the fundamental principles of his doctrinal system. That intent, with whatever degree of consciousness or self-consciousness that A holds it, will shape every aspect of the interaction between A and B.

But just how does a believer believe doctrines? J. P. White says "unshakably," and that is certainly the case with some.[13] But the more interesting cases, I think, are those in which doctrines are held with great flexibility and apparent (only) openness to criticism and refutation. The believer has been taught to defend his doctrines in depth, rather more like Kutuzov than Hidenberg. The intent of the indoctrinator is to prepare his pupil for a world in which his beliefs are always threatened, in which contrary beliefs are seen not as possible truths to enlarge and enrich the mental life but as dangers to be overcome. That intent shapes the pedagogical encounter in its every detail: B's questions must be given immediate and conclusive answers, every vestige of B's doubts must be smoothed over and washed away. When A achieves his intended goals, B learns to be a formidable opponent in debate and hopelessly inept in collaborative inquiry.

(iii) *Method*. The specific techniques of indoctrination are familiar enough to need no recitation here. The question is whether these techniques rest on or presuppose any particular theory of teaching and learning. And the answer is: not exactly—it's really more an extended metaphor, revealed in the phrase one encounters most frequently in talk about indoctrination, used by friends and foes alike: teaching is *implanting beliefs* in the mind of the learner. Within this organic—almost botanical—view of things, if the fundamental beliefs of a doctrinal system can be planted in the mind of the young child, they will take root, grow, and spread, providing the organic structure for later learning. Drilling the child in catechism and credo until memory is instant and letter-perfect may be likened to drilling seeds deeply into fertile soil; properly planted, the life in each seed will transform the nutrients of the soil into more life. Like a tree that's planted by the water, the germ of Truth implanted in children grows into the firm, unshakable conviction of the doctrinally committed adult.

That way of thinking about learning and growth has been with us since human beings have thought about such things, one must suppose. Later efforts to transform that metaphor into a theory which has a truth value have been mostly unavailing, though vestiges of that organic

---

13 J. P. White, "Indoctrination and Intentions," in Snook, *op. cit.*, pp. 117–130.

metaphor persist in the psychology of Froebel and in the ideology of the Open Education movement in England and the United States. Which shows, among other things, that there is no necessary, logical connection between indoctrination and that organic view of intellectual development. It's just that from the Book of Proverbs—"Train up a child . . ." —to A. Pope—"As the twig is bent . . ."—it's been easy to rationalize indoctrinative practices within that organic view. Were it lost, indoctrinators would find a substitute; it's power, not point-of-view, that makes those practices indoctrination.[14]

(iv) *Control.* The literature revealingly is silent on the topic of teacher control as a distinctive feature of indoctrination. The authors, to a man, seem to assume that the distinction between indoctrination and teaching can be made out clearly without any account taken of the social system in which teaching-and-learning are supposed to occur. If the purpose of one's inquiry is to set forth the necessary and sufficient conditions for the truth of a claim, "A is indoctrinating B in X," then it seems strange to ignore the fact of power and control in all those cases that we would unhesitatingly label "indoctrination." Those situations, whether in (old-time) Catholic schools, classes in "Marxism-Leninism" in Soviet schools, or wherever, *do* show the feature of control. More precisely, in those actual instances in which we are most inclined to describe a pedagogical encounter in the form, "A is indoctrinating B in X," it turns out that A is presumed to have the power and (though this presumption is necessarily false) the right to punish and reward B, not only for B's success in taking in X (the beliefs A is trying to implant) but also for B's conduct in general—that is to say, in matters related and unrelated to the beliefs that constitute the ostensible focus of their interaction. But, you rejoin, that's also true of a situation which we would be most naturally inclined to describe as "A is teaching B plane geometry." Right you are —which is why you can never be sure that the latter case is *not* indoctrination. Whereas if A is demonstrating Theorem A to B under conditions that satisfy L and P, we *can* be sure that indoctrination is not taking place.

To sum up: "indoctrination" is not the kind of term, as "teaching" *is* the kind of term, that gets itself rounded off, polished into pretty defi-

14 Soviet educators tend to think of moral education as a function of social variables— qualities in the group to which the child belongs. But they think of other sorts of learning, such as the learning of languages, in terms of the materialist-associationist psychology dominant in the USSR from Pavlov through Luria. Compare P. M. Yakobson, "Studying the Moral Attitudes and Judgments of Children of Different Ages," with D. B. El'konin, "Psychological Study of the Learning Process . . . ," (*inter alia*) in Fred Ablin, ed., *Education in the USSR: Readings from Soviet Journals* (New York: International Arts & Sciences Press, 1964), vol. I.

nite relations to other terms, by constant use in the workaday world. There is little to be gained, therefore, from an attempt to fix our understanding of the concept of indoctrination by careful analysis of linguistic usage. Rather, we should look at the historical conditions that make possible a distinction between indoctrinating and teaching. A culture which didn't recognize the existence of contrary systems of beliefs external to that culture would have neither the practice nor the concept of indoctrination. Nor in all probability, a distinctive concept of teaching: "docere" must have long lain hidden between "dicere" and "ducere." (But that's conjecture; concerning such cultures we have nothing more definite than the somewhat unreliable reports on the Garden of Eden as published in the Book of Genesis.)

The conceptual distinction between indoctrination and teaching appears rather late in the history of the human species. Societies must notice the existence of other cultures; there must be an effort to protect *our* children from *them;* thus emerges the practice of indoctrination, and teaching is wholly submerged in it. Only later, when the distinction between substantive beliefs and criteria for rationality in belief has been worked out in other realms of thought, can that distinction be applied reflexively to teaching. And, finally, before that conceptual distinction can be made into a workable guide to practice, a society must have formalized its educational activities to the point that social decisions can be undertaken on matters of educational policy. Roman legislation regulating the schools of orators shows that distinction clearly; social class, general docility, and intelligence were criteria for the sort of education in which beliefs of some social significance could be held up to rational scrutiny. Frederick the Great would allow the winds of the Enlightenment to blow through the school rooms of the nobility only. And so on.

During the 1930's many American educators were perplexed by the need, or what they took to be the need, to indoctrinate youth in the endangered principles of democracy. The perplexity arose from the paradoxical duty to indoctrinate children in the belief that indoctrination is an evil. In our own more enlightened times we tend to regard our political principles as either immune to threat or not worth preserving; in any event, whatever laws to that effect still remain on our statute books, no one seriously proposes that all future citizens be indoctrinated in the principles of American democracy. In fact, we have reached the end of the line. We no longer designate any beliefs as so central to our social order that we must indoctrinate our youth in them. We no longer designate children of any particular character, intelligence, or stratum of society as peculiarly in need of indoctrination. Obliterating all clear distinctions, we just conform to the institutional mould in which our teaching is carried on. The institutional mould was designed (according to our revisionist historians, rather consciously designed[15]) by men who took it for granted that public school teaching *should* show all four features of indoctrination as described above. It is obviously folly to try to use that mould to stamp out young men and women of intellectual independence and personal responsibility, a folly we persist in year after year at a social cost beyond my power to calculate.

Equally difficult to calculate is the cost of changing the form of schooling so that it is no longer an institution of indoctrination by virtue of its basic structure. But with the aid of the Soo we can see one way in which indoctrination might be eliminated from pedagogical practice. It can be demonstrated that if pedagogy is restricted to lecting satisfying L and P, no indoctrination will occur. The demonstration requires two stages: (i) L eliminates indoctrinative content, and (ii) P eliminates indoctrinative method and control. With the means of acting on it eliminated, indoctrinative intent will cease to be.

**L ENTAILS NO INDOCTRINATIVE CONTENT**

(i) If, in an episode of lecting, A must reveal the grounds on which B is asked to accept that X, then the distinction between substantive belief and criteria has been brought into the interaction. And once in, that distinction cannot be restricted to any given level. The canon Y, which X must satisfy to be rationally grounded, can become itself a substantive belief subject to doubt, requiring criticism and justification by appeal to Z, and so on.

Let me illustrate the point by describing a little pedagogical experiment you can perform in the comfort of your own home, if you happen to have suitable subjects available. Anyone who can perform the elementary operations of arithmetic is a possible subject, though the experiment will abort if the subject is at all sophisticated in mathematics.

The object of the experiment is to demonstrate the difference between

1. A teaches B a proof of "$\sqrt{2} \neq a/b$"

   (where $a$ and $b$ are positive integers containing no common factor) and

2. A proves to B that $\sqrt{2} \neq a/b$.

Providing an instance of 1 is not as simple as it might at first appear. Doing it well requires the kind of skill and insight that we admire in good high school teachers of mathematics. First, you take a proof from a school textbook—about seventh grade for *very* New Math, up to eleventh

---

15 Clarence Karier, Paul Violas, and Joel Spring, *Roots of Crisis: American Education in the Twentieth Century* (Chicago: Rand McNally & Company, 1972).

grade for a traditional sequence—and you study that proof until you've mastered it. Then you find a subject whom you can motivate (coerce or cajole) into playing learner to your act of teaching. And you go through the proof carefully, one step at a time. You have to be alert and attentive to what your subject is actually thinking, where and how his mind is being drawn toward the irrelevant, whether he recognizes the principle by which you justify the movement from one step to another, and so on. With care and cooperation you can bring it about that your subject, B, has accomplished the objective, thus making true

3. B has learned a proof that $\sqrt{2} \neq a/b$

   or even

4. B has learned how to prove that $\sqrt{2} \neq a/b$.

With any luck at all in finding a subject, you will find the experience, if not the most deeply moving in your career, genuinely and immediately satisfying. You should be reinforced with a sense of closure and accomplishment when the subject himself adds the Q.E.D. to the bottom line. It's "neat," as they say.

To provide an instance of 2 is something else altogether. This time the initial step is to find out whether B is inclined to believe, usually without ever having critically examined the belief, that all real numbers *can* be expressed as $a/b$. All the numbers that most of us use in the daily affairs of life can be so expressed. The ancient Pythagoreans believed that to exist was to exist in such a ratio; for them the doctrine "the real is the rational" had a very literal meaning. Just about anyone who doesn't *know* that $\sqrt{2} \neq a/b$ (which is quite different from remembering that one was once the subject of a true sentence of form 3 or 4) and is willing to find out what he is inclined to believe about numbers and ratios will turn out to be inclined to believe that any number that has a definite location on a number line can be expressed as $a/b$; hence, since $\sqrt{2}$ is a number

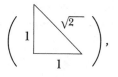

he will be inclined to believe that $\sqrt{2} = a/b$.

The essential condition for accomplishing this first step with your subject, then, is not motivation; it's manners, tact, and consideration. No one is totally uninterested in the (mostly unexamined) beliefs he holds about numbers and their properties. It isn't likely to be an overwhelming desire, but he would be willing enough to pursue the matter, except that he's probably come to believe that his mind has been irremediably confused, that he's therefore incapable of straight thinking in mathematical terms. A great deal has been written about the fact that "teaching" entails severe restrictions on the manner in which one influences the thought of another, but little or nothing about what constitutes good manners in teaching. But it's with delicate tact that you help B to recognize, sans guilt or embarrassment, that he *is* inclined to believe that $\sqrt{2} = a/b$.

All the presupposed conditions for proving something to somebody are now present: the somebody is inclined to believe that $\sqrt{2} = a/b$ while, in truth, $\sqrt{2} \neq a/b$. But proving it will turn out to be an enterprise quite different from just going through the steps. The self-contradiction in the initial step—the false assumption that $\sqrt{2} = a/b$—will be *felt* long before it is actually asserted, even before it is "seen" by the subject. Principles of inference that were not even raised to consciousness in merely teaching B the proof become occasions for controversy. Indeed, the basic, logical principle, $[(P \longrightarrow \sim P) \longrightarrow \sim P]$, which gives form to the pedagogical effort must be tested rather than merely assumed when you're actually using it to prove something to someone.

Now what is the goal of proving to B that $\sqrt{2} \neq a/b$? It must include at least the aim of making true

5. B knows that $\sqrt{2} \neq a/b$.

Still 5 won't do by itself. You could establish 5 by having B calculate the decimal value of $\sqrt{2}$ to 100 places without finding a repeating or terminating fraction. That would establish B's warrant for $\sqrt{2} \neq a/b$ as an inductive generalization, as well as all the psychological certainty anyone would wish. But to prove to B that $\sqrt{2} \neq a/b$ requires making true

6. B knows that N $\sqrt{2} \neq a/b$,

where N means (*notwendig*) necessarily: if the computer gives a terminating decimal fraction for the value of $\sqrt{2}$, then B must know that the computer has made a mistake. Furthermore, you (taking the part of A) must know certain things

7. A knows that N $\sqrt{2} \neq a/b$.

And 7 goes onto the line, subject to refutation, when you undertake to prove to B that $\sqrt{2} \neq a/b$. The goal of the pedagogical endeavor, in fine, is found in the conjunction of 6 and

8. A knows that B knows that N $\sqrt{2} \neq a/b$.

Or, the conjunction of 6 and 8 is entailed by 2.

(I think that 2 entails 7 also, but I don't see any easy way to defeat the counterexamples which imagination brings so readily to mind.)

Now, assuming that your knowledge of the peculiar properties of irrational numbers extends only to what you learned from the textbooks you consulted, I should guess it even odds that you will withdraw your claim to 7 before the demonstration ends. Both you and B may come to know that $\sqrt{2} \neq a/b$, very like you *know* that $E = mc^2$, that the sum of the angles in a non-Euclidean triangle is greater or less than a straight angle, and so on. But neither you nor B is likely to receive the reinforcement you got from the first phase of the experiment when "Q.E.D." wrapped it all up so neatly.

The moral to be drawn from the little experiment is this: when A lects __(\*)__ to B, A puts all of his background beliefs—all of his assumptions, presuppositions, or anything else that makes him take __(\*)__ as lected (proved, demonstrated, explained, accurately described, and so on)—on the line, subject to mutual examination and joint criticism in the interaction itself. Unless B shares those background beliefs, the episode of lecting must terminate short of success. And even when it is successful, it raises to consciousness those background beliefs and makes them liable to future critical scrutiny. It is this logical openendedness that produces the inconclusive endings of the major Socratic dialogues of Plato.

The absence of positive reinforcement in the termini of such episodes means that they cannot be the norm for any institution which relies on reinforcement to condition the behavior that keeps the institution going: one more instance of the conflict between the logical norms of lecting and the psychological bases for school maintenance.

Among the Soo, of course, no such institutions exist. Among them 1 is not, and 2 is, a pedagogical act; for only in 2 can we be certain that no taint of indoctrination appears.

It may be, as liberal advocates of indoctrination inform us,[16] that young children simply cannot come to believe certain things through rational examination, for they lack the necessary background beliefs. It may even be, as Jean Piaget has spent a vigorous and productive lifetime trying to prove, that the age of a child limits the conceptual, or even perceptual, operations of which he is capable.[17] Very well; what the child cannot come to believe on rational grounds, one ought not try to

---

16 "What I propose . . . is that we frankly admit that learning necessarily begins with an authoritative and indoctrinative situation . . ." Willis Moore, "Indoctrination and Democratic Method," in Snook, *op. cit.*, p. 97.

17 Jean Piaget's works fill libraries, and all of them are concerned with the point to which this note refers. Those philosophically inclined might well begin with his recent, small, popularly written *Psychology and Epistemology* (New York: The Viking Press, Inc., 1970), esp. chaps. 2, 3, and 4.

prove to him. What he cannot understand, one ought not try to explain. What he cannot imagine, one ought not try to describe. What he cannot follow, one ought not try to narrate, and so on. But one must be *very* careful not to mistake "does not, right off" for "cannot."

**P ELIMINATES INDOCTRINATIVE METHOD AND CONTROL** (ii) What sort of social relation is established within an episode of lecting? It's probably true that in these pages "A lects (∗) to B" has been taken to suggest a pedagogical context, one in which "A" is the place-holder for a person possessing information, knowledge, understanding, or skill, together with the authority and power that comes with possessing those things, while the place for "B" is to be filled by a person lacking exactly what A possesses, hence subordinate in the relation. But surely that interpretation is adventitious, arising from our tendency to associate teaching with the social relation in the classrooms. But if we had happened to be thinking, say, of a court of law, and the lecting found there, we might begin with rather different assumptions. When a witness describes his experience to the jury, or a defendant explains his conduct to the prosecuting attorney, both instances of "A lects (∗) to B," it is not the case that A and B are related as super- and subordinate, respectively. Or in the practice of medicine: the patient recounts his symptoms *to* the doctor, and the doctor prescribes *for* the patient. Again, the intellectual act as such does not establish any vertical ordering of A and B.

Nor does it establish a relation of debt—the particular obligation arising from an uncompleted exchange. B can ask A for information, instruction, directions, or explanation. By force or trickery, B can extract those things from A against A's wishes; that is, B can rob A of what A knows. But the middle term is missing. B can beg or steal from A, but he cannot borrow the sorts of things that are communicated in lecting. Hence, he cannot be indebted to A, though he may be grateful.

It is true, of course, that lecting under conditions satisfying L and P is among the most psychically intimate relations possible for human beings, hence it does evoke a direct awareness of certain general obligations holding among all self-reflective creatures. Candor, clarity, and benevolence are required of us in every human encounter; it's just that in lecting, momentary lapses from adherence to those canons of conduct are so easily visible on all sides. Even more so is open-mindedness, to use John Dewey's rather pallid term for a powerful idea:[18] as Dewey describes it, opening the mind is more like opening the anus than opening the

18 John Dewey, *How We Think* (Boston: D. C. Heath & Co., 1933), pp. 30–31.

mouth; the latter is done by a direct act of will, the former by putting oneself in the proper posture and waiting till it happens. A is explaining ___(*)___ to B, who has great difficulty understanding it. To be openminded, A may have to give up a belief central to his organized conception of himself and his world—namely, the belief that *he* understands ___(*)___. Can A be grateful to B for having so wrenched his consciousness? Open-mindedness is not necessarily a comfortable attitude, but it's demanded in lecting, more perhaps of A than of B.

From these considerations we may conclude that lecting creates no particular social relation; it requires no particular role expectations; the rules for participating in the act are simply (but insistently) the general canons of ethics and logic. Hence lecting might appear compatible with any social relation, including that we identified above as indoctrination. How can we be sure, then, that no indoctrinative control and teaching methods are employed among the Soo?

One can't always tell by looking whether or not given interaction is indoctrination. Suppose, in conformity with. P, that B wants to know what his ancestors believed about God, suppose that he believes that taking the role of learner in A's pedagogical practices—learning the language, saying the prayers, listening to the sermons, memorizing the catechism and credo, and so on—will help him to come to know what his ancestors believed. Suppose that A knows that B participates in the pedagogical interaction for that reason, and suppose that A tells, shows, recites, chants, preaches, and so on to B in order to help B learn what B wants to know. If B happens to be the same age as children who would ordinarily receive religious indoctrination, an external observer could not distinguish this episode of lecting from one of indoctrination. Are the two therefore indistinguishable?

The only way the distinction can be made is by asking B; and no particular answer, in itself, will determine whether it's lecting or indoctrination. Suppose B is asked why he attends religious instruction and worship so assiduously and suppose he answers, "To learn what my ancestors believed about God"; can we tell whether or not he is being indoctrinated? Not until we ask further, "And is what they believed true or false?" Unless B can understand the point of that question, it would appear that indoctrination is going on. But to understand that question in the sense intended is sufficient to forestall the charge of indoctrination. It isn't necessary that B be able to answer the question; to see the point of the question is to recognize that there are standards of rationality appropriate to beliefs about God, and B need not be able to articulate those standards in advance of testing the beliefs of his ancestors against them.

The outcome of the pedagogical encounter may well be that B has a right to claim:

G: I know what my ancestors believed about God.

The assertion of G does not commit B to any belief about God. That assertion contrasts quite strongly with

G′: I know how my ancestors felt in the act of communal prayer.

B's assertion of G′ can be true only if B has felt the same thing his ancestors felt, but G does not commit him to having believed, nor even to having had the propensity to believe, the same thing his ancestors believed.

(Suppose that B's ancestors believed, as part of their religion and contrary to the weight of evidence available to them, that the sun is a body much larger than the earth. In that case B could affirm

G″: I know what my ancestors believed about the sun.

Needless to say, G cannot be read, as G″ might be read, with "merely" prefaced to "believed.")

Now P, the requirement of pellucidity in lecting, is stated in terms of epistemic intentions. What B wants to know determines what A can try to help B to learn. Now so long as *those* intentions march *pari passu,* A's other intentions are of no pedagogical significance. In the case of B's wanting to know what his ancestors believed about God, A's intention to help B achieve B's epistemic intention is compatible with A's holding any one of a number of further intentions—for example, that B become a true believer, that B regard the whole enterprise as absurd, that B pay for his (A's) services and not bother him about the truth or falsity of the beliefs he is transmitting, or other. I grant that it would be difficult in practice to keep those other intentions from affecting the way A would go about helping B to learn what B wanted to know. But I don't think that matters. So long as the grounds that A holds out to B as reasons for believing that X (that is, that B's ancestors believed so-and-so) are the same as A's reasons for believing that X, and so long as those reasons are presented in such fashion as to make sensible the next-order question ("Are these adequate reasons for believing that X?"), the gravamen of the charge of indoctrination disappears.

Is B's awareness of the significance of the next-order question entailed by P, the criteria of pellucidity? Yes, if taken together with the premise that to *have* an intention is to have criteria for judging whether that intention has been achieved. (That premise is defended in Chapter Two.) To have an epistemic intention is to have epistemic criteria for its achievement. What **P** guarantees (among other things) is that the interaction between A and B will not circumvent B's independent application of his (B's) criteria to whatever happens in the interaction. And that's enough (given L) to guarantee freedom from indoctrination.

**CONSTRAINTS**
**ON THE SOO**

At long last, then, we can return to the question of moral education among the Soo. The digression was necessary to scotch the charge that indoctrination is simply inevitable. It *simply* isn't. Indoctrination may be necessary, given certain other constraints on pedagogical endeavors, such as that a society wishes its young to acquire beliefs that are rationally indefensible, or wishes its young to acquire rationally defensible beliefs at an age before the rational defense of those beliefs would be possible, or wishes all of its young to come to believe things that many would not bother to learn except under compulsion. But it makes no extravagant demands on the imagination to propose a society in which indoctrination does not occur because those constraints do not operate. It's more demanding to imagine a society in which every individual scrupulously avoids conditioning beliefs (that is, conditioning others into behavior which presumptively establishes a belief) without bringing the presumptive belief into critical consciousness. But that rule is logically consistent; it works reflexively (as applied to the conduct of the person who advocates it); it is presupposed in any sensible analysis of "candor" or "sincerity," hence it is a rule which *ought* to be observed universally in interpersonal relations, hence there is no *a priori* reason to hold that it couldn't be followed among the Soo.

The suspicion must be recognized and dealt with: haven't we set up a society which is imaginable (if that) only in the particulars specified? Doesn't it violate what we know from sociology and psychology to suppose that a society thus restricted in its childrearing and pedagogical efforts could, in fact, establish effective relations of production and the corresponding social relations necessary to sustain human life?

From the sociological perspective, little need be said on that point. I know no responsible theory of social structure that even pretends to set such limits of *possibility*. It would be a most interesting and important exercise of the sociological imagination to consider just what consequences we might expect in our social structure were we to adopt the proposed restrictions on pedagogical practices; I cannot imagine any concrete results from such speculation, for the predictable consequences would be politically unacceptable to those who profit from our casual and universal acceptance of false beliefs (for example, that the present distribution of income is morally justifiable).

From the psychological side, more serious challenges arise. The irrational activity of the Superego is held by some psychoanalysts to be a necessary condition for achieving a responsible adult personality. It isn't clear whether or not the Superego's irrational repressions are supposed to reflect (perhaps the better word is "express") irrational *beliefs,* for psychoanalysis starts with a generally disparaging view of the powers of cognitive, intellectual, or rational activity to control the dynamic or libidinal forces in conduct. It is likely, however, that the hard-liners among psychoanalysts would reject the attempt to imagine a society with the proposed restrictions on pedagogy; according to the hard-line Soo individuals could never hold their impulses in check long enough to form a viable society.

The mistake we still make is to hope that more and more citizens will have developed a mature morality, one they have critically tested against experience, without first having been subject as children to a stringent morality based on fear and trembling.[19]

Why would anyone want to accept Dr. Bettelheim's view? It assumes a culturally parochial definition of "mature morality" as a morality that grows out of, rather than apart from, fear and trembling. There is no need to make such a repulsive and counterintuitive assumption. Further, one suspects the moral impulse within the position itself: it seems rather convenient, doesn't it, that psychoanalysis cures what following the hard line causes?—namely, the disabilities resulting from fear and trembling in children. The position starts from the view that morality rationalizes the ever-unresolved internal struggle between fear and self-interest; one wonders which was dominant in Dr. Bettelheim when he wrote the passage. On its own terms, the position has to be examined as a symptom and not as an argument against imagining a different kind of society.

**NECESSARY STAGES IN MORAL DEVELOPMENT**     It might appear less easy to dismiss the restrictions on imagination that seem to be implied by recent field studies of moral development. The long-term research program of Lawrence Kohlberg and his far-scattered associates seems to have revealed that there is a single, definite sequence of stages in moral growth, a sequence from which no significant deviations are now likely to be discovered. And the early stages of that sequence do not fit with the rational, self-critical inter-

[19] Bruno Bettelheim, "Moral Education," in Nancy and Ted Sizer, eds., *Moral Education* (Cambridge, Mass.: Harvard University Press, 1970), p. 87.

action we have envisaged for children of the Soo. This evidence could be read to say that it is not humanly possible to have a society like the Soo.[20]

But limits of possibility can never be drawn from empirical data alone. What is required is a theory that both accounts for the regularities discovered and also leads to hypotheses about what would be discovered under different conditions. (The importance of the laboratory is mostly that: within it, the investigator can establish the conditions to test the hypotheses derived from his theories.) But the theoretical framework within which Kohlberg's research is carried on actually performs neither of those functions exactly and convincingly.[21] To be fair, I should add that I am presupposing, among other things, two rather severe criteria for such a theory. First, it must be formally sound, and it must be empirically tested, which requires that results confirming hypotheses consistent with the theory be shown to be sharply divergent from results confirming competing hypotheses.[22] Second, it must be intuitively plausible: to understand what the theory asserts should lead one to say, "Yes, it *ought* to happen that way." Reinforcement theory in experimental psychology satisfies those two criteria splendidly, and it has nothing to say, one way or another, about the limits and possibilities of stages in moral development.

Lacking any theoretical basis for another view, we should (or so it seems to me) regard the studies of Kohlberg and his associates as contributions to the ethnology of childhood, not as markers on the limits of possibility in moral development. If the sequence of stages they have discovered is, as they claim, the sequence through which *all* children go, no matter how fast or how far they go, no matter what kind of mature character they acquire, no matter how they happen to think about their own progress in moral development—in short, if the sequence is *that* general—then we may presume that Soo children will go through it as

20 The works of Kohlberg and his associates are voluminous. A convenient source is the large, ring-bound collection of photographically duplicated journal articles issued by the department of psychology at Harvard: L. Kohlberg, *Collected Papers on Moral Development and Moral Education* (Spring 1973).

21 See Lawrence Kohlberg, "From Is to Ought: How to Commit the Naturalistic Fallacy and Get Away with It in the Study of Moral Development," in Theodore Mischel, ed., *Cognitive Development and Epistemology* (New York: Academic Press, Inc., 1971), pp. 151–231. For criticism of Kohlberg's theoretical stance, see the essay by Stephen Toulmin, "The Concept of 'Stages' in Psychological Development," pp. 25–60, same volume. Toulmin's comments, pp. 57–60, are particularly apropos to the point of formal shortcomings in developmental theories. See also comment by Kurt Baier in *Journal of Philosophy*, 70:18 (October 25, 1973), 646–648.

22 See Karl R. Popper, "The Bucket and the Searchlight: Two Theories of Knowledge," *Objective Knowledge* (Fair Lawn, N.J.: Oxford University Press, 1972), pp. 341–361.

well, though the actual thoughts and feelings of Soo children, we must imagine, will be very different from those of children who acquire their beliefs in ways that involve fear and trembling.[23]

Or one might take an even less respectful attitude to the current passion for Piagetian-Kohlbergian stages among psychologists. It seems altogether more than coincidental that "science" has found qualitative deficiencies in children's perceptual, conceptual, and moral thinking just as the question of children's rights has penetrated both the courts and the consciousness of sensible men and women. In due time, we shall probably regard "stages of development" very like "penis envy": as ill-formed ideas used by a dominant group to "justify" looking at members of a suppressed group as less than fully human.

Many interesting studies on moral development have been undertaken from different theoretical perspectives in experimental psychology.[24] Careful analysis of these studies would yield constructive hypotheses about the kinds of habits and character traits that Soo children are likely to acquire along with the beliefs they learn from the limited pedagogical encounters they are allowed. But the point for these references to empirical psychology should now be well established: there is no reason to doubt the empirical possibility of a society of the sort we have called the Soo. Nor, quite obviously, is there any (formal) logical inconsistency in the supposal that there is a society in which acts of instruction are limited to lecting satisfying L and P in matters of belief and to supervised practice that also protects the freedom and purposes of learners.

## AN ARGUMENT FROM LANGUAGE?

The toughest hurdle, of course, is the last one. A *really* strong argument against the possibility of imagining the Soo would be the argument from language: if there is a moral sense to the central predicates of normative language, such that no one can feel the force of "right," "ought," "must," and so on in the guidance of conduct unless he has first learned those words by having his conduct externally controlled by their use, then a moral education of the sort we have envisaged for the Soo would be both a human disaster and a linguistic absurdity. Moral language among the Soo would, on that analysis, have the same status as color predicates in the country of the blind: the words might appear in certain vocabularies, but no one would really understand their meaning.

[23] This attitude is, I think, rather like that taken by R. S. Peters, "Moral Development: A Plea for Pluralism," in Mischel, ed., *op. cit.*, pp. 237–267.

[24] A large number of studies from a variety of theoretical approaches are nicely analyzed and summarized by Derek Wright, *The Psychology of Moral Behavior* (Harmondsworth: Penguin Books Ltd., 1971).

With this sort of linguistic foundation, the hard line of Dr. Bettelheim and the developmental sequence of Kohlberg would have to be taken quite seriously indeed.

The trouble with that argument from language is that it's a flagrant case of *petitio principii*. The same words that in one context are taken in a peculiarly "moral" sense, in other contexts are taken as having a merely "technical" sense. Thus "ought" is said to have a moral sense in

A. "You ought to visit your sick friend as you promised you would"

but to have merely a technical sense in

B: "You ought to use a lock washer on the axle nut."

Now there are obvious differences between A and B. But what is not obvious at all is that the difference is accurately characterized by the claim that they represent different *senses* of "ought." There are no logical consequences of A that do not have their counterparts in B; for example, if A is true of the person to whom it it addressed, then it is true of anyone who should be in a relevantly similar condition. But the same is true of B. Likewise, it is hard to see how A would be considered more directive of conduct than B. The same sort of excuses that deflect A deflect B: "I can't get (A) there" or (B) "a lock washer" work equally well. And so on.

It is true, of course, that many people have deep feelings about A and none about B. And it is likely true that those who have such deep feelings learned the sanctity of promises with lots of fear and trembling. But the *petitio* is to claim that the existence of those feelings proves that there is a moral *sense* of the term "ought." There is no logical or syntactical basis for the claim of two senses, not even the limited grammatical basis I have presented for the two senses of "teach"—an argument showing two different classes of verbs fitting two different grammatical paradigms. There is no difference in practice between the two cases; both are instances of language used directly to affect conduct.

Thus farewell to the linguistic basis for claiming that we cannot imagine a society like the Soo. That their children learn without fear and trembling, that they learn without passing through stages of total incomprehension, does not mean that they fail to learn any distinctively moral sense of normative language.[25]

25 This line of argument is obviously a *great* deal more complicated than these few remarks might indicate. Proof that any term is univocal in any language is monstrously difficult, but most of the arguments for the "two senses" view of normative predicates now seem shaky. See Roger Wertheimer, *The Significance of Sense* (Ithaca, N.Y.: Cornell University Press, 1972), esp. pp. 187–201. Incidentally, if my argument is right, Wertheimer's conclusion that attention to *his* arguments is "wasting time" is wrong. It makes all the difference in one's theory of moral education to decide that moral predicates are univocal.

**CENTRAL PROBLEMS**
**FOR ANY THEORY**
**OF MORAL**
**EDUCATION**

Now is the time ("finally," you say) to redeem the pledge made toward the beginning of this chapter that the invention of the Soo would advance the argument with a net saving of time and words. With their aid we shall find it relatively easy to solve the two problems that (almost literally) define any theory of moral education: (i) the ancient and honorable "paradox of moral education" and (ii) the problem of "knowing" in moral education. For it can now be shown that there is an argument which has these two properties: first, it both justifies and is justified by the Soo society, and, second, it solves both the traditional problems within any theory of moral education. Before we turn to that argument, however, let us make sure that we formulate those problems accurately.

## (i) THE PARADOX OF MORAL EDUCATION

As I recall my work with Foster McMurray at the University of Illinois, so many years ago, we used the expression "paradox of moral education" to mean a peculiar imbalance between educational ends and means. The argument went something like this:

Moral education must be either immoral or ineffective. For getting a child to act in the way your moral theory requires that he learn to act requires treating the child in ways your moral theory forbids; while not treating the child in ways that are morally forbidden guarantees that when that child becomes an adult, he will not even acknowledge the distinction between morally required and forbidden.

The paradox is obviously a challenge that no theory of moral education can ignore.

As in so many other points, in this also: the field of philosophy of education is indebted to R. S. Peters for bringing the paradox of moral education into the forum of public discussion. What then is the paradox of moral education as Peters conceives it?

It is this: given that it is desirable to develop people who conduct themselves rationally, intelligently and with a fair degree of spontaneity, the brute facts of child development reveal that at the most formative years of a child's development he is incapable of this form of life and impervious to the proper manner of passing it on.[26]

Put that way, there is really nothing *very* paradoxical about moral education. Suppose frogs had minds and speech and moral education. The

26 R. S. Peters, "Reason and Habit: The Paradox of Moral Education," first published in 1963, reprinted in Israel Scheffler, ed., *Philosophy and Education* (Boston: Allyn & Bacon, Inc., 1966), p. 252.

very wisest of the frogs might say:

> Given that it's desirable to develop frogs who sit around the edge of the pond and catch flies, the brute facts of frog development reveal that at the most formative hours when a tadpole is becoming a frog, he is incapable of this form of life and impervious to the proper manner of passing it on.

Other frogs might lament that revelation, but who could find it paradoxical?[27]

What makes moral education a paradox for us and not for frogs is precisely that the brute *facts* of child development reveal absolutely nothing about a child's capability for participating in a rational, intelligent, and spontaneous form of life. It is only the interpretation of those facts by certain theories which enables Peters to conclude that children are impervious to the *proper* manner of passing on such a form of life, where "proper manner" *must* mean rationally, intelligently, and spontaneously. And that makes the paradox very similar to the formulation given above: unless we were already committed to principles of rationality and freedom in our conduct toward *all* persons, we should not find it paradoxical that we don't extend those principles to our conduct toward children. But we *are* so committed, and children *are* persons (in a way that tadpoles are *not* frogs), and therefore *we* find it paradoxical that we seem obliged *not* to treat children after the manner we know to be proper.

Peters finds intimations of this paradox in Aristotle, but the connection is really rather remote. Aristotle was spared the duty of dealing with the theories of Sigmund Freud and Jean Piaget; thus he never had to work out any alternative theory of how children come to develop the kind and quality of habits which according to *his* theory of ethical conduct, constitute the absolutely necessary background for virtuous action: those habits which are aspects of a "firm and unshakable character" (*Nichomachaean Ethics* II, 4). The paradox in Aristotle is that his ethical theory seems to entail that a man has *to be* virtuous before he can *become* virtuous.

> It is well said, then, that it is by doing just acts that the just man is produced, and by doing temperate acts the temperate man. Without doing these no one would have even a prospect of becoming good (*ibid.*, II, 4).

But just above Aristotle had said that to be a just act, an act must be done as a just man would do it. And that means, among other things, that the act must come from, and be expressive of, a firm and unshakable character. It appears, then, that an agent must possess that sort of char-

---

27 I recall having heard or read this *argumentum ad ranam* someplace, but I'm damned if I can remember where. My apologies to whomever they're due.

acter before he can take the first step to acquire it. Which leaves it a little unclear how a good man is produced. "To *become* a good man is hard, truly," reads Socrates' gloss on Simonides in Plato's *Protagoras* (343e). With Aristotle it seems more a logical impossibility than a moral struggle.

The Aristotelian paradox, as Kazepides (among others) has shown, is rather easily resolved when Aristotle's use of "habit" is correctly understood.[28] Aristotle assumed that moral agents—he called them "men"—could change their habits by thinking clearly about particular acts; for Aristotle's view of practical reason has it that to think clearly about an action *is* to act as reason dictates. No one can change all his habits at once, but no habit is impervious to change. Aristotle recognized what is obvious anyway: the boy who comes to school well equipped with stable habits of temperance and courage is well on the road to becoming a good man. Aristotle, however, wasn't at all interested in *how* the details of maturation and childhood work their effect on character.

But Peters' paradox remains after Aristotle's has been resolved. As Kazepides puts it: "Only a miraculous change in the facts of child development or a drastic change in the requirements of morality will resolve that paradox."[29] Here Kazepides seems to have followed Peters too closely. Exactly where does the paradox lie? In the realm of brute, mute facts? If so, we shall forever be spared cognizance of it. In a logical incompatibility between our moral theory and the facts of human development? If so, the theory is simply wrong: "ought" still implies "can." If our moral theory requires that we treat children in ways that are, in fact, impossible, then we are *logically* obliged to change the theory.

But that's not the paradox we're after. The paradox lies at the very heart of our conception of a civilized life. Note that a psychological theory of moral development is not, whatever Peters and the psychologists may think, a scientific summary (or even reconstruction) of brute facts; it is, rather, a *moral* theory of child development, a *practical* theory of *how we ought to treat children*. The dominant, machismo-infected theories in our culture, from the Book of Proverbs through S. Freud and L. Kohlberg, all regard children as barbarians outside the

[28] A. Kazepides, "What Is the Paradox of Moral Education?" *Philosophy of Education*, 1968, Proceedings of the Philosophy of Education Society, Donald Arnstine, ed., pp. 177–184.

[29] Kazepides, *op. cit.,* p. 182. A very cogent and sophisticated analysis of the paradox of moral education as it arises in the "Open School" movement is found in Kathryn Morgan, "Socialization, Social Models, and the Open Education Movement," *Studies in Philosophy and Education*, 8:4 (Fall 1974), 278–314. I read her article after completing this argument. The difference between us hinges *mostly* on how seriously one should take the research (and theory based on research) from various branches of the social sciences. Perhaps I am as much underly as she seems to me overly impressed by their work.

gates. But the cement that makes possible a civilization of rationality and spontaneity is also the presupposition of any ethical theory: rules apply to *all* persons. And children, from a disconcertingly early age on, are obviously persons and obviously inside the gates. Still and all, to apply some of the moral rules of our present society to children is not to promote rationality and spontaneity. It would require that adults regulate their own actions toward children in ways that would range from inconvenient to absurd. Since our operative moral codes contain many vestiges of barbarism (for example, in the practice of punishment), to extend those codes unmodified to children is obviously unjust. So we invent theories of moral development which show that children are impervious to the proper manner of treating human beings, and thus we try to justify our treating them in ways that are personally tolerable, albeit clearly and unmistakably improper.

The resolution of that paradox is one that each individual who deals with children must work out for himself. It probably won't be resolved at a social level until we have achieved a balance of population and resources such that each child accepted as a member of the society is given full moral status immediately. Those aspects of our moral code that would have to change because they appear ludicrous when applied to children probably *are* ludicrous anyway.

The philosophical point is, in any event, clear enough. The paradox of moral education is in fact a moral problem; it can be resolved only in concrete acts. "But," as Aristotle complained,

. . . most people do not do these but take refuge in theory and think they are being philosophers and will become good in this way (*ibid.*, II, 4).

Some things do stay the same, don't they?

## (ii) "KNOWING" IN MORAL EDUCATION

As with the paradox of moral education, so also with the concept of "knowing" in moral education: in both cases there is a problem only within a theory already committed to rationality as a necessary condition for both moral action and teaching. If rationality were not a necessary component of both teaching and moral action, then moral education could be construed quite simply as a matter of getting children to behave in specified ways under specified conditions. You teach the child to stay out of the street; the child learns to stay out of the street. The pedagogical intent and outcome can be glossed in purely behavioral terms. A theory of moral education based on behaviorism solves the problem of "knowing" by simply eliminating the term.

But that "solution" is unavailable to any theory which takes rationality as a necessary condition for teaching or moral action. For getting the child to stay out of the street does not count as teaching the child to stay out of the street ("teaching" in the specific sense of the term), unless the interaction with the child is constrained by certain fundamental principles of rationality. As Martin says:

Thus we may say that [such] constraining principles . . . have *logical* status: like rules of the game rather than like norms or social conventions, they define the activity of teaching so that if someone violates them, he is not and cannot be teaching.[30]

The theory advanced in this book pushes that general position to its logical conclusion: when teaching in the specific sense is distinguished from its counterfeits, the learning which comes from the interaction entails knowing. But now comes the problem. If you train a dog (and the dog learns) to stay off the street, then you can say that he knows to stay off the street. Perhaps you want to say of the child that he, too, can be trained and thus learn and know to stay off the street. But then you can't take that training-and-learning as any part of moral education. For, to make the contrast clear, we cannot say of any person, child or adult, that he or she knows to speak honestly or knows to judge impartially. We do hold, however, that such virtues are learned rather than innate; it makes sense to say that a person learned to speak honestly or learned to judge impartially; we should think that it makes sense to say that A is teaching B to speak honestly or to judge impartially. But since B cannot know to act so, it follows that A cannot teach B to act so. And it is clear that no one can be conditioned or indoctrinated to speak honestly or to judge impartially, for to practice those virtues is to manifest a quality of action requiring conscious and free choice.

It might be thought that it's purely a prejudice of grammar that the expression "know to X" can be predicated only of unreflective behavior by unreflective organisms; there is, in fact, something a trifle vulgar or colloquial in any use of "know to X." But it isn't *purely* prejudice, for when one tries to think clearly just what the expression might mean, even in matters *like* staying out of the street, it turns out to be a blank. I was once berated for failing to respond to an urgent memo. I pled that I had neglected to empty my mail box, only to be met with: "You *know* to check your mail every day!" But I could not and cannot make out what that might mean. That I know that I *ought* to check my mail every day? I was perfectly willing to grant the value of that habit, which I have since tried to establish in my conduct. But my tormentor meant more than that, I was forced to acknowledge. And surely she meant more

[30] J. R. Martin, *Explaining, Understanding, and Teaching* (New York: McGraw-Hill Book Company, 1970), p. 92.

than to say that I knew *how to* check my mail. But exactly what could be meant by saying either that I did or should have known *to* do something? To say that my dog knows to stay off the street means that he stays off the street or, if forced or enticed into the street, is fearful and anxious to regain the curb. But my neglect and insouciance belied *that* interpretation of her comment. Yet it couldn't be false that I knew to check my mail box, for there was nothing about checking mailboxes I didn't *know* at the time I didn't check it. My supervisor's comment expressed something, no doubt, but it didn't affirm a true or false proposition about my epistemic achievements.

The problem of "knowing" in moral education thus puts us right back to the question with which Meno accosted Socrates. It appears that one cannot know to speak honestly or to judge impartially. From that it follows that one cannot teach (specific sense) those virtues to another, while indoctrination and conditioning are obviously excluded. And surely such virtues are not innate. The *Meno* concludes that it must depend on divine dispensation whether we happen to learn them, and no theory of moral education which begins with a commitment to rationality seems to have come up with a better answer.

**MORAL EDUCATION AMONG THE SOO?** But among the Soo there is no paradox of moral education and there is no problem of "knowing" in moral education; thus, to grant the possible existence of the Soo is to grant a possible solution to both those problems. That conclusion can be broken down into four propositions as follows:

I. There *is* moral education among the Soo.

Now I is simply an instantiation of a fundamental axiom of any social science. Any society that maintains continuous existence across generations succeeds in moral education. Snobs say: "They're just animals, their children receive no moral training of any kind." In times of social breakdown some children, in fact, do not receive moral training of any kind, but we do not believe that such children could, in turn, have children of their own and raise them to adulthood. Such children are rather like Harlow's monkeys.[31] Attempts to rehabilitate such children provide some of the most poignant stories in the history of the human effort to remain human.[32] But the snobs I mentioned above were not talking about the consequences of a breakdown of a social order. The snobs just meant *Them,* members of another race or social class. But

31 Allen M. Schrier, Harry F. Harlow, and Fred Stollnitz, *Behavior of Nonhuman Primates: Modern Research Trends* (New York: Academic Press, Inc., 1965).
32 A. S. Makarenko, *Life and Works* (Moscow: Foreign Languages Publishing House, 1963).

often, perhaps usually, it turns out that people called "animals" by snobs prove to be quite effective in establishing the relations of production and reproduction necessary for promoting human life, while snobs are generally incapable of either.[33]

So whatever else we might mean by "moral education," we mean at least that sort of pedagogical relation between one generation and a second, such that the second can become pedagogue-parent-provider for a third, and so on. Thus to grant that the Soo are a possible society is to grant I.

II. Lecting under conditions that satisfy L and P is sufficient for moral education.

You may wish to retract your provisional acceptance of the Soo as a possible society when you see that you have thereby granted II. But it does follow: if moral education is necessary for social continuity, then social continuity is sufficient for moral education. If the only pedagogical interaction practiced among the Soo is lecting satisfying L and P, and if the Soo constitute a possible society, then II must be true.

The ontological and epistemological status of possible societies is a larger question than we can resolve in these concluding remarks. There are strong interaction effects between the material and psychological conditions under which a society can be imagined or made actual; restraints on the human imagination arise from the material and social conditions under which we live. Thus in one dimension the realm of possible societies is infinitely broader than that of the societies which happen to have been thought of. But not every society which can be imagined is a possible society. A child might imagine a society which adds new members by growing babies among the cabbages. That violates what we commonly understand as a biological law, but even so, we must be careful: if we imagine a society willing to do *whatever* is necessary, given only the constraints of logic and physical possibility, to produce babies among the cabbages, it is hard to rule out the child's fantasy as a literal impossibility. However, a society in which every askable question must be answered Yes is literally impossible, is it not?

Notice that II does not deny the possibility of societies in which no lecting at all occurs; the possibility of such societies entails that they are possible solutions to the problem of moral education. One can imagine a rational theory of totally nonrational societies, in which the entire social significance of every human gesture lies outside the realm of conscious intention. No member of such a society could, *ex hypothesi,* explain his own actions, but we have already postulated that, in that society, moral education occurs without any of the intellectual acts. In

[33] See J. P. Marquand, *Wickford Point* (Boston: Little, Brown and Company, 1939), for a picture of the quintessential snob.

the theory of such a nonrational society the terms "moral" and "functional" would coalesce, as would "immoral" and "dysfunctional."[34] Whether there are insuperable psychological or material barriers against the actuality of such a nonrational society and whether there is a logical barrier against an internally consistent theory of such a society are questions I cannot answer. But it should be clear that, if there were a theory of the totally nonrational society, the "paradox" and the problem of "knowing" in moral education would simply not arise, neither within the society nor within the theory of moral education of that society.

But with the Soo society it is not the case that the paradox and problem do not there arise. It is rather that

III. The Soo society resolves the paradox of moral education.

This does not say that adult Soo never treat the young in ways that would be considered immoral if shown to other adults. They might behave abominably toward their young; but they could not justify their abominations by some presumed psychological necessity, much less mere pedagogical convenience. What Peters says about conscientious educators in our society applies with special force to the Soo:

> It is no use concealing the fact that the activities and modes of thought and conduct which define a civilized form of life are difficult to master. That is why the educator has such an uphill task in which there are no short cuts.[35]

The Soo educator has to accomplish that task within the restrictions of lecting satisfying L and P; conversely, the activities and modes of thought and conduct which define a civilized form of life are restricted to those which can be communicated from one generation to another under that pedagogical restraint. Whether the resulting society would be more or less civilized in general than our own is hard to say, but the Soo would seem infinitely more civilized in at least one respect; no Soo educator would say: "Children . . . start off in the position of the barbarian outside the gates. The problem is to get them inside the citadel of civilization. . . ."[36] Nor could a Soo educator conceive of a child as a *tabula rasa* nor a growing plant nor an unbroken colt. No, the healthy newborn child is a fellow human being whose intellectual powers are exactly equal to the demands put upon them. As the child grows older, his powers will increase, and so also the demands upon those powers. Within that view, it is never necessary to violate the child's rationality for pedagogical purposes.

34 See Dorothy M. Emmet, "Functionalism in Sociology," *The Encyclopedia of Philosophy* (New York: The Macmillan Company and The Free Press, 1962), vol. III, 256–259 and bibliography.
35 R. S. Peters, "Education As Initiation," in R. Archambault, ed., *Philosophical Analysis and Education* (New York: Humanities Press, 1965), pp. 107–108.
36 *Ibid.,* p. 107.

Notice that the theory of moral education among the Soo does not deny the possibility of moral lapses, ακρασία, and so on. A Soo adult might inflict pain or humiliation on a Soo child—in a fit of anger, with absentminded nastiness, for the fun of it, and so on. But, to repeat, the Soo adult could not justify such action by appealing to psychological "facts" nor to some pedagogical advantage presumed to ensue. (Whether such actions could be justified at all in Soo society depends upon other details of the Soo moral code, which we may leave for the Soo to work out among themselves.)

It must be remembered that the paradox we are concerned with arises, and must be resolved, within a *theory* of moral education. Soo society is defined by a theory of education, including moral education. The question arises, within any such theory: "How can we insure that the young will learn the morality necessary for the continuity of our society?" And the answer within the theory defining the society: "By lecting under conditions that satisfy L and P, only." Assuming only the obvious, namely, that lecting under conditions satisfying L and P does not violate other moral rules in Soo society, then the theory is free of the paradox of moral education.

IV. The Soo have solved the problem of "knowing" in moral education.

It might appear that number IV is false, given the astringent resolution of the paradox of moral education. Here is the way it stands: a Soo child might learn to speak honestly and to judge impartially, but in Soo society it does not occur that anyone teaches another to speak honestly or to judge impartially. Let us suppose that the Soo believe that everyone ought to believe that way; if a Soo child happened to want to learn how people in his society feel about honesty and impartiality, someone could explain the moral code to him; and the child could come to know that such beliefs and feelings are standard in his society. Or a child could want to learn how to speak honestly (for example, when doing so might cause pain to oneself or another) or how to judge impartially (for example, when certain interests appear out of proportion because of one's personal involvement), and those skills may be taught, learned, and known among the Soo as among us. A Soo child may be "exercised" by adults in those skills, if the child so chooses, but there doesn't seem to be any place at all in Soo society for the development of a distinctly moral sense, the kind of knowing that we paraphrase weakly as "knowing what I ought to do." How will a Soo child ever know the exteriority and constraint of moral rules, that forum of knowing which Émile Durkheim regards as fundamental to social existence? How will a Soo child ever know the Moral Law, in all its awful majesty, that knowledge which Felix Adler saw as basic to any ethical culture? How can a

Soo child be taught *to care* about moral rules or to have *concern* for standards? Unless the Soo's solution to the problem of "knowing" in moral education touches the deepest springs of human action, then that "solution" is no solution at all; at least it is not a solution to the problem we started with.

**MORAL RULES**         As a result of the kind of education they receive,
**AMONG THE SOO**       or perhaps because of the indoctrination and con-
                        ditioning they *don't* receive, the Soo have a rather
old-fashioned view of moral language. They do not regard words such as "right" and "good" and "obligation" and so on as "Parent" words to be used in the manipulative control of behavior, one's own or an-other's.[37] Instead they regard such language as a very useful way of organizing their beliefs when—individually or collectively—they must de-cide what they want to do, particularly when they feel conflicting im-pulses or desires to achieve incompatible goals. Thus, moral philosophy among the Soo is concerned not only to achieve clarity and consistency among the society's moral beliefs (general beliefs about what actions are desirable and what not), but also to insure that the language in which those beliefs are formulated is readily appropriate to the actual prob-lems faced by the Soo, individually and collectively.

For the Soo child, then, the outcome of moral education is *knowing what he wants to do,* where "I want to X" is the end of an act of reason-ing that began with "I feel impulses to X and to Y and to Z . . . which impulses are (here and now) incompatible." The conjunction: "I ought to X, but I don't want to X," then, represents for the Soo an incomplete act of thought, one in which the active impulses have not *as yet* been thought through. When thinking is complete, "I know what I ought to do" and "I know what I want to do" are synonymous.

Thus, Soo adults who "naturally" tend to use moral language in con-ditioning children's behavior restrain those impulses, for they want their children to learn to use moral language as guides to learning (finding out) what *they* want to do. A Soo adult doesn't say "You mustn't . . . ," "You ought . . . ," or the like. The moral belief guiding the Soo adult is found in the requirement of lecting: one can tell another to do X, but one cannot (either in English or in the language of the Soo) *show* another to do X. But an intellectual act, lecting, requires both showing-and-telling.

---

[37] This use of "Parent" derives from the interpretation of interpersonal relations known as "Transactional Analysis." See, for example, M. James and D. Jongeward, *Born To Win: Transactional Analysis with Gestalt Experiments* (Boston: Addison-Wesley Publishing Co., Inc., 1971), chap. 2.

One psychological premise is concealed, so far, in this account of the Soo. A child who feels conflicting impulses can raise that conflict to consciousness and understand it as wanting to know what he wants to do. When so understood, a conflict of impulse can be the occasion for lecting satisfying L and P. The outcome, if the lecting is complete, is that B has learned (come to know) what he wants to do. With that psychological premise granted, then, the Soo have solved the problem of "knowing" in moral education.

The problem arises because knowing seems so far removed from the springs of action. The goal of moral education cannot be merely to bring it about that B knows what to do, much less (because at even farther remove), that B knows what he ought to do. But such knowing by B seems to be all that A can rightfully intend in his pedagogical acts toward B, for to intend that B actually do X ("know to X") entails violating B's freedom and purposes. But A can rightfully intend to help B discover what B wants to do, if, in fact, B can *want to know what he (B) wants to do.*

A theory of moral education for Soo society must be grounded in an analysis of just what it *is* that B wants to know, such that his wanting to know can become the occasion for lecting under conditions that satisfy L and P. The analysis will not be easy. The logic of desire is complicated enough by itself; here we have an additional mixture of epistemic predicates. Ordinary English already has the distinctions at hand. B says: "I know that I feel an impulse to X, but is X what I *really* want to do?" This is a case of B's wanting to know what B wants to do. B can say: "I believe, on warrant W, that I want to do X." Or "I believe that I want to do X for reasons R." Both of those are (possibly) completed judgments, and they are related, though how I cannot say. That's the sort of thing that needs analysis. "I want to believe that I ought to X, but I know that I ought to Y" is an (as yet) incomplete judgment, leaving it open for B to learn what he wants (ought) to do. In short, there's nothing *obviously* foolish in saying that B wants to learn what he wants.

But what mode of lecting can A bring to the encounter such that he can teach—that is, help B to learn—what he (B) wants to do? The Soo have worked it out in practice, or so we assume when we assume that they constitute a possible society. If the paradox and the problem of "knowing" in the theory of moral education are genuine problems for us—problems we want to *solve*—then we had better follow the example of the Soo. Right?

# FOR FURTHER READING

## BIBLIOGRAPHICAL NOTE

Given the broad conception of philosophy of education advanced here, it is apparent that the literature relevant to the field includes everything ever written. Even if one narrows it down to material devoted specifically to education, the scope is frightening. See

ERNEST, NATALIS, *Un Quart de Siècle de Littérature Pedagogique* (Gembloux: Editions J. Puculot, 1971.)

This survey contains 15,000 entries, and if the inclusion of English language items is typical of all, it comprises only a small and whimsically chosen sample from the field.

But it really isn't impossible to make one's way about in the literature of philosophy of education with some confidence. Harry Broudy and his associates made a prodigious effort to survey and organize that literature during the 1960's. The results of that effort grow more useful as time passes.

BROUDY, HARRY S., MICHAEL J. PARSONS, IVAN A. SNOOK, RONALD D. SZOKE, *Philosophy of Education, An Organization of Topics and Selected Sources* (Urbana: University of Illinois Press, 1967).

A smaller, handier starting point is

POWELL, JOHN P., *Philosophy of Education, A Select Bibliography*, 2d ed. (Manchester: The University Press, 1970).

The *Encyclopedia of Philosophy*, edited by Paul Edwards, 1967, contains several articles on philosophy of education and references to the most important works in the canon of historical writings.

The periodical literature is immense and scattered, but even so, not impossible to survey. *Studies in Philosophy and Education* (Francis Villemain, ed.) is devoted exclusively to this field. The concluding issue of each volume of *Studies,* called "Reviews and Rejoinders," contains reviews of recent works in the field and responses by authors reviewed. It also contains a current bibliography (prepared by T. Whitsun Nelson) of books and essays from other journals. The preparation of an "R&R" issue is an immense task, and it appears somewhat irregularly.

*Educational Theory* (Joe R. Burnett, ed.) is the official periodical of the Philosophy of Education Society. As its title suggests, however, *Educational Theory* publishes not only philosophy of education but also essays from other theoretical disciplines concerned with education. It lacks the continuity of argument that is carefully promoted in *Studies,* but it does open more lines of philosophical argument than any other periodical. It also concentrates some issues, such as Vol. 24, No. 1 (Winter 1974), specifically in this field. This same pattern of mixing philosophy of education with other theoretical disciplines is found in other journals, such as *Educational Philosophy and Theory,* published by New South Wales University in Australia, and *Journal of Educational Thought,* University of Calgary.

Journals of general interest in education, notably *The Record* (Teachers College, Columbia University), *The School Review* (University of Chicago), *Harvard Educational Review,* and *The Review of Education* (H. J. Perkinson, NYU, ed.), contain occasional essays in philosophy of education. Journals in general philosophy publish articles in this field as a matter of course, and some sometimes devote special issues to particular topics in philosophy of education. References to all such publications are available in standard indexes.

Continuity in philosophical argument is among the major goals of the various associations and societies devoted to philosophy of education. These arguments can be followed through the pages of *Philosophy of Education,* the *Proceedings* of the Philosophy of Education Society's Annual Meetings, which are edited by a member of the Society and published for the Society by Studies in Philosophy and Education, Inc., Francis Villemain, editor. Since 1967 the Philosophy of Education Society of Great Britain has published the *Proceedings* of its annual conference. The Far Western Philosophy of Education Society now publishes its annual Proceedings through Arizona State University in Tempe. Other regional associations in the United States and other English-speaking countries publish occasionally when money, energy, and quality of available materials permit.

The National Society for the Study of Education (NSSE) devotes its yearbook to philosophy of education on a longer cycle. *Philosophies of Education* appeared in 1942, *Modern Philosophies and Education* in 1955, both edited by John S. Brubacher. *Philosophical Redirection of Educational Research,* edited by Lawrence G. Thomas, D. B. Gowin, and H. B. Dunkel, was published by the NSSE in 1972. The changing perspectives in the field are, I believe, reflected rather accurately in those volumes.

Like other branches of the parent discipline, philosophy of education has been well served by anthologizers. Those essays that are published (or republished) in standard anthologies are called the "classics," and those anthologies that include the classical articles become the standard anthologies. But mostly it's a matter of who is writing interesting things and encouraging others to do so. R. S. Peters from London, Israel Scheffler from Harvard, and B. O. Smith and Harry Broudy from the University of Illinois have been notable on both counts. Directly or indirectly, at least one of those gentlemen has been influential in the preparation of the following anthologies, each of which concentrates on a particular topic or follows a rather specialized, analytical style of doing philosophy.

## SPECIALIZED ANTHOLOGIES

ARCHAMBAULT, R. D., ed., *Philosophical Analysis and Education* (London: Routledge & Kegan Paul Ltd., 1965).

BANDMAN, BERTRAM, and R. S. GUTTCHEN, eds., *Philosophical Essays on Teaching* (Philadelphia: J. B. Lippincott Company, 1968).

BARNETT, GEORGE, ed., *Philosophy and Educational Development* (Boston: Houghton Mifflin Company, 1966).

BROUDY, H. S., R. H. ENNIS, and L. I. KRIMERMAN, eds., *Philosophy of Educational Research* (New York: John Wiley & Sons, Inc., 1973).

CHAZAN, BARRY I., and JONAS F. SOLTIS, eds., *Moral Education* (New York: Teachers College Press, 1973).

DEARDEN, R. F., P. H. HIRST, and R. S. PETERS, eds., *Education and the Development of Reason* (London: Routledge & Kegan Paul Ltd., 1972).

GUTTCHEN, ROBERT S., and BERTRAM BANDMAN, eds., *Philosophical Essays on Curriculum* (Philadelphia: J. B. Lippincott Company, 1969).

HOLLINS, T. H. B., ed., *Aims in Education: The Philosophic Approach* (Manchester: The University Press, 1964).

KOMISAR, B. P., and C. J. B. MACMILLAN, eds., *Psychological Concepts in Education* (Chicago: Rand McNally & Company, 1967).

MACMILLAN, C. J. B., and T. WHITSON NELSON, eds., *Concepts of Teaching: Philosophical Essays* (Chicago: Rand McNally & Company, 1963).

MARTIN, J. R., ed., *Readings in the Philosophy of Education: A Study of Curriculum* (Boston: Allyn & Bacon, Inc., 1970).

MISCHEL, THEODORE, ed., *Cognitive Development and Epistemology* (New York: Academic Press, Inc., 1971).

PETERS, R. S., ed., *The Concept of Education* (London: Routledge & Kegan Paul Ltd., 1967).

PETERS, R. S., ed., *The Philosophy of Education* (Fairlawn, N.J.: Oxford University Press, 1973).

SCHEFFLER, ISRAEL, ed., *Philosophy and Education*, 2d ed. (Boston: Allyn & Bacon, Inc., 1966).

SIZER, N. F., and T. R. SIZER, eds., *Moral Education* (Cambridge: Harvard University Press, 1970).

SMITH, B. OTHANEL, chmn., *Education and the Structure of Knowledge*, 5th Annual Phi Delta Kappa Symposium on Educational Research (Chicago: Rand McNally & Company, 1964).

SMITH, B. O., and R. H. ENNIS, eds., *Language and Concepts of Education* (Chicago: Rand McNally & Company, 1962).

SMITH, RALPH A., ed., *Aesthetic Concepts and Education* (Urbana: University of Illinois Press, 1970).

SNOOK, I. A., ed., *Concepts of Indoctrination: Philosophical Essays* (London: Routledge & Kegan Paul Ltd., 1972).

VANDENBERG, DONALD, ed., *Teaching and Learning* (Urbana: University of Illinois Press, 1969).

————, ed., *Theory of Knowledge and Problems of Education* (Urbana: University of Illinois Press, 1969).

More general anthologies are a tricky business. They can become pretty shoddy affairs, a way of getting one's name on the cover of a book and a royalty check from a publisher without earning either. The following are, I believe, not liable to such charges. Each represents a distinctive principle of selection, each contains some selections not readily available elsewhere. (*Disclaimer:* There are also, I'm sure, lots of other general anthologies worthy of respect.)

## GENERAL ANTHOLOGIES

BURNS, HOBERT W., and CHARLES J. BRAUNER, eds., *Philosophy of Education: Essays and Commentaries* (New York: The Ronald Press Company, 1962).

CAHN, STEVEN M., ed., *The Philosophical Foundations of Education* (New York: Harper & Row, Publishers, 1970).

MORRIS, VAN CLEVE, ed., *Modern Movements in Educational Philosophy* (Boston: Houghton Mifflin Company, 1969).

PAI, YOUNG, and JOSEPH T. MYERS, eds., *Philosophic Problems and Education* (Philadelphia: J. B. Lippincott Company, 1967).

STRAIN, J. P., ed., *Modern Philosophies of Education* (New York: Random House, Inc., 1971).

Because of its close connection with teacher training programs, philosophy of education is taught *mostly* at an introductory level to students whose only contact with the field will be that one course. A natural consequence is that an overwhelming proportion of all publishing in the field is devoted to introductory texts, which themselves may follow any one or combination of different patterns of organization, along historical lines (Bowyer's), "schools" of philosophy (Brameld, Pt. I), or problems (Beck). Or the text may work through the author's personal scheme of concepts for understanding the world; in that case, the more interesting and integrated the person, the more integrated and interesting the text. The following list contains a sample of texts I've found useful for one reason or another.

## INTRODUCTORY TEXTS

ARNSTINE, DONALD, *Philosophy of Education, Learning and Schooling* (New York: Harper & Row, Publishers, 1967).

BECK, CLIVE, *Educational Philosophy and Theory* (Boston: Little, Brown and Company, 1974).

BOWYER, CARLTON H., *Philosophical Perspectives for Education* (Glenview, Ill.: Scott, Foresman and Company, 1970).

BRAMELD, THEODORE, *Philosophies of Education in Cultural Perspective* (New York: Holt, Rinehart and Winston, 1955).

————,*Toward A Reconstructed Philosophy of Education* (New York: The Dryden Press, 1956).

BROUDY, HARRY S., *Building a Philosophy of Education* (Englewood Cliffs, N.J.: Prentice-Hall, Inc., 1954).

BROWN, L. M., *General Philosophy in Education* (New York: McGraw-Hill Book Company, 1966).

BRUBACHER, JOHN S., *Modern Philosophies of Education*, 4th ed. (New York: McGraw-Hill Book Company, 1969).

CURTIS, S. J., *An Introduction to the Philosophy of Education* (London: University Tutorial Press, 1965).

DUPUIS, A. M., and R. B. NORDBERG, *Philosophy and Education: A Total View* (Milwaukee: The Bruce Publishing Company, 1968).

GREEN, THOMAS F., *The Activities of Teaching* (New York: McGraw-Hill Book Company, 1971).

KILPATRICK, WILLIAM H., *Philosophy of Education* (New York: The Macmillan Company, 1951).

MACDONALD, JOHN, *A Philosophy of Education* (Glenview, Ill.: Scott, Foresman and Company, 1965).

PHENIX, PHILIP H., *Philosophy of Education* (New York: Holt, Rinehart and Winston, Inc., 1958).

SCHOFIELD, HARRY, *The Philosophy of Education: An Introduction* (London: George Allen & Unwin Ltd., 1972).

Critical studies of educational philosophies are found in abundance in other European languages and in earlier times in English. The "Classics in Education" series from the Teachers College Press performs a valuable service in keeping the materials for such studies readily available. Each of the following works is pretty much *sui generis*. A sustained critical, historical literature is yet to be achieved.

## STUDIES OF EDUCATIONAL PHILOSOPHIES

BRAUNER, CHARLES J., *American Educational Theory* (Englewood Cliffs, N.J.: Prentice-Hall, Inc., 1964).

BRUMBAUGH, R. S., and N. M. LAWRENCE, *Philosophers of Education: Six Essays on the Foundations of Western Thought* (Boston: Houghton Mifflin Company, 1963).

CHILDS, JOHN L., *American Pragmatism and Education, An Interpretation and Criticism* (New York: Holt, Rinehart and Winston, Inc., 1956).

MASON, ROBERT E., *Contemporary Educational Theory* (New York: David McKay Company, 1972).

MEHL, BERNARD, *Classic Educational Ideas from Sumeria to America* (Columbus: Charles E. Merrill Publishing Company, 1972).

PRICE, KINGSLEY, *Education and Philosophical Thought* (Boston: Allyn & Bacon, Inc., 1967).

General histories of educational thought have inaccuracies of scale, inherent limitations of the genre. Older works are often to be preferred; a scholar will treasure his copies of Boyd (1921), Hoyt (1910), or even Compayré (1888!). Better than some other recent examples is

FROST, SEVERE E., JR., *Historical and Philosophical Foundations of Western Education* (Columbus: Charles E. Merrill Publishing Company, 1966).

The most sensitive soft spot in the literature of philosophy of education is in extended monographs dealing with the central concepts in educational theory. The following are worthy examples of a literature that needs strengthening.

## MONOGRAPHS

DIETL, PAUL J., "Teaching, Learning, and Knowing," *Educational Philosophy and Theory*, vol. 5 (New South Wales University Press, 1973), pp. 1–25.

HARDIE, C. D., *Truth and Fallacy in Educational Theory* (New York: Teachers College Press, 1962). First published in 1942. Cited edition contains excellent bibliography prepared by B. P. Komisar.

HIRST, P. H., and R. S. PETERS, *The Logic of Education* (New York: Humanities Press, 1971).

MARTIN, J. R., *Explaining, Understanding, and Teaching* (New York: McGraw-Hill Book Company, 1970).

PETERS, R. S., *The Concept of Motivation* (London: Routledge & Kegan Ltd., 1958).

————, *Ethics and Education* (Glenview, Ill.: Scott, Foresman and Company, 1967).

SCHEFFLER, ISRAEL, *Conditions of Knowledge, An Introduction to Epistemology and Education* (Chicago: Scott, Foresman and Company, 1965).

————, *The Language of Education* (Springfield, Ill.: Charles C Thomas, Publisher, 1960).

————, *Reason and Teaching* (London: Routledge & Kegan Paul Ltd., 1973). (A collection of essays, not a unified argument.)

SOLTIS, JONAS F., *An Introduction to the Analysis of Educational Concepts* (Reading, Mass.: Addison-Wesley Publishing Co., Inc., 1968).

SNOOK, I. A., *Indoctrination and Education* (London: Routledge & Kegan Paul Ltd., 1972).

WHITE, J. P., *Towards a Compulsory Curriculum* (London: Routledge & Kegan Paul Ltd., 1973).

WILSON, JOHN, NORMAN WILLIAMS, and BARRY SUGARMAN, *Introduction to Moral Education* (Baltimore: Penguin Books, 1967).

It probably won't be much longer that a work in this field can make even a pretense to scholarship while citing only English-language sources. We shall have to practice our powers of reading other languages, our translators will have to get busier, and our retrieval systems will have to go international if we are to continue serious work in philosophy of education. Ready?

# INDEX*

Anscombe, G. E. M., 98n
Aristotle, 91, 157–159
Arnstine, Donald, 8n, 158n
Asch, Solomon E., 138n
Assertive risk, 43

Baier, Kurt, 153n
Bateson, Gregory, *et al.*, 127n
Benedict, Ruth, 13
Bereiter, Carl, 18–21, 122–127, 130
Berger, M. I., 11n
Bettelheim, Bruno, 152–155
Black, Max, 15
Bromberger, Sylvain, 110–113
Broudy, Harry, 8n, 17
Burckhardt, Jacob, 60

C. I. A., 124
Christians, 11
Connely, John B., 128n
Cremin, Lawrence A., 11n

Darwin, Erasmus, 63n
De Pew, 31–33
Dewey, John, 11, 64, 91–93, 148
Dietl, Paul J., 72
"Double-bind," 127

Edwards, Paul, 56
El'Konin, D. B., 142n
Emmet, Dorothy M., 132n, 163n
Encyclopedias, 56
Epistemic logic, 109
Ethics, 3

Evidence-translation, distinction between, 60

Fascism, 17
Flew, A. G. N., 140
Formula Q, 59–64
Freud, Sigmund, 91

Green, Thomas F., 4n, 29, 96
Greene, Maxine, 94n

Hardie, C. D., 53n
Harlow, Harry F., *et al.*, 161n
Haynes, Emily, 4n
Hilgard, Ernest, 55n
Hill, Winfred F., 56
Hirst, Paul H., 19, 100n
Hook, Sidney, 63n

James, William, 137
Johnson, Mauritz, 8n

Kant, Immanuel, 126
Karier, Clarence, 144n
Kaufman, Arnold S., 5n
Kilpatrick, William Heard, 95
Kimball, Solon T., 132n
Kimble, Gregory, 56, 59
Kissinger, Henry, 52
Klein, Jacob, 25n
Kohlberg, Lawrence, 152
Komisar, B. P., 7n, 35n, 74, 76–77, 94n, 96–98, 102–105
    Komisar's Law, 35, 42
Konorski, J., 133n
Kuethe, James L., 58, 86n

* Does not contain references to sources listed in "For Further Reading." More complete topical references are found in the Table of Contents.